Marathon Man

Marathon Man

**MY 26.2-MILE JOURNEY FROM UNKNOWN GRAD STUDENT
TO THE TOP OF THE RUNNING WORLD**

Bill Rodgers
and Matthew Shepatin

THOMAS DUNNE BOOKS
ST. MARTIN'S PRESS ❦ NEW YORK

THOMAS DUNNE BOOKS.
An imprint of St. Martin's Press.

www.thomasdunnebooks.com
www.stmartins.com

Library of Congress Cataloging-in-Publication Data (TK)

ISBN 978-1-250-01698-0 (hardcover)
ISBN 978-1-250-02312-4 (e-book)

St. Martin's Press books may be purchased for educational, business, or promotional use. For information on bulk purchases, please contact Macmillan Corporate and Premium Sales Department at 1-800-221-7945 extension 5442 or write specialmarkets@macmillan.com.

First Edition: April 2013

10 9 8 7 6 5 4 3 2 1

BILL RODGERS:

*To Karen, you have a
Heart of Gold*

MATTHEW SHEPATIN:

*To Merel and Chris, the
proprietors of the Monaco
"Writers' Retreat"*

Contents

To give anything less than your best
is to sacrifice the gift.

—STEVE PREFONTAINE

The long run is what puts
the tiger in the cat.

—BILL SQUIRES, MY COACH

Marathon Man

Relax, Mr. President

I'm lucky to have a big brother like Charlie, for many reasons, including this one: For thirty-five years, he managed the Bill Rodgers Running Center—our shoe and apparel store in Faneuil Hall, Boston. Charlie took over the responsibility of running the store so I'd be free to put in the long miles each day that serious marathon training demands. (In my prime, I was churning out up to 170 miles a week.) Over four decades, the store organically evolved into an informal museum, cluttered with memorabilia covering my running career: old newspaper clippings, framed pictures, bib numbers, racing shoes, gloves, and jerseys. The store also displayed a treasure trove of photos and artifacts celebrating the achievements of past running greats who inspired Charlie and me since we were kids. The walls were additionally plastered with items paying tribute to the 116-year history of the Boston Marathon, which, for my brother and me, has always been more than a famous road race that takes place on the third Monday of every April. It's been a big part of our life, of who we are, and of who we've become.

As Charlie's beard gradually turned white and grew down to his belly button, he became the keeper of this little temple to runners past and present. My brother, who has given thousands upon thousands of personal tours, was always happy to show off our framed *Sports Illustrated* cover of American running legend Steve Prefontaine. He was happy to divulge how we got our hands on a signed racing glove from immortal Czech distance runner Emil Zátopek. He was happy to tell you the tale behind a newspaper clipping of the infamous $10,000 Marathon Derby of 1908, when the "marathon craze" swept cities from London to

New York. He's happy to do all of this because, just like me, he loves running.

Hanging among these prized mementos could be found a T-shirt with my most famous quote written on it: The marathon will humble you. But the truth is, sometimes it will do more than humble you. Sometimes it will break your heart.

It was the 1936 Boston Marathon. Ellison "Tarzan" Brown, a brash young Narragansett Indian from Rhode Island, ran at a record pace through the first seventeen miles. Despite trailing Brown by three minutes, defending champion John "the Elder" Kelley remained ice cool. He knew the impulsive rascal would pay for his fast start now that he'd hit the series of Newton Hills—or what my coach, Bill Squires, called the Killer Chain. Sure enough, Brown started to tire through the treacherous hills. Kelley smelled blood. He blasted away over a three-mile stretch, erasing Brown's entire half-mile lead. He pulled even with the fading leader. As Kelley passed him, he reached out and gave Brown a friendly pat on the shoulder, as if to say, *Good try, kid. But you're out of your league.* I'll take it from here. Brown was awoken by the gesture. He stormed back up to Kelley on the last and most daunting of the Newton Hills. As Brown surged past him on the steep climb, Kelley could only look on with helpless horror. Brown cruised to the finish line and was crowned Boston Marathon champion, while Kelley faded back to finish fifth. The late *Boston Globe* sports editor Jerry Nason, who witnessed the incident on the final hill from the press vehicle, described it as "breaking Kelley's heart." The spot has been known as Heartbreak Hill ever since.

Here I was, forty-three Patriots' Days later, trying to avoid my own heartbreak at the very same spot along the 26.2-mile course to Boston, only in my case, I was going head-to-head with Japan's twenty-two-year-old phenom, Toshihiko Seko.

I first noticed Seko shadowing me as I charged into the hills near the sixteen-mile mark, but, in fact, he had been on my heels the whole time. He was employing the same clever tactics he had used four months earlier at the prestigious Fukuoka Marathon in Japan, the unofficial world championship for marathoners: stay tucked in safely behind me. Wait . . . wait . . . wait . . . Attack on the home stretch. Blow me away with his strong finishing kick. This is how he beat me on his home turf, handing me my one marathon loss in 1978, after I'd netted victories at Boston and New York.

I glanced back at the silent runner hovering just off my shoulder, like a predator patiently stalking his prey. As we ran a foot apart in the pouring rain, we looked radically different in appearance: I wore big white gardening gloves and a thick light-blue wooly cap, complete with a Snoopy patch. Seko was a sleek stealthlike figure with a neat crew cut and all-white uniform. (Author Robert Johnson once wrote, "If Bill Rodgers was the marathon's Peter Pan, forever young and enthusiastic, Toshihiko Seko was Boston's Mr. Spock—focused, businesslike, and humorless.") Seko's face was hard to read, but his steady, relaxed breathing, compact arm swing, and fluid strides told me he felt strong. My right arm swung wildly across my body, my stomach hurt, and I had to pee. Up the hills I began to waver. Seko passed me. I tucked in behind him and watched his form. I adopted his stride—a much shorter, quicker stride. I suddenly felt more at ease. I flashed back to Fukuoka. I couldn't let him outkick me again in the end. I had to get rid of Seko now. I saw Coach Squires in the crowd and gave him a wink. It was the time to make my move.

Through the twisting stretch of hills, where so many runners have hit the wall and so many dreams have been trampled, I poured it on. But I wasn't only trying to burn out Seko, I was trying to catch the leader, Garry Bjorklund. That made me run harder and faster. I didn't feel fatigue when I was in pursuit of another runner. I didn't think about Seko breathing down my neck as long as I had Bjorklund to chase down. I charged forward, all my focus on the one man in front of me.

I finally caught Bjorklund at the base of the second Newton hill. As I overtook him, he glanced over to me and said, "Go for two-oh-eight." But I was concerned with the win, not the world record. I glanced behind me. Seko was still there, still dogging me every step of the way. I had to shake him off. Up the hills I pushed, even harder now. But Seko wouldn't go away.

We reached Heartbreak Hill—the single most significant hill in all of road racing. I knew this would be my last chance to drop my rival. I thought back to the story of 1936—would this be where I'd have my heart broken? Would I watch victory slip through my fingers like John "the Elder" Kelley or soar ahead to victory like Tarzan Brown?

I summoned my strength and roared up the hill. As I crested the top of the mighty hill, I looked over my shoulder. For the first time, Seko had dropped back a few yards. I couldn't believe it. He was fading. That last climb had done him in. This was his first Boston Marathon. He didn't know these hills, but I did. I trained on them sometimes twice a day. I knew why Coach Squires called this stretch the Killer Chain. Not because of their severity, but because of where they began—at mile 16, when legs start tightening and spirits begin to break—and how they culminated. On Heartbreak Hill. Welcome to my home turf.

Up until that point, I had been running scared. But now, I had a little lead on Seko and a straight shot downhill all the way to the finish line. I felt gung-ho. Maybe I can win this thing, I thought to myself. I exploded down the hill, flanked by hordes of wild, screaming fans, the corridor between them barely wide enough for me to pass through. Ahead of me, an escort of three police motorcycles fought to keep the surging crowd back. In the madness, a policeman's horse reared up, taking out one of my motorcycle escorts. I kept running, light as a breeze. I didn't look back.

An ear-splitting roar went up as I passed a huge party of friends and family, gathered outside the running store I had opened with my brother, Charlie, and wife, Ellen, two years earlier. In that moment, I tried to fathom how our little basement store had become the epicenter of the late-1970s Boston running boom, and how a skinny, wide-eyed misfit like me had become a big part of the sport's explosion in popularity across the country.

As I soared past the Eliot Lounge, where for years I'd shared many a good time with my runner pals, I caught a glimpse of Seko. He was about two hundred yards behind. I could taste victory. All along the course the multitudes chanted my name, "Go, Billy, Go!" I lifted my soaked wool Snoopy cap from my flowing blond hair and waved it to the cheering fans. It lifted me up to know this was my city, my streets, my people. They were on my side. The wave of my cap was my way of saying "thank you."

Over the last thirty yards, I sprinted with all my effort, my arms pumping, legs churning, sweat flying off me. The announcer shouted over the PA system: "Ladies and gentlemen, the greatest runner in Massachusetts, the greatest runner in the United States, the greatest runner in the world and the history of the world!" But all I could hear was the roar of the crowd.

As I broke through the finish line tape, I gritted my teeth in a triumphant snarl, still holding my Snoopy cap tightly in my hand. Newspapers were snapping my photo. People were chanting my name. I had captured my third laurel wreath at Boston, broken the course record, and, after four years and many hard races run, set a new personal best time in the marathon—2:09:28.

Moments later, I was packing up my clothes in the chilly, dank confines of the Sheraton Hotel garage. I grabbed a traditional bowl of beef stew, all the while signing autographs for as many people as I could. After a while, Ellen tried to tell everybody that I had to go home, warm up, and rest. "That's okay," I told her. "I can sign a few more."

The rain continued to pelt the streets as Ellen and I slowly made our way up Chestnut Hill Avenue toward my store. Despite the steady hum of raindrops falling on our heads, I didn't exactly feel like sprinting. We reached Cleveland Circle, and walked unnoticed through the meandering crowd. But, all of a sudden, a few people spotted me. More and more heads began to turn. All at once, people started shouting out, "Way to go, Boston Billy!" By now, even runners were pausing in the middle of the course to applaud me on my journey home. Embarrassed by the attention, I hurried to the entrance of the basement store. Up above in a balcony, a bunch of young revelers with beer bottles hand saluted me with cheers of "Boston Billy." I quickly ducked inside and locked the door behind us. Standing there with Ellen, soaking wet and exhausted, I could still hear the people chanting for me outside. I thought to myself, How in the world did I end up here? But what happened next would really blow my mind.

It was the next morning. April 17, 1979. I listened to the rain patter outside the store while I drew a warm bath, where I'd soak my sore muscles. I was already half naked when I heard the phone ring. Ellen picked it up. Ellen always answered the phone. She was my gatekeeper, standing between me and the constant stream of requests from race directors wanting me to come to their races, people asking me to speak at their event, reporters and television producers seeking interviews. I heard her voice rising in annoyance, "Who's calling? The president? The president of what?"

There was a long silence. Then, Ellen called out to me, "Bill, you need to come out here."

I threw on a robe and came out of the bathroom. "It's the president," Ellen said in a shell-shocked kind of daze. "Of the United States."

When I picked up the phone, a presidential aide was on the other end. He asked me my name, and if I was somewhere I could talk. I replied "yes." The phone suddenly went silent. I turned to Ellen, eyes wide, mouth agape.

A minute or two later, a voice came on the phone. It was President Carter. He congratulated me on my third victory at Boston, and then we started chatting about the marathon. He told me he read lots of running magazines.

"I grind out five miles a day," President Carter said to me. "So I really admire what you marathoners do."

I told him to keep it up. He was doing a good job. As a runner. And a president.

He ended the conversation by asking me if I was doing anything May second.

Ellen rushed over and flipped open my appointment book. She gave me the thumbs-up.

"Looks good," I said.

"Great. We're having a state dinner for Japanese Prime Minister Masayoshi Ohira and I'd love for you to come."

"The woman who won the race. Joan Benoit. She's a senior at Bowdoin College in Maine. She set the American record."

"Yes, yes. I'll make sure she also receives an invite."

"Thank you, Mr. President."

The next day, we received the engraved invitation in the mail. It was black tie. I only owned one suit. Most of the time I wore race giveaway T-shirts and sweatpants. I would have to go and rent a tux.

Future presidential candidate Paul Tsongas, then a Massachusetts senator, invited Joan Benoit Samuelson and me down for a luncheon the day before our dinner at the White House. At lunch, we put on a "running clinic" for the large group of senators that were there, including Senator Strom Thurmond, who was then in his seventies. He boasted that he had recently run six miles, and then asked me if I ate the white or yellow part of eggs. After lunch, the press corps took pictures of us shaking hands with the senators. They also snapped photographs of Joanie and me pretending we were jogging on the Capitol steps with Senator Tsongas.

When venerable House Speaker Tip O'Neill, from my home state, heard we planned to take a cab to the White House, he gave us use of his chauffeur and limousine. On the ride over to 1600 Pennsylvania Avenue, I sat in the back of the limo next to Ellen, fidgeting in my tuxedo.

I was looking out the window when I saw a big sign that read FIRE-WORKS. I told the chauffeur to pull over. Moments later, I came out of the store in my tux, carrying a giant box of fireworks. I gave Ellen a big smile. She sighed and quietly shook her head. I knew how excited my dad would be when I showed him the bounty. He was a bit of a fireworks fanatic. So was I. In retrospect, bringing a stockpile of highly explosive fireworks to the White House might not have been the brightest idea.

We were greeted at the entrance by a team of aides in military dress uniforms. They ushered us into a reception room. One of the aides briefed me on the strict protocols. He then told me a story about how he was strolling up to the White House one day when he spotted all these men leaping into bushes and ducking behind trees. He had no clue what was happening. In an instant, he caught sight of President Carter running by on his daily run. The Secret Service agents were leaping from tree to tree and bush to bush on the White House lawn, secretly keeping an eye on Carter while he was running.

I was nervous as hell as I waited to go through the receiving line. I kept grabbing flutes of champagne off the passing silver trays and quickly downing them. Ellen was like me—she came from a regular, middle-class family—and I could see this was all a little nerve-racking for her, too. Finally, we were escorted to the receiving line. A second later, I was shaking hands with the president. He was very friendly. He kissed Ellen. He asked the photographer to come over and take a picture of the first lady, himself, Ellen, and me. He introduced us to Prime Minister Ohira, who spoke excellent English, and I told him what an honor it had been to race in his country, and that Japan produced some of the toughest marathoners in the world. He smiled.

The dinner was being held on the west terrace of the White House, for the first time ever, and it was a beautiful night. When we sat down at our assigned table, the only other person there was Joan Benoit. A moment later, the President and Mrs. Carter and Prime Minister Ohira and his wife walked up to the table. Joanie and I kind of sunk down in our seats, the light sound of violins wafting in the air. I realized this was probably bad form, so I popped up nervously out of my seat. This was mind-boggling. What were Ellen and I doing sitting with the president?

Fireworks were going off now—only they were exploding inside my stomach. Here was the president of the free world sitting directly across from me. I was frozen with nerves. I've always been one of those people who doesn't say anything at parties unless someone says something to them. I listened to the President tell Peter Falk of *Columbo* fame that I ran a marathon at a sub-5:00 pace and that Joanie ran at a sub-6:00-per-mile pace. Peter Falk was nodding with a smile while smoking a Kool cigarette. He asked if I cared for one of his Kools. I said, "No, thanks, only Winstons." Of course, the last Winston I puffed had been over six years ago. Back when I was riding around on my motorcycle, drinking in bars with my pal Jason, and working a menial job at the hospital. I wasn't running at all. I was a society dropout. No money, no life, no future.

Now here I was, answering questions about running from the president. He asked me if he should be breathing through his nose or his mouth.

I said, "Just relax."

"But how many breaths per stride is it normal to take?" he asked. "I start off taking maybe three breaths per stride, but it gets up to four when I'm tired."

"Don't worry about all that. Keep a steady pace. Breathe naturally."

Which was something I was having a seriously hard time doing at that moment. As the courses flowed—avocado with a seafood salad, suckling pig from Georgia—I started to relax more. It helped that the president was so down-to-earth. I was having fun. After dinner, we were escorted back inside to a grand room where pianist Bobby Short entertained us. I could see from the big smile on President Carter's face that he was having a good time. It was a happy occasion. I smiled back.

I never in a million years imagined I'd be standing where I was, the president's honored guest, or that I'd be giving him running advice. Just as I never imagined that in six years time, I'd win four Boston Marathons, four New York City Marathons, and three number-one world rankings. Never imagined I'd end up Boston's golden hometown boy, and the most popular marathoner in the world. Never imagined I'd wind up twice on the cover of *Sports Illustrated,* or that Ellen and I would be profiled in *People* magazine. Never imagined my rivalry with Olympic champion Frank Shorter would capture the world's attention, or that I'd carry on America's reign of marathon domination that Shorter began at the Munich Games in 1972. Never imagined my lasting success in the Boston and New York City marathons would launch road racing into the brave new world of professionalism. Never imagined I'd become a symbol of the running boom that seized the country in the late seventies, inspiring a lot of people, for the first time in this country, to make running a normal part of their day.

It all just kind of happened, but for the life of me, I don't know how. I was just a guy who liked to run. Same as my brother, Charlie, and my lifelong best friend Jason Kehoe.

It's true. The marathon will humble you. But sometimes it will do more than humble you. Sometimes it can change your destiny.

Here's the story of how it changed mine.

ONE

The Teachings of Amby Burfoot

April 21, 1975
Hopkinton, Massachusetts

For weeks, I had prayed for mild conditions on race day, but prepared mentally for any type of weather. There was nothing more fickle than Mother Nature around April in New England. Would I have to run the Boston Marathon in a snow squall like those poor racers in 1961? Would I have to brave a torrential downpour like the one that greeted competitors in 1970? Or would I have to endure the sweltering heat that brutalized runners in 1909—a race that earned the nickname "the Inferno" after the mercury soared to 97 degrees?

"Bill," said my big brother, Charlie, standing beside me on the town green.

"Uh-huh," I said, not really hearing him. Feel that brisk wind, I thought to myself. The heat will not bring me to my knees today, not like it has before. My prayers had been answered—a cool, overcast spring morning. The perfect day to run a marathon.

It was here of all places, in the sleepy New England village of Hopkinton, Massachusetts, that I gathered with some two thousand top-flight (I can't stand the term "elite") runners for the start of the Boston Marathon. On the town green, I loosened up and prepared for the race, amid spectators milling about and other competitors warming up.

The marathon has turned the center of this quaint small town into a bustling scene of excitement. You could feel the electricity in the air. Swarms of people passed by me on the green. Locals carried lawn chairs to set up along the course. Runners paced in nervous anticipation. A man in a clown suit sold colorful balloons. I heard the Hopkinton High School marching band playing nearby. For a big kid like me, it was heaven. For a racer with undiagnosed attention deficit disorder, also me, it was dangerously distracting. But not today. Not today.

"Bill!" My brother's loud Boston accent snapped me out of my gaze. "Well? Do you want some gloves?" he inquired.

"Yeah, that's a good idea," I said. "Did I bring any?"

"Of course not," Charlie said in a teasing sarcasm.

I blinked at him a couple of times.

"Don't worry. I'll run down to that little hardware store," he said, pointing to the row of stores farther down the center of town.

"Okay," I said.

Charlie cut off down the street, straight at the statue of the World War I doughboy soldier, rifle on shoulder in midmarch. He stopped dead in his tracks as if the doughboy, suddenly springing to life, had aimed a rifle at his forehead. Charlie swung around to me and shouted, "Stay there!"

I admit it. I've been known to get lost easily. And forget stuff. And lose track of time. But come on, Charlie. My mind was focused like a laser beam on one thing today. For countless months, I had trained like a man possessed, running over a 150 miles a week, spending solitary hours circling the dirt path around Jamaica Pond. I'd punished my body on the very hills I would soon face, pushing everything else in my life to the periphery. For so long, I'd thought about nothing but winning this race. And standing there, moments before the gun sounded, I felt ready for a battle.

Speaking of battles, the race has been held every Patriots' Day in

April since 1897, in part to commemorate the anniversary of the most famous run of all, Paul Revere's midnight ride on April 18, 1775, to warn the patriots in Lexington and Concord that the British were coming. Fifteen runners participated in that first race in 1897; ten finished. John J. McDermott of New York emerged victorious, crossing the finish line in a new world record time of 2:55:10.

Boston oozes prestige and tradition. It's the oldest continuously run marathon in the world, held on almost the exact same course for over a century—a course that was patterned after the ancient route from Marathon to Athens. It's also famous for being the only marathon in the world in which all runners have to qualify. Many families over many generations have returned annually to run the race, or to watch the drama unfold from their go-to spot along the road, creating a festive row of lawn chairs and barbecue grills. Stroll around Boston on Marathon Monday and you'll know why they call it the world's biggest block party, or what's known around these parts as "a seriously wicked ragefest."

Truth be told, I didn't always grasp the romantic, almost mythical, attraction that runners have felt toward the race, going back to the early 1900s. In those days, hundreds of immigrant workers came from far and wide to the city for a shot to prove themselves worthy of the greatest honor a runner could achieve—the laurel wreath crown of the Boston Marathon. Some of these dusty-faced dreamers would hop freight trains to Boston with nothing but a pair of sneakers in their knapsack and a few cents in their pocket. What made the marathon different from many of life's other competitions is that sometimes this was all a man needed to come out on top.

Take Frank Zuna, a wiry, 150-pound plumber from Newark, New Jersey. In 1921, the twenty-seven-year-old man of Czech Bohemian descent jumped the train to Boston, wearing his racing gear under his dirty work clothes. Zuna conquered the field in a record-shattering time of 2:18:57, then almost skipped the public celebration in his honor. He told the BAA officials he had to grab the next train home or else he would be late for his plumbing job the next morning.

To this day, runners from all over the world, from remote parts of the Ukraine to the mud-hutted villages of Kenya, grow up dreaming of running just one race—the Boston Marathon. Given all the lore, the tradition, the epic stories of athletic triumph and tragedy, the one-of-a-kind personality of the course, the city where it takes place, and the people who make up the huge crowds along the way, it's no wonder many consider this the Holy Grail of marathon running in America and the world over.

There I was, a pale, drifty grad student, warming up on the town green, same as Frank Zuna and all the other dirt-poor, skinny-legged dreamers who had come before me. I hopped up and down a little in my lucky, faded gray Camp Wonderland warm-up sweatshirt, blowing on my cold hands. Just then I felt a hard slap on my shoulder. It was my friend Tom Fleming. He was wearing a smart-aleck grin, along with a white mesh T-shirt that exposed his nipples, and could easily have come from the closet of wrestler Randy "Macho Man" Savage.

This was Tom—a Jersey dude, amped to ten on the dial, ready to go toe-to-toe with anybody, anytime. If I glided swiftly over the road like a gazelle, Tom charged down it like a bull. Hanging on his bedroom wall was this sign: SOMEWHERE IN THE WORLD THERE IS SOMEONE TRAINING WHEN YOU ARE NOT. WHEN YOU RACE HIM, HE WILL WIN. Tom wasn't about to let that happen; he put in more hard miles than anybody I knew. But under all that hot-blooded, chest-puffing drive, Tom was a nice guy with a big heart.

"Hey, Bill," said Tom. "How do you plan to see where you're going with all that hair in your face?" Before I could respond, Tom threw a white sweatband over my head, causing my hair to cover my face and blind me.

With my long hair, skinny frame, ratty sweatshirt, and discount tube socks, I certainly didn't look the part of the typical track athlete. Then again, none of the guys in our little crew—the Greater Boston Track Club—fit the picture of dedicated, word-class competitors. Alberto Salazar, an eighteen-year-old kid from Wayland, Massachusetts, used to tag along with us on our workouts (hence his nickname, "the Rookie"). He described us as "oddball hippie outcasts" and me in particular as a "sweet, friendly ragamuffin guy; a hippie with a dirty-blond ponytail."

We might have been a bunch of rogue runners with our long hair and free-spirited lifestyle, but good luck finding a more hardcore group of athletes in 1975. We ran more miles in a week than most people drive in their cars. Day in and day out, we trained to the point of exhaustion, through bone-chilling New England winters and sticky-hot Boston summers.

None of us made any money road racing because there wasn't any to be made—if you won a race, you were thrilled to come home with a new blender. It was an amateur, *Chariots of Fire*–style situation: We ran for the love of the sport and the thrill of pushing the boundaries of what could be done in that day and age. Roger Bannister, the Oxford medical student who became the first man to break the four-minute mile in 1954, a feat previously thought to be humanly impossible, called it "a challenge of the human spirit." That's exactly how we saw it. (Coincidentally, 1975 was the year Bannister would suffer a near-fatal car accident that forced him to give up running.)

I parted my hair out of the way so I could see again. Tom was staring back at me with a cocky grin

"Looking good," Tom said. He held for a couple more seconds, then took off toward the high school, which had been turned into a makeshift staging area for the top runners. As I watched him disappear into the crowd, Charlie returned with a pair of white gardening gloves.

"Try these on for size," he said.

I slid on the gloves. Almost instantly, my hands started to warm up. I was lucky to have Charlie there to support me. It was nice to have the company. Kept the nerves calmer.

As for my girlfriend, Ellen, she'd camped out somewhere along the second half of the route. She had the idea to write BOSTON—GBTC in black marker on the front of my singlet the night before in our apartment. She felt, even though the crowds lining the course had no clue who I was, they'd be moved to cheer for me once they saw I was a local kid. I thought it was worth a shot. Besides, I took pride in representing my team and my city in the world's most famous footrace.

I had found my mesh singlet a month earlier in a Dumpster outside our housing complex in Jamaica Plain. I loved that it was so light-weight—it felt like I was wearing nothing—and it didn't chafe while I ran. What in the world a perfectly good shirt was doing in the trash, I have no idea, but I've always had an eye for finding treasure among the discarded.

I found my shirt in a Dumpster, my water bottle was an old shampoo bottle, and my racing gloves came from the gardening aisle. As for my footwear, I assumed I would be running the marathon in my beat-up Asics with the holes and rips and broken-down arches. But a week or so before the race I received a mysterious package at my apartment with this letter attached:

April 9, 1975
Mr. Bill Rodgers
Jamaica Plain, Mass. 02130

Dear Bill,

First of all congratulations on a fine race in Rabat. You have really improved this last year and hopefully will continue to until the Olympic games.

The reason I'm writing is because Jeff Galloway told me you were interested in training in our shoes. I'm sending you a pair of Boston '73s and a training shoe. Any comments would be greatly appreciated. Just feel free to drop me a line and let me know what you think.

Wishing you continued success for '75.

Sincerely,

Steve Prefontaine

I was awestruck to get a personal letter from Prefontaine, then America's biggest track and field sensation. While I had never met the middle-distance rock star runner from Oregon, I felt a kinship with him. Maybe because we were both skinny scrappers, each with one leg longer than the other. Like me, you could count on Prefontaine to run from the front, to push the pace, and to give it everything he had from start to finish. The whole country loved Prefontaine for the same reason I did—he left it all out there every time he raced, heart and soul. As he once said, "Somebody may beat me, but they are going to have to bleed to do it."

I admired that Prefontaine brought the same gutsy determination to his battles off the track that he did on them. He took on the over-bearing rule enforcers of our sport at a time when few dared to do so. He knew it was wrong that the AAU dictated where and when U.S. athletes could compete. He was sick of these corrupt old men who maintained the belief that no matter how much time and passion a runner devoted to his sport, he should be barred from making a decent wage doing what he loved. According to them an American runner should make his own way, perhaps as a part-time bartender, like Prefontaine, but still compete against the best athletes from other nations like the Soviet Union and Finland who were fully funded, could train year-round, and, in some cases, were doped up on steroids. It bothered him that he had to turn down a $200,000 pro contract in 1975, then the largest ever offered to a runner, to maintain his amateur status for the

1976 Olympic Games. Instead, the world famous athlete was forced to live in a trailer with his dog, Lobo, and survive on food stamps while maintaining his tireless training program, which included grueling runs alone in the winter in Eugene, Oregon.

While Prefontaine was busy racking up records and winning titles at the University of Oregon, his legendary track coach Bill Bowerman created a shoe for his star runner by pressing lightweight foam rubber into his wife's waffle iron. The result was the first modern athletic shoe sole. In 1972, Bowerman added a "swoosh" logo to his sneakers, modeled after the wings of the Greek goddess Nike, and the rest is history. Meanwhile, Prefontaine became the face of Nike, as well as American distance running.

I had never before owned a pair of shoes that felt this light. They weighed zilch. Maybe five ounces. The waffle soles also provided better traction. They were made for running fast on the road. I loved them. The only problem: When I put the shoes on, they were slightly too big.

"Well, they're better than anything else you've got," Charlie said.

He was right, of course. I was a poor grad student. My running life offered no financial opportunities, and even if it did, I'd have to forgo them in order to maintain my amateur status, just like Prefontaine had. I didn't have money for state-of-the-art racing shoes. If Prefontaine hadn't sent me those Boston '73s a week before the marathon, I'm not sure what I would have done. After all, I wasn't likely to find a pair of brand-new, light-as-air, waffle-soled running flats, not even if I searched every Dumpster from Jamaica Plain to Dorchester.

Charlie walked with me to the starting line. The scene bordered on total chaos. There were no race officials, no volunteers to help corral the eager spectators. No ropes to hold anybody back. Just a feisty, bald, seventy-one-year-old barking out orders in a thick Scottish accent. This was Jock Semple. Longtime unofficial caretaker of the Boston Marathon. He alone arranged all two thousand racers, like some crazed conductor.

Jock spotted me and wildly signaled for me to come over. A serious long-distance runner himself in the 1930s, he was a tough, irascible Scot who saw it as his personal mission in life to preserve the tradition of the Boston Marathon. Jock had the final say on all matters pertaining to the event. He had no patience for anybody who didn't have the utmost respect for the race and its runners. To Semple, the Boston Marathon was a serious athletic contest for noble and daring men—and men only—willing to sacrifice body and soul to achieve excellence. Jokesters like Johnny "Cigar" Connors, who in 1935 ran the first couple of miles while toking on two cigars at the same time, and in 1937 crossed the finish line in pink panties, causing Jock to blow his smokestack. I was fortunate that Jock took a shine to me and gave me such a low number—#14, to denote my 1974 finish—ensuring that I was up front with the top runners.

Just before Jock whisked me to the front, I looked back at Charlie. For the first time, I saw a little fear register on his face. Maybe he was worried that the gloves, which I'd never worn before in a race, would irritate me. Or perhaps he was frightened that my feet would slide right out of my running shoes in midstride, revealing Prefontaine's gift to be a curse. Or maybe it was worse than that. Did he fear that I wouldn't finish? Was he thinking how I'd run out too fast in my first Boston Marathon and wilted on Heartbreak Hill? Or how I'd burst away too early last year and flamed out again on the brutal incline? I'm sure he wished he could tie a rope around my waist; that way he could hold me back when he felt I was running too fast a pace. He was not alone. Everybody in my life, all of whom were rooting hard for me today— Charlie, Ellen, Coach Squires, my GBTC teammates—wished at times they possessed a device with the power to settle me down. My parents sure could have used a device like that when I was a kid. Then again, knowing me, I would have found a way to break free. My brother knew this better than anyone. I always found a way to break free.

As I established my position at the starting line, I thought about my brother and how he might be competing alongside me if it weren't for his asthma. When he was a kid, his chest would tighten on long runs. Charlie also liked to point out that he got the short legs and long torso while I got the long legs and short torso. But I don't know about all that. I did know that I was glad to have a big brother like Charlie. I knew he would do anything for me, but there was nothing he could do for me at this point. He gave me the gloves and now my hands were warm. That might not seem like much help—not when it comes to competing in a marathon against a bunch of world-class runners looking to skin you alive on the roads—but for some reason, Charlie's small gesture of support meant the world to me. I didn't know if I could win, but I was not going down without one hell of a fight.

Jock Semple was the only person who thought I could win, or at least, the only person who dared state this opinion to the press. The reporters chalked it up to the wistful longings of an old man. After all, everybody knew it was Jock's dream to have a local runner win the Boston Marathon, which hadn't happened since Arthur Roth's victory way back in 1916. When the press scribes asked my GBTC coach, Bill Squires, about my chances for victory he'd told them: "Don't pick him. He's too inexperienced. A year from now, he'll blossom into the marathoner he should be, but not this soon against this field."

Jock's wishful thinking aside, there was no reason for the reporters to focus any attention on me—some kid who'd won a few local road races. Instead, the media trumpeted the course record holder, Ron Hill, the only British man to ever win the race. At age thirty-six, Hill was on the downside of his career, but he felt in his heart he had one last great Boston Marathon in him. Before the race, he told reporters that if he got a tailwind—watch out—he was going after his own record. He was talking about breaking 2:10. Coach Squires has set a goal for me of 2:15. I knew this would be a stretch. Last fall, I tried to break Tom Fleming's course record of 2:21:54 at the New York City Marathon and ended up finishing in fifth with a time of 2:35:59. A short time later, I did win the Philadelphia Marathon in the low 2:20s. And just a month ago, I had won the bronze medal at the World Cross-Country Championships, an international competition on par with the Olympics. Everybody from the world's best milers to the best marathoners competed in this single winner-take-all event. Claiming third against the best runners across the globe gave me a ton of confidence. I felt like if I had a great race that 2:16, maybe 2:15, was possible. At this stage in my career, hitting under 2:20 would be a huge accomplishment.

Tom caught my eye a few runners to my left. He wore a look of fierce intensity. Nobody wanted to win at Boston more than Tom or punished himself more training for it. The heavy mileage had paid off as Tom looked fit and strong. In his mind, nobody could beat him. All the top marathon runners felt this way. They were right to have felt this way. You need to have some cockiness to think you can pull off a win of this magnitude. But the truth is, no long-distance runner is invincible, no matter how good they think they are. The marathon will humble even the fittest competitor. It's what makes this race so exciting. It's as unpredictable as the weather in New England. And that's a good thing—at least if you're a spectator.

Pent-up energy wafted through the air as the runners waited to explode out of the gate like hostile wolves. At every marathon the runners were quiet and tense at the start line, but the feeling here was amplified. The reason was right before our eyes: a narrow stretch of country road, no more than fifty feet across, enough room for twenty runners at best, that dropped off the earth. Well, it only looked like it dropped off the earth. In truth it was just a steep, harrowing decline, roughly thirteen stories down.

I stood in the ready position, boxed in on all sides by runners, crouched and tense-faced in their racing bibs and short shorts. The pack drew in a collective breath. You could hear a pin drop as we all waited for the sound of the gun to pierce the silence. The excitement rushing through me threatened to spoil into nausea. This was it. We were like a huge time bomb about to explode. *Bang!*

The moment the gun fired I felt the soles of my Boston '73s hit the pavement. In twenty-six miles and 385 yards from now my life would be changed forever. Here I go.

EIGHT YEARS EARLIER
WESLEYAN UNIVERSITY, MIDDLETOWN, CONNECTICUT

When I entered Wesleyan University in the fall of 1966, the farthest I'd ever run was twelve miles and that was on a lark. I usually never did more than two or three miles in high school. One day, in late spring of my senior year of high school, I was out on a training run with the other members of the cross-country team, which included my big brother, Charlie, and best friend, Jason. I spotted a sign for the next town, six miles away. Without giving it any thought, I took off for it. Once I arrived there, I turned right around and ran back home. I didn't think anything of my long-distance dash. I wasn't looking for attention. I did it just to see if I could do it, and because I loved the feeling of floating along when I ran. Lo and behold, one of the reporters at the local newspaper caught wind of my accomplishment and all of a sudden it was in the paper: "Local Boy Runs 12 Miles!" That's how bizarre it was back in the early sixties to run long distances. Run twelve miles and people start checking behind the barbershop for your Klingon spaceship. Back then, doctors warned that you could drop dead from running that far. They theorized that we all have a certain number of miles in us—if you used them up too soon, you would die. Too much activity was bad for your heart; meanwhile, cigarettes were good for you. Seriously, this is what doctors were telling people in those days.

In my freshman year, I was a member of the varsity track and cross-country team. Wesleyan was a small New England liberal arts college—far from some track and field powerhouse like the University of Oregon. In fact, our freshman cross-country team had to default a couple of dual meets after failing to field five men. At Wesleyan, the focus was squarely on academics.

Although I won most of my dual-meet races my first year, there were half a dozen guys on the team who were faster than me. Still, nobody came close to touching our two standouts—Amby Burfoot, a junior from Groton, Connecticut, and Jeff Galloway, a senior from Atlanta, Georgia. I first met Amby Burfoot when I was a high school senior in Newington, Connecticut. It was a chance encounter. His younger brother was my main competitor in the Connecticut high school cross-country championships, and Amby came down from college to cheer him on.

I remember it was a beautiful fall day to race. From the start, I ran with a carefree abandon but I was also going for the win. Around the halfway mark, I broke away from the rest of the pack. Amby stood at the edge of the route, which ran along the fairways of a local golf course, and waited for the runners to come racing by. He suddenly saw me approaching, a good fifty yards ahead of the rest of the field. As I powered ahead down the rain-soaked path, I was too focused to hear Amby yelling from the side of the course: "Come on, Gary! You can catch him! Rodgers is fading!"

Amby's impression of me before the race was that I was this spacey blond-haired runt with a goofy running stride. Therefore, he was left stupefied as he watched me pull away from his brother, Gary, and the other top high school runners in the state, to finish first. I didn't know it at the time, but my convincing win is not what peaked Amby's curiosity, it was the way I floated along the course, almost with a vacant look in my eyes. To Amby, I wasn't so much running as gliding over the grass. Amby came up to me after the race and tried to sell me on coming to Wesleyan to run for the track team. And that's what I did.

While the rest of us on the team was gearing up for our next dual meet against some similarly small, academically minded liberal arts college like Trinity and Williams, Amby was pursuing a far greater and more daunting mission—to win the Boston Marathon—which no college student had ever done. Amby devoted his entire life to this one solitary goal. He was committed with a capital C and refused to let anything interfere with his strict training regimen, which stood in stark contrast to the relaxed and informal running program the others of us on the team followed. Amby would practice with us every afternoon, but he'd also take extra runs on his own, usually twice a day, one early in the morning, one after practice. He averaged up to fifteen miles a day; twenty on weekend days when he didn't have classes. He also would go out for a twenty-five-mile training run ever Sunday, a ridiculous distance as far as I was concerned. For the week, he ran anywhere between 120 to 150 miles. In 1968, you were more likely to come across Bigfoot than somebody putting in over a hundred miles of road work each week, let alone a college student. I'd never known anybody to work that hard for anything, least of all me.

I was amazed by Amby's drive and maturity. I was in awe that he knew what he wanted out of life, and that he was determined to go to any lengths, physically and mentally, to get it. Amby was always trying to get other runners on the team to join him on his daily training runs along the outskirts of campus. He wanted the company. Few people ever agreed to go with him. I loved the feeling of running outdoors, I had since I was a kid, and Amby's single-minded quest to conquer the marathon intrigued me so that I agreed to start going with him on his training runs.

If the Boston Marathon was Amby's Mecca, the place he could find running nirvana, then his local church was the trails that crisscrossed the periphery of the Wesleyan campus. Generally, we would go between seven to ten miles once a day.

Within minutes of leaving campus, we were moving side by side through the stunning countryside. Amby kept a nice, steady pace that was a delight to follow, whether we were climbing hills or cruising along flat, wooded trails. Amby would lead me over every type of terrain imaginable. We'd run loops around lakes. We'd go along cliffs. We'd climb up over rocks. Our runs felt like unchartered adventures.

Amby would take me out in every kind of weather. I discovered the exhilaration of running over snow. I got to know the beauty of running through spring showers. He was also responsible for completely changing the way I viewed running. My coach in high school was Frank O'Rourke, a tough, no-nonsense Irish Catholic whose infamous junkyard bark easily carried from one end of Newington to the other. Beneath his old-school bluster, however, he was a kind and paternal man who cared deeply for his players.

Coach O'Rourke, a former high school half-mile state champion, made it his mission in the fall of 1964 to turn our scraggly team of misfits and perennial losers into a powerhouse on the track. He had his work cut out for him. For one, none of us had any formal training. We had no clue about pacing. We ran full-out. And then the moment we crossed the finish line, we'd all collapse on the ground in a heap. Guys would get sick and throw up.

I recall him saying something to my parents when I joined the track team. He said to them, "Don't expect too much." I think Coach meant that I didn't really have a lot of genetic fast-twitch muscle fibers, i.e. I was scrawny. Or he might have just thought I was just too spacey, disorganized, and cheerful a kid to excel at sports.

Every afternoon in high school, Coach O'Rourke put us through vigorous calisthenics—push-ups, sit-ups, jumping rope—followed by interval training, a mix of high-intensity speed work and light jogging. We were expected to run as fast as the sprinters. He didn't make us chase chickens like Rocky's pugnacious coach Mickey Goldmill, but he did have a similar loud, gravelly voice that cut through our boyhood chatter faster than a blade. Also like Mickey, he never ran with us. Instead, he'd yell out splits in his gruff but encouraging way.

Coach worked us hard, at least harder than any track coach thought of training his team of runners in 1963. But he also infected us with his passion for running. He managed to get more out of me than anybody else had my entire life. I was the type of kid who was always making excuses not to run—too cold, too rainy, not feeling well, stomach issues. But I liked Coach O'Rourke and was willing to work hard for him. He showed interest in me. When you're young, you're looking for somebody who believes in you.

Our views did occasionally clash, however. I remember Charlie, Jason, and I started wearing our hair longer in high school. This drove Coach crazy. As Charlie would say, "It was a little too long for a good Spartan organization like the Newington track team." One day, O'Rourke decided to set us straight. He gathered us in his office and ordered us to cut our mangy mops. Jason pointed out to him that Tom O'Hara, an American kid, had broken the world indoor record in the mile in 1964 in Chicago. And he had long hair. "Long red hair!" I interjected. After that, Coach O'Rourke never bothered us again about our locks.

When I arrived on the Wesleyan campus, I carried with me Coach O'Rourke's views on running. Workouts should be tightly scripted. They should leave you exhausted and drenched in sweat. Beating people on the track over a distance of one or two miles is what mattered. But then something happened. Amby took me under his wing.

As I copied his easy and relaxed strides on our long runs, I began to discover what he already knew. Training need not be an all-or-nothing battle, involving punishing track practice, grueling calisthenics, and wrenching interval sessions every afternoon. It could be a fun and easy cruise through the gorgeous New England countryside. It could be an act of freedom by which I could step outside myself and my racing mind. A long run in nature could even be a way to connect my physical body with the unseen spirit of the universe. As much as I enjoyed my German literature class, that's not something that ever happened during a lecture.

Amby and Jeff never crushed us during our team's daily training runs, which they could easily have done. Instead, we always moved together through campus as a cohesive unit. Many of the top runners on the teams we faced had an aggressive, macho, cutthroat attitude. Which isn't to say that Amby and Jeff were not tough competitors, because they would go out there and annihilate you in a race. But generally speaking, Amby and Jeff had a far different perspective on running than most people in those days. They saw it as a fun thing to do. It was relaxing. It was social. It was a lifestyle.

From months of following Amby on his training run, I had slowly built up my mileage. He worked me up to the stage where I was running seventy-five miles a week. I was dedicated to a point, but nothing like him. I did the required workouts with the team, but I would sleep in on the weekends and miss runs, unless Amby woke me up and pulled me out of bed. I was a freshman in college in 1967—I was interested in exploring the social aspects of college life. I'd go out on the weekends and party. I started drinking alcohol for the first time as a freshman. I wasn't a big drinker in college. I only remember getting drunk once—as a freshman. I threw up.

I was enjoying all these new experiences (well, maybe not that last one). On the weekends, I would go with my friends to dances, maybe drink a few gin and tonics, smoke a few cigarettes. Nothing crazy. Normal college stuff. I liked my new social life and had no intention of curtailing the fun in an effort to excel as a runner. Why would I?

The rest of the week I focused on my academics, which I found to be much more demanding than they were in high school. I was never in danger of flunking, but I was at the bottom of my class. Jeff was the kind of generous person who would help me with my homework when I got behind, which was often. As I grappled with the demands of working part-time in the cafeteria and my tough coursework, my attitude toward running changed. While I was still motivated to do well in my dual meets, the main reason I ran was because it was a fun thing to do, and it relieved the stress that came from balancing a strenuous academic workload with a part-time job.

Running mile after mile along the tree-lined roads near campus with Amby was great. I knew I couldn't beat him—I never thought I could—but I'd try and stay with him. By just looking at Amby, you might not think he was a strong person, but I knew from running, side by side with him, just how incredibly fit he'd become. Sure, he looked like he was running on stilts, but he had developed terrific strength in his upper body and core. There was not a single imbalance in Amby's movements. His posture bordered on robotic. He was a machine.

The thing about Amby, he didn't have a lot of genetic inborn speed, meaning that at a hundred meters he was nothing special, but he had built up great cardiovascular strength from all the training he did. Amby didn't get tired. At least, I don't remember ever seeing him get tired. Most importantly, he had built up a psychological strength. The marathon is in the mind. Just because you can run eight or ten or even twenty miles at high speed doesn't mean you can do it over a full marathon. What the mind can conceive, the body can achieve. Maybe not in all cases—you need some natural talent to run a four-minute mile. But the marathon has a lot to do with willpower. You might not have thought it, looking at his Tin Man frame and nerdy glasses, but inside, Amby was tough as hell.

He reminded me of a modern-day Abebe Bikila, who'd begun running as a sheepherder's son in the remote mountainous village of Jato, Ethiopia. Years later, he stunned the world when he won the 1960 Rome Olympic marathon running barefoot, becoming the first black African to win a gold medal. He then broke the world record at the Mexican games before a car accident left him in a wheelchair. Both of us completely idolized this foreign athlete who we didn't even know. We always called him by his nickname, Abebe the Lionhearted.

Amby had the same tall, rail-thin frame at Bikila. But it was his solitary running life on campus that echoed the qualities of the Ethiopian champion—the stoic detachment, the fierce pride. Bikila's running coach once said, "Abebe was made by Abebe, not by me or anyone else."

Over many New England seasons, I had watched as Amby had made Amby. Herein lies the true power of running: With every mile you run, with every stride you take, you do more than reshape your body—you reshape your destiny. It would be a long time before I came to understand that myself.

Amby thought I showed real promise as a runner, which is why he was a little disappointed with my lackadaisical, half-assed approach to the sport. In Amby's world, I was a party boy. He would never chastise me, or pressure me to put forth more effort than I was willing, but he would always say things like, "You'd be a good runner if you ever became serious about it," or "Hey, Rodgers, you still drinking a bottle of gin tonight?" I didn't think there was anything wrong with my carefree lifestyle, or my lax attitude toward running. I was in college!

Amby was always trying to get me to go out with him on ten-to-fifteen-mile runs on the weekend. Once, during my freshman year, Amby managed to convince me to go with him on a fifteen-miler. It was my first long run (unless you count that fluky twelve-miler that made the local news). Here's what I recall: We ran at a nice, easy pace. Amby always set a moderate pace for himself, between six and a half and seven-minute miles, and I stayed with him for over an hour, but then my legs locked up on the fifteenth and I had to walk the final mile. So this is what it felt like to go beyond myself. Interesting.

As I mentioned, Amby would wake up every Sunday morning and run twenty-five miles as part of his preparation for the Boston Marathon. Amby knew there was zero chance of dragging me out of bed early on a Sunday morning, especially not after I'd been out partying late the night before. I needed some time to recover from my hangover before even beginning to consider lacing up my running shoes. So we struck a compromise. Amby would wake up before me and run the first ten miles on his own and then I would join him for the final ten miles. Call it the Burfoot–Rodgers Running Accord.

Amby would say to me, "Bill, I'm going to be on campus at ten, so why don't you meet me out in the middle of the football field or on the track around the football field." I would be waiting there and, sure enough, at ten o'clock to the minute, I'd see a tall, angular figure striding stiffly toward me. Amby was like clockwork. Blew my mind.

Amby had mapped out our course just as precisely as he had mapped out everything else in his life, from the moment he woke up at 6:30 a.m. to the time his head hit the pillow at exactly 9:30 p.m. Amby's actions were never without purpose. Even inviting me to join him on his training runs was about more than giving me a gentle nudge to grow up. Running with a partner helps you run faster and maintain focus. It also kicks boredom. In that way, I was a big help to Amby. Also, since I hadn't already run ten miles, I was fresh and could push Amby a little bit on the last half. If he had been out there by himself, he might have started sagging.

After leaving campus, we ran three or four miles uphill along Route 66, a country road without much car traffic. We ran at a good clip, tackling some serious hills, hilly enough that there was a small ski slope nearby. On the way back we would sneak off the road and run along wooded trails for a couple of miles. I loved following Amby through the winding and rugged dirt path, the sound of our footsteps trampling leaves and small branches. I loved the challenge. I would think: *Can I do this? Can I stay with him?* I wasn't afraid of pushing myself too far. It was fun.

Of course, our heads couldn't have been in more different places. The lanky figure running next to me was focused on being the first American in a decade to win the Boston Marathon. He was aiming to compete against the world's best marathon runners. I was aiming for my next college dual meet. His competition would be the mighty Finns, the fanatical Japanese, the world-class Mexicans; mine would be a kid named John Vitale from the University of Connecticut.

We would talk the whole way on our runs.

"How was your trip home?" I asked.

"Great. I went on some long runs through the countryside with Johnny. We ran hours through these amazing Indian trails near Mystic. After that, we went back to his place. We sat in the living room and chatted over tea and cookies. Well, actually, he talked; I listened. He's a wild guy to listen to . . . one of these great old Irish storytellers. He talks about Thoreau and Vonnegut and quotes Dylan lyrics. He talks about the dangers of the military-industrial complex. He talks about finding one's own place in the universe, even if it puts you at odds with the rest of society. He's just the best guy ever."

As fate would have it, Amby attended the Fitch High School in Groton, Connecticut, where his track coach was Young Johnny J. Kelley, who in 1957 became the first American to win the Boston Marathon since John A. "the Elder" Kelley, no relation, in 1945. The younger Kelley was a Running God in the fifties and not just in Boston, which was his home for a while, but around the world. He ran on two American Olympic teams and won eight consecutive national marathon titles at Yonkers, New York. Many consider him the first modern American road runner.

As the years passed, however, Kelley's great accomplishments faded in people's memory. Meanwhile, the one-mile race had become a national obsession, thanks to running sensation Jim Ryun, who in 1964 became the first high school runner to break the four-minute mile. As for the great American marathoners of yesteryear—seven-time Boston Marathon champion Clarence DeMar, John "the Elder" Kelley, Young Johnny Kelley—by 1968 they were all but forgotten. When no American came along to duplicate their success, the marathon went from having little visibility around the country to practically none. For the next decade, the Europeans and the Japanese would dominate the Boston Marathon. It looked like an American might never win there again.

Amby's father had died in a car accident early in his life, and in high school, Johnny Kelley became something of a second father to him. And just as John "the Elder" Kelley had taken a sixteen-year-old

Johnny Kelley to his first local road race, Johnny Kelley introduced young Amby into the secret and sacred world of New England long-distance running. In Amby, he found an eager pupil to lead on long runs through the countryside. Together, the tiny, gregarious Irish teacher and his tall, shy, Germanic student would traverse hilly pastures, splash through streams, and bound over rough old Indian trails, the locations of which were known by Kelley alone. Through his mentor, Amby became part of a tradition of rebellious New England road warriors who went back to that original long-distance racer, Paul Revere. And now he was taking the wisdom he had learned from the older runners who lived around the area—Johnny Kelley; Norm Higgins was another—and passing it down to me.

"How was your weekend?" Amby asked, the conversation moving as leisurely as our strides.

"Jason and some other friends came up to visit. We played some poker."

"Drank some beers," Amby added.

"Yeah, we might have had a couple," I said with a shrug.

"Sure. Just a couple," Amby replied with a dead-pan grin. "So, you thought about this summer?"

"What do you mean?"

"You should run five miles a day. If you do that, you'll come back in the fall, guns blazing in cross-country."

"That's a good idea," I said.

I meant it, too. It was a good idea. To my way of thinking: You do cross-country in the fall, then indoor track in the winter, and outdoor track in the spring. The summer was for goofing off with your friends. It was for relaxing, and going to the beach, to the movies, and to dances. If I was feeling particularly motivated, I might run five miles every third or fourth day. Amby subscribed to a slightly different philosophy. He'd be living and breathing running that summer.

As we ran shoulder to shoulder down the road, we could see the dorms in the distance on Foss Hill.

"I heard the girls there are having a mixer up there tonight," I said, sarcasm dripping.

"Should we go up there now and make dates?" said Amby. "I'm sure there's a couple of beautiful brunettes waiting for us."

"I think I see them right now. They're waving at us from the quad."

This was a common joke between us—the total absence of females at our all-male school. In fact, we spent many hours on the road discussing the opposite sex. What else is there really to talk about? Unfortunately, we had a lot more experience talking about girls than actually dating them. I remember having a crush on a gal in middle school. I think she knew I had a crush on her, too. I wanted to ask her out, but never followed through. Honestly, I was a terrible social misfit. I would go to a dance and sit in the stands and watch the more aggressive jocks talk to the girls. I remember wearing a clip-on tie to my first dance and one of my pals came over, yanked it off, and threw it away.

Between Charlie and me, he had far more success with girls in high school. Charlie was into cars, which was a cool teenage activity. (I was into collecting butterflies and running—not cool at all.) He was more outgoing. He was handsome and the girls liked him. In high school, he had a girlfriend. As for me, I was trying to meet somebody but without too much success—my silly glasses and scrawny build notwithstanding. No, I wouldn't be called a hunk by anybody's description. I was definitely a bit of a nerd in high school and during that era, it was not good to be a nerd, in any way, shape, or form. Running retarded me even more socially. Charlie and the rest of the cross-country team used to go to his girlfriend's to hang out when they were supposed to be out on workouts. They would do this right under Coach O'Rourke's nose. While they were drinking soda pop and making out in closets, I was out doing the entire workout by myself. I just enjoyed the sensation that running outdoors gave me.

Here, running alongside Amby through the trails and streams beyond campus, I was once again granted that same soaring rush of freedom. The part about those runs that Amby remembers most is how differently I ran along the road than he. Amby ran with this narrow focus, like some automaton, looking straight down the road. He ran inside of himself. He focused hard on his running effort and didn't see things in the environment around him. I was able to run with a more relaxed stride—"flowing" is the word Amby always thought of when he watched me run. I gazed all around me as I ran, whether it was at clouds drifting in the sky or birds nestling in the trees. I was always finding stuff that Amby never noticed: money on the road and things like that. I'd stop to pick up items on the side of the road, which I think drove Amby crazy. Running never felt like a chore to me; it was the opposite. Pure fun. I would run along the country road, singing the words of my favorite song to myself. "Here comes the sun, here comes the sun, and I say, it's all right."

Amby studied me closely, like I was some rare species of bird. For all his dedication and hard work, he was cursed to never know what it felt like to run effortlessly. He had to maintain his concentration as he ran and focus hard on every step he took. As he moved alongside me, he wondered, how was it that I could float along the road the way I did? I had no idea. I was just doing what I'd always done. I didn't know any other way to be. Ever since I was a kid, running felt as natural to me as breathing.

When we were boys, my brother, Charlie, and I would spend entire days running wild, or as wild as possible in our quiet, leafy suburban town of Newington, Connecticut. Our best friend, Jason Kehoe, who lived down the block from us on Thornton Drive, and who we'd known since we were two years old, always joined us on our boundless adventures. We were the three amigos, the Three Musketeers, inseparable.

We hiked trails, fished ponds, and played out our childhood fantasies in the thick woods behind our house. These woods were made for pint-size cowboys, junior pirates, and intrepid explorers. I'd bound over logs, rocks, and bushes. Sometimes we'd run around with bows and arrows, hunting for turtles, frogs, and snakes. We were like the tribe of rag-taggle Lost Boys in *Peter Pan*. God knows how many miles we covered! I've heard that Kenyan children are very active. It's normal for them to run to and from school and the market. No one walks, everyone runs. That's the way we were. We were always moving.

I think I enjoyed running even more than my brother and the other neighborhood kids. It suited my personality. I had all this energy and wasn't so good at directing it. I was always bouncing off the walls and hanging from the rafters. I found it difficult to sit in a classroom for eight hours each day. I preferred to be outdoors where I could burn off energy. I definitely had some form of ADHD. Today, I would have been given Ritalin. But back then, I was just a kid who couldn't sit still. My family and friends would just sigh and say with a little grin, That's Bill for ya. Always getting into something.

Charlie was the oldest among us, and the leader of our group. He was often cautioning Jason and me not to carry through with whatever dubious, high-flying action we were about to undertake. He might, for example, say to us, "Well, the farmer is rapidly approaching us on his tractor and he doesn't look too happy about you eating his corn, and maybe you shouldn't be taunting him as he bears down on us." Charlie would sprint away while Jason and I would continue to make faces at the farmer for another thirty seconds, before getting away by the skin of our teeth.

I was a notorious teaser, Tom Sawyer style. Sometimes I pushed too far, like the time I stood on my front lawn, taunting our neighbor Gerald with goofy faces. He stood glowering back at me across the street on his lawn. At once, Gerald marched over. There was a look of murder in his eyes. He clearly intended to punch me in the face. Gerald sprang on top of me, sending us rolling on the ground. Out of nowhere, Charlie rushed over and said, "You gotta get off, man! You're not gonna be hitting my brother!" But Gerald paid no heed, and was acting fairly crazed, so Charlie let him have it in the side of the head. Gerald got up and staggered away. That was the end of it. Although I had probably asked to be punched, it meant a lot that Charlie had come to my defense. I knew I could always count on him to make sure that no harm came to me, and it made us closer than any two brothers could be.

It seemed like I was always running afoul of some authority figure in our town. One time, the cops drove me up to my house after busting me for setting off fireworks. Another time, store detectives chased me out of a Sears Roebuck. Charlie, Jason, me, and Gerald used to sneak into a private pond to fish and someone would always end up chasing us away. We'd also go hunting with our BB guns in Stanley Park in nearby New Britain. Obviously, we weren't supposed to be doing that.

One time, we were having a grand time chasing after squirrels and ducks in Stanley Park. All of a sudden, we heard sirens. A police car pulled up. The four of us instantly bolted in different directions. So much for inseparable. I had a good hormonal system for moving when I needed to, and this definitely qualified. I must have set a personal record for running through whippy brush and prickers. They weren't going to catch me. I dove into a nearby pond and hid waist-deep in the safety of the thick reeds. Poor Gerald wasn't so lucky. He got nabbed.

As a boy, my favorite activity was chasing butterflies in the huge field near our house. It was here, dashing through the tall grass, wielding the homemade net I'd made with a pillowcase and broomstick, that I discovered my love for running. I'd spot a butterfly to add to my prized collection—perhaps a giant swallowtail or a red admiral or a luna moth—and chase after it like a bird of prey. Charlie and the other kids watched in awe at the speed with which I ran down the elusive, winged creatures. They couldn't fathom how, long after they had collapsed in a sweaty heap, I could still be charging back and forth through the field, armed with a butterfly net, a happy grin across my face. For some reason, I alone had been given the gift of being able to chase the fluttering butterflies for hours straight without tiring. I didn't understand it, and neither did my parents, Charlie, or anybody else close to me, but running outdoors for miles and miles felt like the most natural thing in the world to me.

I remember running through the field one day with my friends, the warm summer sun baking our scrawny limbs as sweat poured off us in sheets. I caught sight of Charlie zeroing in on a beautiful tiger swallowtail. I was about eighty yards away and broke into a tremendous sprint. At the last second, I swooped in with my net and snatched the fluttering creature just under Charlie's nose. For the first time in my life, I felt that fiery, competitive spirit overwhelm me. I knew then that nothing could ever match the thrill of running as fast and as far as my feet could take me.

As Amby and I continued to move in perfect stride along the quiet country roads on the outskirts of campus, chatting about silly stuff like girls and music, I took in the beautiful colors of the New England foliage and smiled. I couldn't believe that training could be like this; that I could feel like I did as a kid chasing butterflies with Charlie and Jason. Happy. Free. Flowing. "Here comes the sun," I sang to myself, soaring along the road. "Here comes the sun. And I say, it's all right."

Little did I know of the storm clouds gathering in the distance.

TWO

The Full Twenty Miles

APRIL 21, 1975
ASHLAND, MASSACHUSETTS

The spectators erupted in wild cheers as the field of two thousand runners broke from the starting line. It was like we had been shot out of a cannon—like dynamite going off. Adrenaline propelled the swarm of runners around me thundering down the straight, narrow road. In the mayhem, there was pushing and shoving and grabbing of shirts.

I was in a full sprint now. It was like the entire race was only three hundred yards, which is insane because it's actually a bit farther than that. I knew from my first two times here that I needed to reach the tight corner ahead of the swift-footed pack if I was to negotiate the steep turn down the hill. At the same time I was making a beeline for the corner, the crowds, with no rope to hold them back, pressed forward into the road. I weaved my way through the gauntlet of fire and managed to scramble up to the front of the ragged stampede.

The main thing now was to keep my wits as I fended off the horde of hell-bent runners nipping at my heels. To panic would have meant certain disaster. All of a sudden, the road in front of me took a sharp ninety-degree turn. The savage yells of the spectators were still ringing in my ears as I navigated the blind turn and started down the steep hill.

As I made my way through the crowded traffic, I watched some guy with absolutely no chance of winning go flying down the hill ahead of us. This happens at every marathon. He was somebody who wanted to be in the limelight—who wanted to be on TV. Or he was somebody who was just totally incapable of pacing himself. Every race I've ever run, there's been that guy.

I had learned from my past two experiences in the Boston Marathon to stay under control. Be the captain of my own ship. Let adrenaline and nerves take over and I'd be road kill before I reached mile one. That goes for all top runners. And there will be no use in bellyaching later to Jock Semple that the other runners nearly trampled you to death. Boston is Boston and you have to be able to handle what it throws at you.

At that moment, this meant fighting my way through a frantic barrage of flying elbows amid the noise of pounding footsteps. Yet my mind remained calm in order to clearly see what was going on around me; that way I could avoid danger in a split second. Nimbly sidestep a competitor about to step on my foot; duck out of the way of another guy about to trip and crash into my rib cage. Run calm, stay focused, and breathe, Bill. It's the only way to survive.

I emerged from the dicey start, alive and kicking. Only twenty-six miles to go!

Pace-setter Bernie Allen took the lead early in the race. I ran close behind with Tom Fleming and the other race favorites. We had shot down that first hill at a pretty high speed. This wasn't a day for hanging back and conserving too much energy, not with an overcast sky and a cool tailwind. For a New Englander like me, hot weather meant bad news, but on a perfect day like this I knew I could push it.

I was breezing through these early miles. I was feeling my way through the race. This is what the top marathon runners do. They are careful with it. I finally got this. It took getting beat up my first two times at Boston, and getting wrecked in the New York City Marathon the previous fall. But as I ran here through the first miles, I didn't try to go beyond myself. I was pushing it, but at the same time I was watching

it, making sure to run with the competition. I was actually staying behind the other top runners.

I spotted Tom Fleming wailing down the road. No surprise there.
Everybody knew Tom was a front runner. He liked to be out ahead,
pushing the pace, challenging anyone to duke it out with him, mentally
as well as physically. As I said, Tom trained hard. Now he was going to
find out just how hard the rest of us had trained. He was betting it
hadn't been as hard as he.

The lead pack started to spread out a little as we climbed the slight
incline heading out of Hopkinton. Contrary to popular belief, there are
more grades to Boston than just the Newton Hills. As a matter of fact,
few sections of the Boston Marathon course are totally flat. Here I was,
setting up exactly how I was going to run the race. Who were these runners pouring it on in front of me? Did it matter? Not to me. I didn't care
who was up there. They weren't going to run away from me.

As the rural road started to flatten out a bit, a small group of runners took off. I tucked in behind them. I didn't try to break away too
early. I didn't try to take the absolute lead. Some people need to be in
the lead. They need to control the pace. I don't know why. All top runners like to be near the front. But most times the winner doesn't take
the lead. Usually, the winner comes from the pack just behind the front
runners. It's a terrible position to lead. It makes you vulnerable. You
have a bulls-eye on the back of your skull. You are the hunted. Better to
be the hunter. Also, you can't draft anyone. You can't see what's going
on behind you.

I was not conscious about time. I was not looking at my watch constantly. I don't even think I was wearing one. I was concentrating on my
opponents, watching for signs alerting me to their state of mind. I
couldn't afford a momentary lapse in judgment; you wouldn't believe
how the outcome of such a lengthy footrace could turn on a dime, but it
can. It usually does.

We hadn't gone out more than a mile or so and the lead pack was already turning this into a race. I was not worried. I was so psyched I could hardly stand it. It was on. The question was: How much are these other runners willing to gamble? A better question: How much am *I* willing to gamble? Will my past flameouts here, caused as a result of going out too fast, hold me back? Or do I go for it? My mind considered this as I kept a nice even pace behind the leader.

I reached Ashland in the second mile. It's not a heavily populated area so there were less people cheering me on from the roadside. At that stage of the race, I was not going that hard; rather, I was running within myself. It was not unusual in the old marathon days for runners to push themselves from the gun. Runners would run as hard as they could and then keel over at ten miles. Only a small number of people had ever run a marathon, and so people didn't know how to train for them, or race them.

I was right where I wanted to be, floating comfortably behind the leader. The race was unraveling well, at least better than my previous ones. I took stock of my body. I was moving smoothly, landing softly on the balls of my feet, my head bobbing ever so slightly. I consciously held my form, which was flawless, unless you counted my right arm swinging freely across my body to compensate for a slight foot imbalance. I was breathing easy and feeling good. The new shoes felt great—light as could be—and I'd like to believe Prefontaine's gift guided my feet forward with each strike of the ground. It's at this point I locked into a rhythm, which I would stick to for the next several miles.

I think I might have passed by a couple of nurseries heading into Ashland. The thing is, I didn't care too much about the scenery around me. It was a simple foot race, you know. I didn't see the cheering spectators, or the fields and farms, or the sporadic homes that lined the road. I saw only my competitors and the ground zipping by under my feet and the minuscule section of world lying directly ahead of me. A week later, I could care about the nurseries and look through them and buy a plant.

As I wound my way through Ashland, I continued to evaluate my competition. Who am I racing? Who's in the lead? Who's this guy crowding me in the Mexican singlet? Right away, I could see he was a very good runner. Only top runners wear their national symbol on their chest, like the American flag or the maple leaf or the rising sun, or the Russians way back would have a Soviet symbol. The other guy wearing Joe's Pizza Shop? Not as much a threat.

No doubt the man pounding the pavement next to me—who happened to be Mario Cuevas, the top Mexican marathoner at the time—took one look at me in my handwritten BOSTON singlet, gardening gloves, and kooky headband and thought I posed as much danger to him as a puddle.

Everything I knew about Mario Cuevas I could glean running elbow-to-elbow with him. That's a whole lot more than you might think. The serious marathoner must be part superathlete, part Sherlock Holmes. Was Cuevas's running style smooth or awkward? It was smooth. Was he breathing light or heavy? Light as a breeze. Was the sweat pouring off his body? It wasn't. Did he look fit? He did. As fit as me? Well, we'd see about that.

The lead group—which comprised about eight of us—passed through the quick-alternating ups and downs that marked our route. We continued to flex our muscles in the cool tailwind. The temptation to try to push it in these perfect conditions was almost unbearable. It was the unspoken thought going through all of our heads: I may never again in my whole career have a perfect day like this to run a marathon. What are the chances it should come on the day of the Boston Marathon! The course record is just sitting there, waiting for one of us to break it. Why shouldn't it be my name etched forever in history? Or be spoken in the same breath as great past champions like Clarence DeMar, Tarzan Brown, Gérard Coté, John "the Elder" Kelley, and Johnny Kelley? Victory doesn't come any sweeter than that!

But this was also going through all our minds: Push my body too hard and too fast and it might rebel against me. Maybe not after five miles or ten miles, but the deeper and deeper you go into the race, the greater the chance you'll suddenly find yourself drained of any more fighting energy. One mile you're in the lead, the next mile you're zapped like a bug in a microwave. Limping to the side of the road, crippled with cramps, doubled over in pain. That's why there's no sport like the marathon. It's a little over two hours of unexpected twist and turns in the plot; a twenty-six-round fight in the ring while moving at a five-minute-mile pace.

Believe me, there's a lot of wishful thinking going on before the starting gun fires—and some serious self-deluding. We're all hard-striving athletes who think we can do it. We can conquer the beast. This makes it difficult at times to hear what our intuition is trying to tell us. It's only once we're out on the course that the numerous pitfalls of running that hard for that long come to light. Only then do we become achingly familiar with how the race can weaken our body and tear at our spirit.

The race is a great unveiling—an unfolding of how we feel, psychologically and physically, on that given day. And 26.2 miles is a long way to run, and no matter how well we think we've prepared, situations will arise along the course that weren't in the brochure. A lot can happen to the body—and the mind—over a distance of 46,145 yards. I knew this. I also knew the race wasn't over until I actually crossed the finish line.

No matter how fit or strong we all thought we were, the course could pound any one of us into flaming wreckage. Maybe the heat does you in. Maybe it's severe dehydration that forces you to stop. Maybe it's a pulled hamstring that derails your quest. Or it could be somebody just ran better than you.

Yet we all hold out hope that on this Patriots' Day the stars will align for us—my body will respond to all the hard training I've done, Mother Nature will hear my heartfelt pleas, I'll put together the race of my dreams. In this way, preparing for a marathon is a bit like planning for a miracle.

The marathon is the essence of the unknown transforming into the known; there's always as much potential for destruction as there is creativity, as much chance of misery as there is elation, as much room for heartbreak as there is for triumph. That's the fun of racing a marathon. It's about seeing if you can go to the very edge without going over the cliff. Can you handle twenty-six miles at the same blistering pace as the guy next to you—in this case, a lean and muscled Mexican wolf named Mario Cuevas?

I was about to find out.

SEVEN YEARS EARLIER
BOSTON, MASSACHUSETTS

The year was 1968. Most people remember it for the turbulent presidential election that brought Richard Nixon to power, the shocking assassinations of Martin Luther King Jr. and Robert F. Kennedy, and the wave of student protests that swept across American campuses, as well as around the globe, from Paris to Prague to Mexico City.

While these events deeply altered my reality, what I remember most about 1968 was my college roommate Amby taking me into the mysterious, unknown world of long-distance running. Amby taught me everything there was to know—from how to build up my endurance to taking care of my body. "Don't overrace," he would tell me. "And get a lot of sleep." But he did more than that—he acted like a big brother, which was lucky for me, considering that for the first time in my life, I didn't have my own big brother, Charlie, to watch out for me.

Starting my sophomore year, Amby and I roomed together. Our dorm room was split down the middle. Amby kept his side very neat, and almost completely bare, other than textbooks, lots of running shoes, jars of vitamins, wheat germ, and Tang—all under the bed. As for me, I slept on a mattress on the floor, had a turntable stereo, a candle lamp made from a red wine bottle, and all sorts of odds and ends—press clippings, loose change, used matchboxes—floating haphazardly around.

Personal grooming habits aside, we had both been raised in lower-middle or middle-class families and now we were at a preppy school. The other kids had a lot more material stuff than we did. We both worked at the cafeteria to help pay for our tuition. Sometimes at night in our dorm room, I would flip on my stereo and play Simon and Garfunkel. I loved the soaring harmony of that one song: "I am a rock, I am an island." I'd call out to my roommate: "We've gotta be a rock, Amby! We gotta be hard! Go it alone!"

Amby would run eight miles before coming to work at around 8:00 a.m. I would be buttering toast in the kitchen as he came through the cafeteria line. We always ate breakfast together. Amby ate like a Buddhist monk. I couldn't do that. I was brought up eating meat and potatoes and putting butter on everything. Of course, I've always been an oddball when it came to food. I'd put ketchup on brownies, peanut butter on eggs, and mayonnaise on hot dogs. Amby would go to the cafeteria in the morning and pile whole grains, fruit, yogurt, and about eight glasses of fruit juice on his tray. For a six-foot-tall guy of 140 pounds, he consumed healthy food like a rhinoceros. Sitting together in the cafeteria, Amby would look over at his plate and then over at mine and shake his head in mild repulsion.

In all the time I roomed with Amby, I never saw him put anything bad in his body, negative in his mind, or take a day off from his training regimen. He bordered on monklike in terms of how he lived. He didn't drink, he didn't smoke, and he was a vegetarian. Nobody was a vegetarian in those days. But if Johnny Kelley didn't eat meat, then neither did Amby. If Johnny Kelley ate wheat germ, then so did Amby. If Kelley believed in going on *two* long runs a day, an insane, even dangerous notion at the time, then it was two-a-days for Amby. You wouldn't find

Amby's radical training regimen in any running guides because, well, there weren't any running guides. What he was doing didn't have a name. It was that cutting-edge.

Amby was always trying to get me to compete in a local road race with him, but I resisted. With good reason, too. The races Amby was talking about me competing in were ten, fifteen, sometimes twenty miles long. I couldn't imagine racing that far. It was insane. But Amby thought I was a natural for longer distances. I disagreed. My goal was winning my dual meets in the two mile. That was hard enough.

In February of my sophomore year, Amby finally convinced me to run my first long road race: a half marathon in Durham, Connecticut. I could only hold out against Amby's positive encouragement for so long, and who knew, maybe it would be fun.

By the time Amby and I arrived at the starting line a blizzard had swept down on us. The blowing snow felt like pinpricks on my face as I took my place at the start with the other runners. I stood there, shivering on the middle-of-nowhere country road, wearing a pair of baggy gray sweatpants and my grandpa's red woolen Monmouth College football sweater. To complete the absurdity of my outfit, I didn't have a hat or gloves on.

Once the race got under way, I sprinted to the front with Amby and the lead pack. I should have run conservatively, considering that this was my first time racing over five miles, and I practically needed a Sherpa to guide me through the raging snowstorm. But I was an aggressive cross-country runner, through and through.

I charged along the hilly back road, snow pelting my eyes. But, try as I might, I didn't have the firepower to hang with Amby. His pace was too fast. All of sudden, I lost sight of him in the icy whiteout conditions. One by one, the more experienced runners passed me on the snowy, desolate road.

I had no idea how many miles I had run—there were no mile markers—but I knew exactly how many water stations I'd seen. Zero.

As for the plow guy who drove past me in his truck, he had no clue what I was doing running in a blizzard. To be fair, at that moment, neither did I.

As the miles wore on, my grandpa's letter sweater with the big M on it had become soaked through with snow and sweat and then froze. I felt the full brunt of the swirling winds—what I couldn't feel were my fingers. My biggest worry, besides hypothermia, was running clear off the course and tumbling into some icy ditch. See, there were no volunteers on the side of the road to guide my way. No spectators to cheer me on. It was just me out there, alone and miserable, hoping to reach the finish before I froze to death.

When I staggered across the finish line, my ears were stinging red, my lips cracked, my legs cramping badly. What was Amby thinking? I was not a natural long-distance runner. I couldn't compete against these serious road racers. It would be five years before I tried racing that far again.

Of course, I had made a mess of things. First, I should have dressed in layers, and worn lightweight clothing and a winter hat and mittens. Of course, this was 1968, outdoor sportswear such as Gore-Tex didn't exist. That stuck with me, the need for better equipment in our sports. What's more, I'd gone out fast and hard, like it was another high school cross-country race. I ran the way I'd always run; it had worked for me in the past. I had always won my races before. I was still too young and foolish to heed Amby's lessons: Build your strength in training, strategize before each race, go in with a plan, pace yourself during the race, read your opponents, feel out their weaknesses, know when to attack and when to hold back, and move with steady, relentless focus. Basically, race smart.

Unlike most of the students who went to Wesleyan, I hadn't been at the top of my class in high school. I wasn't a natural scholar like my dad. Nor was I anything like Amby, who not only dominated on the track, but also thrived academically. I remember once walking by Amby's desk and seeing a psychology paper marked with an A. I had never gotten an A. I was struggling to maintain a C average. I took religion, Russian literature, German literature. I loved reading, so those were enjoyable subjects for me. For a little while, I started majoring in economics. But math scared me. I struggled with statistics. Then I became interested in sociology. I enjoyed that. It gave me something to sink my teeth into. But I only ever got by.

I used to think I wanted to become a lawyer because my mother's father had been a prominent judge in Hartford. He was this feisty Irishman who'd graduated from law school in 1906. If you were Jewish or Irish, good luck getting into the world of law. But he did. He was definitely not part of the establishment; he was an independent thinker of the New England variety. They called him the "human dynamo." He used to take stairs two at a time. That was just his mentality. Of course, I also used to take stairs two at a time.

I remember he had a heart attack and Charlie and I went to visit him in the hospital. He was flittering around the room like a butterfly trapped in Tupperware, and shouting, "Get me out of this place!" I understood his panic and frustration at being restrained from motion. As a boy, I spent many days struggling like crazy to get loose, flapping my wings frantically to fly off.

I know I inherited my feistiness from my mother, who got it from her father. She was a nurse's aide at Newington Hospital and an Irish Catholic of the highest order—she had me in December of '47. Charlie was born exactly twelve months before and my sister, Martha, showed up thirteen months after. Our mother was a tiny bundle of wound-up energy. Back then, she was a proud five feet and one quarter inches. Today, she's down to four feet, ten inches and eighty-five pounds and you know what? She still has more energy than most twenty year olds.

In addition to giving me the gift of a nonstop motor, my mother also passed on to me her profound sense of empathy for the sick and less fortunate. My cousin Paul had cerebral palsy and I remember feeling sympathetic toward him. I'd ask myself, What if that was me? What if I couldn't run through the woods chasing after squirrels with my friends?

For some reason, I always gravitated toward people like Paul. I found those who were off to the side more interesting than those in the mainstream. I remember one guy in high school named Arthur. He was very bright but severely disabled. He couldn't join the track team with us, that's for sure. I would call him "Arturo" because we used to practice our Spanish on each other. Back in those days, there wasn't much concern for people like Arthur. But I liked him and we became best pals.

I suppose I was like my father in that way. He'd talk to anybody and everybody. I've been known to talk to winos on the street for twenty minutes and then give them a dollar bill. Charlie will be telling me, "Now, Bill, don't give him any money. He's just going to get drunk and fall down on the ground." But I can't help get into a personal interaction with these guys. My mother wouldn't give them one second of her time, but my father would. He'd be sitting there, having a long conversation with them, like me.

My dad is a far more methodical, slower moving character than my mom, who's as easy to track as a bumblebee. He started as a professor at Hartford State Technical College and rose to the position of head of mechanical engineering. I never saw where the man worked, nor did I have a clue about the theoretical math he taught. I'd understand my dad much better as I got older, but as a kid, all I knew about him was that he worked a lot. Even in the summer, he'd write books and travel to New Mexico on research projects. My brother and I sometimes didn't understand his solemn devotion to his career. Later in life, I would meet people who were his students, including my brother-in-law. They would tell me: "Your dad was a great teacher. He changed my life." I didn't know of this kind of thing. My dad was not a bragging kind of guy. He had strong opinions, for sure, but he shied away from talking about himself. I suppose a lot of fathers were like that back then.

While I got my rambunctious energy from my mom's side, I had a quiet persistence, which came from my father's side of the family. Our paternal history traces back to a seventeenth-century bagpiper from Crieff named Patrick Rogie. The ancestor who came over to the New World from Scotland was a Protestant minister and a medical doctor. He went out and settled in the woods of Virginia. He educated all his sons. They became good writers and readers. Many of my father's colonial ancestors attended college in the middle of nowhere. I don't think there was any braggart stuff going on back then—you did the job and that's all. Charlie and I descended from these tough, hard-working, and quiet Scottish people.

I remember my dad taking Charlie and me down to the Peabody Museum of Natural History at Yale University to show us just how far along we'd evolved as humans. But seeing the diorama of cavemen bursting into a high-speed footrace to chase down their prey, I knew my need to move was nothing new. We were meant to move. We were meant to run. We had been for thousands of years.

My father was also fascinated with flying—Charles Lindbergh, World War II airplanes, the aviation industry. He grew up building remote-control planes and sometimes he would take us out with him to fly his plane. In some ways, his thinking was very nuts and bolts, but he also had a larger worldview. He passed that on to Charlie and me—a certain sense that anything is possible, that you could do anything.

Open, friendly, easygoing, optimistic, spacey—I would say that I shared all these attributes with my father. Charlie would always say, "Dad's off in quasar land again." I guess that I, too, was prone to getting lost in the clouds. Once, I remember playing some game out in the front yard with Charlie, Jason, and a few other neighborhood kids, and I said, "Well, I'm going to go in and use the bathroom."

They were all waiting outside for me to return so they could resume the game. A good amount of time passed by. "Where the hell's Bill?" everybody asked. Finally, Charlie went in the house and walked upstairs, and there he found me lying on the bed, reading a book. I'd completely forgotten about the game.

My dad and mom were not too happy with all the trouble I conjured up for myself as a kid. I was lucky to have good, loving parents. They showed a lot of patience with me—and they sure needed it. Then one day Charlie, Jason, and I joined the track team. We were no longer Lost Boys running wild in the woods. We returned to school new men. We were runners. And once I found running, everything changed. Imagine pouring water on the ground. Goes all over the place, right? Pour that water into a channel and suddenly you have a stream and then a river and then a raging, powerful body of water that can't be stopped. Running was my channel and I poured myself into it full force.

While I was a productive member of the Wesleyan cross-country and track team, I didn't train nearly as hard as I did in high school. I wasn't like Amby, living by the "devote everything to your running" creed. I'd go out partying with my buddies on weekend nights and get back at around four in the morning. As I carefully crept into the dorm room, I'd know that Amby had been asleep since 9:30.

While I saw two days without classes as an excuse to party, Amby saw it as an opportunity to get in longer runs. The notion of sleeping in Sunday morning was as absurd to Amby as, well, me waking up early on God's day of rest to go on a little twenty-mile run.

Almost every weekend, Amby would go home to run with Johnny Kelley. His departure was my cue to ring up my high school buddies and tell them to drive up for the weekend. Jason and a couple other high school pals would show up with a few beers already in them and we'd have a miniparty in my dorm room. We listened to rock music on my stereo, killed some beers, maybe stopped by a mixer in the vain hope of meeting girls.

I made sure that nobody did anything in Amby's room or touched any of his stuff. I knew he would know if so much as a strand of wheat germ was out of place. Of course, Amby would return to find me on the mattress on the floor, curled up under my blanket. I don't think it was that he was mad at me for throwing my little parties or missing runs. But I could sense his frustration that I didn't do more with the gift I had.

In the eyes of Amby, I was a party boy. And I never even thought of trying to get my roomie to come out with me on the weekend. Hit a Saturday night keg party? No way. Amby detested beer and, more importantly, he had to rouse himself at 6:30 a.m. for his ritual Sunday morning 20-miler. A weekend skiing trip? Not a chance. Skiers twisted their knees and broke their ankles and risked countless other injuries. Go on a simple dinner or movie date? Not those either. Amby had no time for flirtations or anything that might muck up his marathon ambitions.

Through the open door, I'd hear Amby listening to "The Impossible Dream" from the famous Broadway musical *Man of La Mancha*. In that year, 1967, Red Sox fans adopted it as their theme song when the home team made its miracle run to the World Series. I knew that to Amby the words struck a more personal note: *To dream the impossible dream. To fight the unbeatable foe. To bear with unbearable sorrow. To run where the brave dare not go.*

There was no question that winning the Boston Marathon was Amby's impossible dream. I did look at my roommate as if he were slightly mad, like the figure of Don Quixote, attacking windmills that he believed to be giants. Maybe it was because I didn't possess my own "impossible dream"—I never wanted anything with the passion that Amby possessed for conquering the Boston Marathon. He had a yearning in his blood to fulfill his quest. I didn't understand it, but it fascinated me.

On a Sunday morning in March of 1968, the Burfoot–Rodgers Running Accord was broken.

We were three weeks away from the Boston Marathon, the race Amby had been training for since the day we met, as if his life depended on it. He wanted to get in one last, hard workout before Boston.

He decided that he'd run twenty-five miles that Sunday—he also decided that his training partner would be joining him, whether or not he was working off a hangover.

It was around eight in the morning. I was fast asleep on the mattress on the floor. The whole campus was sleeping. That is, except my roommate. With the stale smell of pot still wafting down our hallway, Amby sat at the edge of his bed, his coins stacked perfectly beside him on the sparse dresser. He reached down his spiderlike arms and laced up his running shoes. He'd already had a bowl of granola, around ten glasses of orange juice, and a shot of wheat germ.

Next thing you know, I felt a hand rousing me from my slumber. I wiped the sleep from my eyes and saw Amby towering over me like a gangly willow tree. He had a look on his face that I'd never seen before, and I knew what it meant—lace up your shoes, soph, because today you're running the whole route with me.

Moments later, we were running stride for stride through the empty quads, while the early morning sun crept over the treetops, and the smell of wet, thawing grass filled our nostrils. The slanting rays of the sun hit our frames as we passed between each massive stone building. I could have sworn that Amby was starting out at a faster pace than normal.

We turned on to Route 66 and ran a few miles uphill, the elms and oaks that lined the country road passing by us in a blur. We then headed into the larger Middletown area, toward the banks of the Connecticut River. I was a little groggy, a consequence of my seriously low threshold for gin and tonics, but as we got moving I felt good.

Amby veered off the main road and onto a rough-and-tumble dirt trail. Instinctively, I swung in behind him. I was up for the adventure. I followed Amby as we traversed the trail, weaving around streams and rock formations. Racing up steep hills and banks, coasting down the other side, I felt a rush of adrenaline. The emotions flooding my body were a link back to my childhood in Newington and those aimless summer days chasing around with Charlie and Jason. By the time we reached a small lake, twelve miles from campus, I had a tight hold of that wild, free-roaming spirit of my youth.

As we roared around the shimmering water on that warm spring day after a long winter, I took it all in: birds chirping, blue skies, tranquil breezes. I passed some wild apple trees, their swelling pink buds ready to burst. It was the kind of day that made you glad you were alive—warm and still and sweet.

I was so lost in the world around me I didn't realize we had covered the first thirteen miles at a 6:30-per-mile pace. Or that Amby was running with an aggression that he'd never shown before on a training run. His eyes radiated intensity as he stepped up the pace. I think he was fed up with seeing me drift effortlessly on his shoulder while he attacked the road with focus, with precision, and with perfect form.

After we finished the loop, we started on the twelve miles back to campus. Amby asked if I was doing okay. I told him I felt great. In fact, I felt exuberant. I'd never thought of running this far and fast before. Suddenly I was doing it.

We were moving at a good clip now over a constant stretch of rolling hills, flying by old stone walls and ridges dotted with family farms. Amby kept running faster and faster, trying to drop me the whole way. He upped the pace to six-minute miles. But to Amby's disbelief, I wasn't fading.

Around Mile 18 I surged ahead of Amby for a moment. Amby's jaw nearly scraped the ground. After all, he had been training about 120 miles a week; I was putting in maybe forty. He had completed numerous twenty-five-mile runs; I had almost never gone beyond ten miles. Amby had done a full year on the New England road racing circuit from Cape Cod to northern New Hampshire without ever losing a race. He was the best long-distance road racer in New England and here I was, this part-time runner who'd run a couple of five-mile road races, challenging him every step of the way.

We hit Mile 23 and Amby and I were running elbow to elbow. I felt great. I always ran on emotion and at that point the adrenaline was pumping. Amby was a methodical runner; he relied on patience and experience. I didn't know what I was doing!

Amby picked up the pace again.

It couldn't be happening, but there it was—I was still there, floating easily alongside Amby. This was more than he could take.

With two miles to go, Amby, without so much as a glance in my direction, said, "Hey, Bill, I'm gonna pick it up now." I was welcome to tag along if I wanted. All at once, Amby kicked into another gear, one I'm not sure that even he knew he possessed. He ran those last two miles as hard as he could go—as if it were the end of the Boston Marathon. I sped up just enough to stay even with him.

Amby was moving now at a five-minute-mile pace, and I was determined to match him stride for stride. All of a sudden, a cramp shot up my leg like a bolt of lightning. Just like that, my muscles waved the white flag. I was instantly reduced to a hobble. I watched Amby disappear down the road, leaving me in the dust.

Perhaps Amby had wanted to simulate the big race coming up, which is why he ran those final two miles back to campus with all his might. Or maybe my roommate needed to teach me one last lesson. He had to show me that I had a natural gift for distance running, a gift that he himself had been denied. But that unlike me, he was willing to put in the long, hard miles, to endure the pain, to make the sacrifices, to test the limits of his heart. For this reason, he was on the road to becoming a marathon champion, while I was on the road to nowhere. His story would be one of hard-thought victory. Mine would forever be one of squandered talent.

THREE

Blown off Course

Perhaps the only thing more difficult than winning the Boston Marathon is describing the journey—what you see at this or that mile. It's like asking a Kentucky Derby jockey to describe everything he sees outside the rails while he's racing around the track. "The only time you can be with God is in the immediate moment," a pastor once told legendary jockey Pat Day. "You can't be with him five minutes ago, or five minutes from now. Only now, this instant." I would add: The only time you can run your best race is in the immediate moment. The trick is staying in that present state of mind over two hours and 26.2 miles. Few succeed.

No doubt I passed by thousands of spectators, historic clock towers, railroad stations, storefronts, factories, homes, farms, but my eyes zeroed in on something far more crucial. The man running silently in my shadow.

I couldn't read his eyes—he wore dark sunglasses that hid them. I couldn't read his face—he wore a mask of emotionless stone. Even his thin, black mustache was inscrutable. All I knew was that he was a Canadian. He wore a giant maple leaf on his singlet. After the race, I would learn his name: Jerome Drayton. To this day he is Canada's greatest marathon runner—incredibly, he still holds the national marathon record he set thirty-eight years ago.

I glanced over my shoulder again. Drayton was no longer shadowing me. While I sensed I hadn't heard the last of the cryptic man in shades, my immediate concern was the man pulling even with me. I instantly recognized him: Britain's greatest marathoner, Ron Hill. The 1969 European champion. The 1970 Commonwealth champion. The man who zapped me in the San Blas Half Marathon in Puerto Rico. The man who hasn't missed a day of running since December 20, 1964. That kind of personal commitment is what his fellow British runner Roger Bannister meant when he spoke of "the challenge of the human spirit."

In 1970, the people of his tiny hometown of Accrington, England, passed around a collection cup and raised enough money to send Hill to Boston to compete. Running in a 40-degree downpour and nasty headwind, Hill won the race in a course record time of 2:10:30, becoming only the second man ever to break the 2:10 barrier. "I had no idea what time I was running—I didn't have a watch and the mile markers were weird, like the one that said '4¾ miles to go.' I couldn't believe it when I found I'd run a 2:10 personal best. For winning, I got a medal and a bowl of beef stew." That's right. No prize money at Boston. To be fair, it was delicious stew.

I greeted Hill's arrival with silence. Our shoulders were practically rubbing, but I let my ground-devouring strides do my talking. He was hard to miss as he ran. He was shorter than the other racers with his stout legs, coal black hair, handlebar mustache, and cheeky shorts emblazoned with the Union Jack, which he had designed himself. It irked me that he owned the course record. I felt an American should hold the course record. It irked me that foreign runners had dominated the event since the 1930s and the days of American champions like Clarence DeMar, Les Pawson, Tarzan Brown, and John "the Elder" Kelley. (In the previous three decades, a mere trio of Americans—my roommate Amby Burfoot in 1968, his coach Young Johnny Kelley in 1957, and fellow conscientious objector Jon Anderson in 1973—had captured the ultimate prize in marathoning.)

As we approached Framingham, the crowds continued to dwindle and for miles we passed only a small number of spectators on the road. It was quiet and calm now. Side by side, Ron Hill and I swung past Bracketts Pond and followed the course as it snaked uphill through the mostly wooded area. The way Hill was matching me stride for stride, I felt compelled to respond to the challenge. The adrenaline was flowing and I had plenty of fight. I refused to shrink in the awe-inspiring presence of the course-record holder. I was thinking feisty. There's "Ron the Hill." I told myself. As in "thirty-six years old and over the hill." He's had a legendary career but his best days have come and gone. This is my time.

In many ways, I ran best when I was right next to somebody. My competitive instincts kicked in and I went into another mode of being. "When he wasn't running, Bill seemed like the gentlest—and spaciest—guy in the world," Alberto Salazar once said. "But once he laced up the training flats, the starling turned into a swooping bird of prey. Bill just soared on a breathtaking, light-footed stride."

Sometimes, in the thick of the battle, I overreacted to the competition and let my primitive brain run riot. In other words, I raced stupid. Too much from the gut. But reacting emotionally to a situation is a part of who I've always been, ever since I was a scrawny runt, battling Charlie and Jason to catch elusive butterflies in the fields, or a little later, running my heart out through the forest trails as a member of my high school cross-country team. At times it's gotten me into trouble—big trouble—but other times my feistiness proved to be a great weapon. In order to win the race, sometimes you have to go a little berserk.

I can't tell you the exact time in a marathon race to succumb to that animalistic nature—to lose *a bit* of control and fight with fury. But I promise you, it's not after the first mile, or the second, or the fifth, or even the tenth. There's too many tough miles left to withstand such an early release of aggression. Even squandering a little of your energy reserves early on can spell doom later when the race toughens up, when it takes every bit of energy you can muster to outlast your opponent. How about Mile 16? Maybe you can lay the hammer down with a surge of speed and break away from the competition. Just maybe. You still have ten more miles to go, so you'd better know you have the strength and stamina to finish strong. It's easy to confuse bravery with foolhardiness. With that said, if your goal is to win the race, and not just finish it, then at some point you need to trust your talent and your instincts and go for it. Three miles into the race, running stride for stride with Hill, I told myself to be patient: You'll know when the time is right to make your move. It's not now.

I attacked the upgrade going from Ashland into Framingham. If you're feeling bad here, something has gone horribly wrong for you. You did not run smart, you went out way too fast, or whatever you ate the night before isn't agreeing with you. Regardless, you're probably not going to finish. You're definitely not going to win. I know because this is what happened to me my first time. Ran too fast. I was in too much of a hurry. I had no clue what I was doing. That's a bad way to run a marathon. It's a bad way to go through life.

Hill and I remained shoulder to shoulder as we sped along the road to Framingham, about five miles into the race. With a stiff wind at our back, neither of us was willing to yield to the other. We flew past a nondescript stretch of the course that, eight years earlier, had been the scene of a brief but historic confrontation. Back then, women weren't allowed to run in the marathon. Twenty-year-old college junior Katherine Switzer showed up and registered as K. Switzer, fooling the race officials, who assumed she was a guy. Karl or Kevin perhaps?

Once Jock Semple got wind of the interloper on his course, he jumped on the press bus and took off in a rage. Jock spotted Switzer. He couldn't believe that somebody would have the gall to engage in subterfuge to get a number. He felt tricked. He thought she was another prankster in the vein of Johnny "Cigar" Connors, out to make a mockery of his serious athletic event. What Jock didn't understand was that

Katherine Switzer was a serious athlete, who had been training hard with a coach for the past year.

A crimson-faced Semple leaped off the press bus, chased after Switzer, and tried to rip the bib off her gray sweatshirt. "Get the hell out of my race and give me that number!" bellowed Jock. Her hulking boyfriend, Tom Miller, a collegiate hammer thrower who was running beside her, threw a body block that sent the sixty-four-year-old flying through the air. The photographers on the press bus captured the altercation and the next day the pictures of this crazy little Scotsman attacking a woman runner were featured in major media outlets around the world.

Overnight, Switzer was held up as a defiant hero. When she crossed the line in four hours and twenty minutes, she didn't just become the first woman to officially finish the marathon, she had broken down a major barrier for all female athletes. It was a big moment for women's sports. Unfortunately, poor Jock was portrayed as some women-hating Neanderthal. To his credit, after the incident, Jock took steps to make amends. After Switzer ran Boston in 1972, the year that woman were finally welcomed to run, he congratulated her with a kiss in front of the cameras. The pair formed an unlikely friendship that endured until Jock's passing in 1988. On his deathbed, he laughed and told Switzer, "Oh, I made you famous."

It's a pity that Jock Semple is mostly remembered for trying to pull Switzer off the course that day in 1967. He was one of the race's top competitors during the 1930s, and, as *Runner's World* put it, "a one-man volunteer staff (with Will Cloney as race director) for decades during a period when no one else cared much about the marathon." Simply put, nobody did more to preserve the heart and soul of the Boston race than Jock.

Just past the five-mile mark, the mysterious Canadian Drayton opened a small gap on the lead group, which included me, Ron Hill, Tom Fleming, Mario Cuevas, Steve Hoag, Richard Mabuza from Swaziland, and Peter Fredriksson of Sweden. I love marathoning when this happens. A small group of leaders jockeying and rejockeying for position, watching and waiting to see who is going to make their move. The eight of us were within arm's reach of one another as the course led us through a small residential area. I felt the wind in my hair as our powerful strides devoured the road under us. I knew we were moving fast. Did I know we were twenty-four seconds behind Hill's all-course record? How could I?

SEVEN YEARS EARLIER
WESLEYAN UNIVERSITY,
MIDDLETOWN, CONNECTICUT

It was the spring of 1968. I was hoping to survive my final exams, a major challenge under normal circumstances, extratricky amid the noisy chaos of radical political protests happening right outside my classroom window. That March, seventy-five students and faculty marched on North College to protest the visit by a representative of Dow Chemical, which produced napalm for our fighting forces in Vietnam. Then, in May, several people gathered for a ceremony honoring 170 Wesleyan students who'd refused to go to war.

I supported the student demonstrations, but I found it hard to throw myself into the cause while dealing with the busy demands of running my dual meets, working at the cafeteria, and floundering academically, all the while being filled with a jumpy, impending sense of dread. My nonconfrontational demeanor did not equal complacency. Every day, I watched images on the news of hostile campus uprisings, engulfing schools like Columbia, where students seized five university buildings and barricaded themselves in for six days. My reaction was: Could I be excused to go chase butterflies in the field with my brother, please?

It was going to take a miracle for me to squeeze through with passing grades. Amby, meanwhile, had finished his term papers two weeks before they were due. He'd scheduled every minute of his final two weeks of training before Boston and wasn't going to let anything interfere with it. Not classes, not campus uprisings, not a giant meteor hurdling right for Earth. When everybody else would be hiding in underground bomb shelters, Amby would be galloping along his twenty-mile loop.

On April 20, 1968, Ambrose Burfoot crossed the finish line to win the Boston Marathon. My twenty-one-year-old roommate had just become the youngest champion of the oldest and greatest marathon in the world. He had single-handedly carried forth the mythic New England running legacy of Clarence DeMar, Tarzan Brown, Les Pawson, John "the Elder" Kelley, and, most touchingly, his mentor and friend Young Johnny Kelley.

Sixty-year-old Johnny Kelley didn't just run the race that year; midway through the race he was still up with Amby and the other lead group. He was still fighting like a champion, even when he shouldn't have been. He finally faded the last half of the race. I've always suspected that the reason Johnny Kelley ran so hard that day was that he wanted to get to the finish line as fast as possible to congratulate Amby. Sure enough, Kelley came through the plaza, crossed the finish line, and made a beeline to Amby. And even though he was several inches shorter than his pupil, he gave him a big hug. "I know how happy you are, Amby," Kelley said. "But you can't be any happier than I am. I think I finished fifteenth, but it doesn't matter. I think the only reason I kept going was so I could be here to exult with you."

While Amby was in the midst of becoming the first American in eleven years to earn the title Boston Marathon champion, I was two hours away at a dual track meet in Middletown, Connecticut. Amby had felt guilty about missing the race—he didn't want to let down the team—but Coach Swanson, who had watched, as we all had, Amby train like no man alive, reassured him that it was okay. I liked Coach Swanson for that.

How could I have missed seeing Amby win the Boston Marathon? You have to understand, the event wasn't even televised at that time. I had no idea what the race looked liked, how the city transformed into this huge parade, or how the city's inhabitants, from the banker down to the street sweeper, were swept up in the excitement of hosting the most famous and prestigious marathon in the world.

I didn't get the mystical attraction it held to runners from all over the world—Europe, Japan, Africa, South America. I didn't get how hordes of people, unable to control themselves, would rush onto the course behind the lead runner when he made his final push to glory. I didn't get why the race meant so much to so many. Nobody on our team did. I just knew that 26.2 miles was a very long way to run.

For some odd reason, the city didn't rejoice in Amby's victory the way they should have. The media did not sing his praises, give him a clever nickname, hold him up as a beacon of hope. They should have, but they didn't. Of course, nobody could refute his groundbreaking accomplishment—the first home-grown talent to win at Boston in over a decade! A twenty-two-year-old student! And yet it didn't give birth to a running boom. The universe, as usual, was working on its own internal timetable.

Back at Wesleyan, there was no giant banner awaiting Amby like some conquering hero, no big party thrown in his honor. I don't even remember him showing me his medal. Amby wasn't like that. Life went back to normal, although I think perhaps Amby stopped playing "The Impossible Dream."

After Amby graduated, I was no match for the social stimuli of college: the parties, the discos, that girl sitting across from me in the library. Another mental distraction for me was our country's escalation in Vietnam. The war had become this strange theater from which no American who owned a television could escape. It was the first war to be televised, which meant nightly news reports that took you to the battlefield. But although I could see what was going on with my eyes, I couldn't wrap my mind around it. As Emile de Antonio put it: "Every day we saw dead Americans, dead Vietnamese, bombings, all kinds of rather interesting things, but never one program on why; never one program on the history of it; never one program attempting to place it in context."

I tried very hard to put it in context, consuming all the information I could on the war, poring through newspaper articles, engaging in political debates with classmates on the way to and from class. I gathered that the basis of the government's decision to take us deeper into war was to stop the spread of communism in Asia. I didn't buy into that theory.

By my junior year, our team had lost its backbone—Jeff and Amby. I guess it was my turn to step up and be the leader, but that was never me. Charlie was the leader; I, along with Jason, had always been a good follower. I was still the fastest two-miler on the team, but for the first time since I was a sophomore in high school, my times got slower instead of faster. I'm the kind of person who, if there's somebody to aim high with, I can do it. I looked for others to lead the way for me, like Coach O'Rourke or Amby. I didn't have the motivation to excel on my own. I wasn't self-directed in that way. Without Amby around to drag me out of bed for a morning run, I slumped.

With another lazy summer looming on the horizon, I could hear Amby's refrain, "Train over the summer, Bill. Keep up your fitness. It will pay off big time when you return in the fall." In years past, I ignored his advice. But I truly felt the urge to lift myself out of this rut. So, for the first time in my life, I trained over the summer. I was back home in Newington, running five miles every day in the bright, hot sun. I'd come bounding up the front porch after a long run, dripping buckets of sweat, and Charlie would be looking at me with a warm, puzzled smile. He recognized a certain toughness in me that I'm not sure he saw in himself. But I knew from watching Amby what it took to be a distance runner—you've got to be one tough dog.

I started to get my fitness back. I set a new goal for my senior year: run the two mile in under nine minutes. I'd never hit this mark before so that put a charge in me. I continued to struggle academically, which only fed my desire to succeed on the track. At least then I'd have one reason to feel good about myself. Same as in high school, really.

I was also motivated by a challenge to my position as the best two-miler on the team. A freshman arrived at Wesleyan that fall—a Frenchman whose name escapes me. He ran a 9:05 in high school, so he was a really strong runner. I was determined to put this young hotshot in his place just as Amby had been with me.

As I worked toward my goal in the two mile, I continued to throw in longer runs. I was averaging seventy-five miles per week. I felt good about that. Sure, Amby averaged around 130 miles a week his senior year, almost double my amount, but he was training for the Boston Marathon. The thought never crossed my mind to enter a race longer than five miles. Five miles felt long!

In December of 1969, I had one last chance to break nine minutes in the two mile—at the final indoor race of the season at the Coast Guard Academy. It didn't look good. In spite of all the work I had put in, my fastest time in the two mile up to that point was 9:24. Taking that big of a chunk off my PR would not be easy.

I lined up beside the young Frenchman. I got off to a great start and took an early lead over the field. From there, I maintained my torrid pace. We came up on the second mile and that's when the Frenchman made his move. We were running neck and neck. I kept pushing the pace, but he hung right on my side. We came up on the final stretch and I knew it was time to pounce. With a final powerful kick, I surged ahead of the Frenchman and held him off as I sprinted across the finish line.

My winning time was announced: 8:58. I had broken nine minutes!

That's the way our sport is. You train and train, and sometimes you don't feel like you're making any progress, and then suddenly you do. You rest a little and suddenly, whoa, you're up at another level. The body always responds, but sometimes it takes a while. It takes you by surprise. And that's what happened to me that day. I was psyched.

A couple of weeks after setting my PR at the Coast Guard Academy, my draft number came up. I can't recall what it was; Jason remembers his was 151. But our numbers bought us both six months. Around the same time, the Supreme Court had ruled that people could apply for conscientious objector status, not just on the basis of their religious beliefs, but due to their moral objections, as well. That decision opened the door for a lot of young people who were against the war to apply to become a CO—Charlie, Jason, and I jumped on that bus.

The application process was very involved. You had to show your objection was based on your religious and moral beliefs and not because you were afraid to fight. You had to get letters of support, testifying to your character, and your parents didn't count. Jason recalls getting a bunch of hawks to vouch for his sincerity. Amby and Charlie each wrote a letter on my behalf. So did Coach O'Rourke. I owed them a debt of gratitude.

Amby had also filed for conscientious objector status in the spring of his senior year. Prior to going in for his draft board review, he worried they were going to grill him on his religious and moral beliefs. Amby went in and the first thing he said to them was, "Okay, yeah, I'm a conscientious objector, but, by the way, the *red, white, and blue* Olympic marathon trials are this summer and I would like to compete in those and so maybe you could give me four or five months off to go for the gold." And then they could come after him. They said yes to that. By the time he got back from his dismal failure in the marathon trials, Amby had secured a draft-exempt position as an elementary school teacher in Groton, Connecticut.

I knew that no matter how the draft board decided in my case, I wasn't going to Vietnam. I'd heard lots of antiwar activist were heading to Canada. For some strange reason, I thought about going to New Zealand. Don't ask me why New Zealand. The idea that in six months I might no longer be in America was tough to handle. I didn't want to go. I decided I wouldn't. I'd either be granted objector status or go to prison, like Muhammad Ali did. No matter what, I wasn't going to do something that I thought was hurting the country. It was tough because a lot of people felt the exact opposite. Some of them were my friends.

It was a very tricky time to come out against the war; one day I was a regular, all-American kid from the suburbs and suddenly I was a commie-loving draft dodger. An outsider in my own country. The splitting apart of the nation I felt occurring within myself.

All of a sudden, running didn't have any meaning to me. I had reached my goal—I had broken the nine-minute barrier in the two mile. What else was there? I had never been a great talent; I was a solid runner at a Division III school. What avenues were there for a track and cross-country runner after college anyway? The answer was none. Nobody took marathon running seriously. At Wesleyan, a school of seven thousand, there was one: Amby Burfoot. And he knew, as well as I did, that there was no way to make a living as a long-distance runner.

Graduation was coming up and I had no idea where I was headed. So I retired from running. I was done. A footnote in my life. Something I told people I did back in college.

I didn't resent Amby for being the athlete I'd never be; I didn't have his drive. I was okay with that. It was another fact of life. The Charles River would always flow into Massachusetts Bay; no matter how much I ate, my frame would always be more Woody Allen than Steve McQueen; Triumph motorcycles would always be cool and catching butterflies would always be hard; and life would always have a way of working out the way it's supposed to work out. Most of the time, anyway.

That spring, a student strike turned the Wesleyan campus upside down, just as similar strikes were doing all over the country. More than four hundred American colleges were shut down as a result of these student uprisings. On May 4, National Guard troops shot four unarmed students at Kent State. Hundreds of thousands of people converged in front of the reflecting pool at the Washington Monument. The protest had gone national. And it wasn't just four million students who had started to question our country's leaders. Now, mainstream America started to say, "Wait a second. What's going on here?" This question was being asked all over the country. Although I was moved by the injustices, I didn't belong to any movement. I didn't fit in with my peers who repudiated and raged anymore than I did with those who embraced free love and psychedelic drugs. (Oddly enough, sometimes they were one in the same.) This I believed: People got hurt in war. The opposite was true of running. In running you got healed.

I went into the preinduction physical and passed all the tests. Some people tried to fake their physicals. You'd hear all kinds of stories about people losing weight or getting sick or something. Amby told me about this easygoing, long-haired California runner named Bob Deines, who finished sixth in Boston in 1968. He was very much against the war. He scheduled his preinduction physical a few days after running a marathon and when they came in and saw this beat-down, skeletal figure crawl in on his wobbly last leg, they determined him unfit for service. I wasn't going to do that. I just believed what I believed in. That was that.

In late winter of 1971, Charlie, Jason, and I were granted conscientious objector status. We now had to find a job to fulfill our two-year alternative service requirement. That meant we were limited to work "deemed to make a meaningful contribution to the maintenance of the national health, safety, and interest."

Before starting our job search, Jason and I decided to take a trip to Key West, Florida. Jason was a big fan of Ernest Hemingway and so we spent a lot of time drinking his favorite drink, the daiquiri, at his favorite watering hole, Sloppy Joe's. We rented a couple of poles and fished off the end of the pier. It was heaven.

I returned home to Newington and entered a whole new kind of reality—as a substitute letter carrier at the local post office. What could be a more meaningful contribution than working at the bottom rung of the U.S. Postal Department? My "radically" long hair stereotyped me as being against the war. And I was against the war. I remember the older guys at the post office, many of them veterans, yelling stuff like, "Get a haircut!"

My uncle had fought in World War II but he was too nice of a guy to get on my case about my long hair or my objection to the war. I do remember him saying to me once, "Why don't you go into the National Guard?" That's what President Bush did. He had the connections to become a pilot in the guard, but he never went to Vietnam. Yet he was seen as patriotic because he was serving in the military. I had a different perspective. I thought I was patriotic by not serving. I felt in my heart, This war is not good for us. This is not smart. It's going to hurt us in every way, shape, and form. We have to think long and hard about this.

I think we took a lot of grief for our beliefs, but hopefully some older people changed their minds. In the end, I think many did. Of course, none of that changed a simple, sad fact: Our people were taking a beating over there.

That March, I got a call from Jason. He told me he'd found a job working at the Peter Bent Brigham Hospital in Boston as a grounds-man, and if I wanted, he could try to get me a job there, too. I came up two months later and got a job as an escort service messenger. It meant I was no longer running on the track, but racing to the morgue.

FOUR

Racing to the Morgue

In Framingham, Jerome Drayton, with his dark sunglasses and steely expression, ran a few yards ahead of the lead pack. Without any warning, he blasted off. I followed. It was no struggle to match his pace. I was so fit that I could go with anyone. I didn't care who it was—Tom Fleming, Ron Hill, Jerome Drayton—didn't matter to me. I could race with anybody, at any pace. And that's what it was all about. This wasn't a race for third place or fifteenth place or 1,000th place. It might be for somebody else. That's cool. I'm not interested in that.

I expected Ron Hill and Tom Fleming to go with us, but they hung back—albeit for different reasons. Let Billy take off, Fleming thought. There's twenty miles still to go. He'll burn himself out on the hills like he did twice before. Let him run Drayton into the ground. While Tom Fleming didn't stay with us for strategic purposes, Ron Hill didn't give chase because he was already smoked. When Fleming caught up to Hill, he said in his typical, joking tone: "How're you feeling, Ronnie boy?" to which the thirty-six-year-old Englishman panted, "Bloody knackered; I'm hanging on to you." I'd left Ron Hill in the dust. This gave me a huge shot of confidence.

Running along with Drayton, I felt I was setting myself up for the real battle ahead, cruising along, getting into race mode. The other runners trailed off behind us. That included Tom Fleming. There was no time to feel bad for him. He was a friend, but on the course he was a foe. A powerful foe who lived and breathed the marathon, and who ran every single race like his life depended on it. I know Tom thought of me as this easygoing space cadet who got along with everybody. Okay, I did get along with everybody. But I had another side of me that came out when I raced. Make a tactical error, I pounced. Let your guard down for a second, I went for the jugular. And I wouldn't think twice. I was waiting for you to show your weakness—maybe I detected your breathing was slightly more labored than it was a mile earlier—and that's when I'd push the pace. And I'd keep pushing harder and harder, increasing the severity of your pain, until I'd annihilated your soul, your spirit, your body. And after I'd left you on the side of the road clutching your side, I'd be on to my next opponent, or the finish line. Once the race was over then we could go to the Eliot Lounge and be friends again. I'd even buy the first round of blue whales.

Drayton and I poured it on through the streets of Framingham. Suddenly, we were out of the woods of Ashland and Hopkinton and running down this big, wide commercial street. There was no shade, which could be rough on hot days. We ran almost touching elbows through the industrial town, breezing past gas stations, little taverns, and factory buildings. I wouldn't describe it as the most scenic part of the course. Of course, the surrounding area had no meaning or power, except that it was flat and I knew I was a quarter through the race. It was always a significant feeling to hit the first 10K of the race. What it meant was "you were making progress." You'd gone a quarter of the way and now this race was starting to crank up. The marker allowed you to calibrate your pace, if need be. I don't recall plugging figures into my head. With no official clock to check my splits, I didn't have any idea as to my time at that stage. I knew Hill's course record was 2:10:40. I knew that was out of reach for me. I was a 2:18 marathoner. I sensed I could run faster than that. I didn't think about my prerace goal of 2:15 once the race began. After all, it was pure speculation.

Near the seventh mile, Drayton and I came upon an intersection where I could hear the noise of the crowd in the distance. We came around the bend and all of a sudden we were greeted by the cheers of spectators stacked several deep. In a lot of other sports, the crowd is in a stadium set way back, but here they were right on us, up close and personal. The pace was slow enough to be able to see the people and to feel the electric current surging through them, and more importantly, into me. As the crowds increased along the course, so did the intensity of this sensation. I knew, here in Framingham, the crowds were not nearly as crazy as they were going to be later on.

As we approached the train station in Framingham, my eyes widened. More people! A huge crowd of people cheering crazily in the distance. I'd run several local road races where a couple of local folks would stand on the side of the road in front of a rolling cow pasture, clapping for me as I passed by. But I had never experienced anything like this. Passing within arm's length of the crowd, they unleashed a torrent of cheers and war whoops.

It was here in 1907 that the lead pack of ten runners came through just as the freight train was approaching. The runners put on the afterburners and raced across the tracks as tons of steel passed only feet behind them. The story goes that Tom Longboat, a nineteen-year-old Canadian kid from the Onondaga tribe, leaped through the open door of the passing train and out the other side, and kept running. At any rate, the train severed the lead pack from the remaining 114 runners, who had to stop and jog in place for a minute while the train rolled across the road. Longboat went on to capture the laurel wreath in record time while the other race favorite, Hank Fowler from Cambridge, complained bitterly that getting stuck behind that train cost him his chance at victory. Thankfully, I made it over the train tracks without having to jump through any train cars.

I crossed the train tracks, waving happily to the crowd gathered outside the train station. Funny thing, I don't remember doing that.

This was the other side of my ADHD, the good side, especially if you happen to be a distance runner. Most normal people could not run for over two hours without a single break in concentration, but my condition gave me an abnormal talent for immersing myself in a single activity I enjoyed, in this case running. Once I went into this zone of hyperfocus, I shut out the rest of the world. I could have been running through an artillery range with live mortars going off around me and it wouldn't have bothered me. Being able to lock it down for 26.2 miles while disregarding the messages of worry, confusion, and insecurity that can infect the mind and deplete the body gave me a special edge. Which was kind of funny because, the rest of the time when I wasn't running, my mind was all over the place. Everything has a flip side, I suppose.

Drayton and I were the first runners to reach the first checkpoint, which read 6.5 MILES. The arbitrary marker was of no use in terms of keeping track of your pace. Why have a marker at 6.5 miles? Why not 7.5 miles? The answer: It was close to the train, allowing officials in the old days to quickly monitor the progress of the race before quickly jumping back on the train and going to the finish in Boston. Without markers set at regular intervals, I had to gauge my pace on feel alone.

Drayton was running very easily next to me at the same record-setting pace. I was in a steady rhythm, my feet kissing the pavement. If I ran at this roaring pace at even a slightly reduced fitness level, or on a much hotter day, I would be sure to dump out in the Newton Hills. Our footsteps hit the ground at the same interval. How fast were we moving? Who knows? All that mattered was the race, the course, and how I felt. All that mattered was that I had just run a two-hundred-mile week. It lifted me up. I felt sort of like a running Superman. I don't think there's too many others doing this, I'd think to myself.

I had a gut feeling that Drayton was one of them. He was a true amateur like me—training on his own without any financial or scientific assistance. Working a full-time job. Waking up early in the

morning to run ten miles before his job, then putting in another seventeen miles after. The amount of time and effort we put into training for
the marathon could be seen as a clear sign of madness, but we both
knew the quest for greatness in this sport required a single-minded, almost obsessive dedication. As Drayton once said: "I never really liked
the marathon to begin with, but when it really felt like a chore, I'd just
say to myself, Somewhere in the world, one of my competitors is out
there running right now. He's got to do it, so I've got to do it."

Drayton and I didn't exchange a single world as we ran in perfect
unison. Drayton wasn't a real talker. He was assessing me, and what I
could do. He didn't know what I could do. That was my advantage. On
the other hand, I had no idea what he could do, either. Who was this guy?

It turns out he was born Peter Buniak in 1945 in Germany. His
poor Russian-Ukrainian parents gave him his name, and not much
more. As an infant, he survived on frozen potatoes and icicles. By the age
of six, he was put in foster care. Recalls Drayton: "I learned how to
fight, how to throw stones when it was three against one, and how to keep
to myself." Amid the background of a ravaged city, a teenage Drayton
found momentary escape as a runner.

When he was eleven, Drayton emigrated to Toronto, Canada. In
order to cut ties with his bitter youth in postwar Germany, he gave himself a new name. Like most things about Drayton, the origins of his
adopted identity are shrouded in mystery. While it's hard not to notice
that former Canadian world-record holder Harry Jerome and American
Paul Drayton both medaled at the 1964 Tokyo Olympic Games, he
claims he came up with "Jerome Drayton" by flipping through a European phonebook.

In 1969, Drayton showed up at the Fukuoka Marathon in Japan, the
unofficial world championship for marathoners, with his new identity,
complete with dark shades and mustache. He refused to speak to virtually
anyone before the race. Drayton was angry that he had not been invited
to run in the prestigious race, despite posting the third-fastest time of the

year at the Motor City Marathon in Detroit. Not only that, he had to plead with the Canadian government just to help pay for his flight over.

A day before the race, a reporter asked Drayton to assess his chances against the fastest marathoners in the world, including 1968 Olympic marathon champion Mamo Wolde; 1969 European marathon champion Ron Hill; and 1969 Boston marathon champion Yoshiaki Unetani. "In spite of recording the third fastest time of year, 2:12:00, I was not invited to the race," said a stone-faced Drayton. "I will win the race tomorrow."

As soon as the race got under way, Drayton rocketed out to the lead. The experienced runners knew to let him go. Let him burn himself out. By the halfway mark, Drayton had built a thirty-one-second lead. The top runners weren't worried—it was only a matter of time before this party-crashing Canadian would crash back to Earth. Drayton responded by increasing the pace. He led wire to wire, becoming the first Western athlete to come to Japan and win their coveted marathon.

Immediately after shocking the racing world, Jerome celebrated with nobody. No teammates were there to throw him a party. No girlfriend was there to leap into his arms. He sent a telegram to his parents in Toronto to inform them of his victory, and that was all. You can be sure the next day he was back out there. Training hard. Running alone.

FIVE YEARS EARLIER
BOSTON, MASSACHUSETTS

In 1971, President Richard Nixon said, "Emptying bedpans has as much dignity as the presidency." It was a winter earlier and I was emptying bedpans as part of my daily routine as escort messenger at Peter Bent Brigham Hospital. I was also disposing of soiled linens, washing dishes, and taking lifeless bodies down to the morgue. You know, dignified stuff.

I was one of eight escort messengers. Almost all of us had signed up for this inglorious job in order to satisfy our alternative-service requirements as conscientious objectors to the war. We would wait in a little area off to the side of the nurses' station for the bell to ring. Long-haired Quakers, Catholics, Mennonites, Amish—well, maybe no Amish—in wrinkly white uniforms objecting conscientiously to the war, one mindless errand at a time.

The part I liked about the job was that I was always moving and interacting with people throughout the hospital. I'd constantly be running through the long maze of corridors, traveling from one department to another, picking up X-rays in Radiology and delivering them to a doctor's office or rushing blood from the blood bank to the operating room or taking a patient up to Pathology to get tested and then returning them to the main ward.

I hated sitting still for too long. I was too impulsive. I got bored too easily. Luckily, I never had to wait long for the nurse's bell to ring, alerting me that I was needed.

Brring!

"Orderly!" the head nurse would call out to me. I'd pop my head up like a rabbit. "Take Ms. Graham up to Imaging. Right away."

The second the words flew out her mouth, I was off. I wheeled Ms. Graham through the hospital's labyrinth of long white halls, teeming with doctors and nurses and sick patients. I had never been in a hospital before, except once when I was a kid and I'd had my appendix taken out. In college, when I ran along the country roads with Amby, I'd gaze around in every direction, but as I moved through the hospital, I kept my eyes fixed directly ahead. By not dwelling on the horrible things going on around me, like the sight of people dying among strangers, I could keep my sanity.

I thought it best to present a positive and cheerful attitude to the patients, no matter how disturbed I was by their condition. I wheeled Ms. Graham around the corner, and up the elevator we went. Within seconds, we arrived at the next floor and I whirled Ms. Graham out the door and rolled her down the hallway, the humming bright lights passing one after the next. We reached the end of our journey—the Imaging unit—and I brought Ms. Graham into the room, where a nurse was scribbling something on a clipboard. She didn't bother to look up at me as I rolled Ms. Graham to a stop and exited out the door.

I didn't bother to check my watch. I don't think I was even wearing one. But I'm sure the time it took me to bring Ms. Graham up to Imaging wasn't far off the American record . . . for Brigham Hospital escort messengers. Yet when I returned to the nurses' station there was no thunderous applause from the hospital staff, nor did the head nurse lay a wreath of garland upon my head.

I sat back down in the escort messenger office, where we would all be smoking cigarettes, which was allowed in hospitals back then. Things would really be cranking in the hospital. I was there for no more than five or ten minutes before another call came out. "Orderly!" I heard a voice bark. "Bring Mr. Finkelburg up to Hematology to get blood work."

And I was off!

Who knows how many miles I covered in a day. It was a big hospital and I walked all around it during my shift from 3:00 to 11:00 p.m. It must have been over five miles. One time, I was rolling a gravely ill patient to an operating room. The guy was dying of emphysema. We got to the OR and I waited with him for the doctor to show up. All at once, the guy jumped up off his stretcher and said, "You should quit smoking those." He lumbered over to my backpack, sitting in the corner of the room, and snatched the pack of Winstons from the front pocket. He put the smoke in his mouth and, holding the lighter as steady as he could in his sickly hand, he lit the tip. Watching him with sad astonishment, I thought, quietly: I should quit smoking those.

As I sat around the bare room with the other escort messengers, waiting for the bell to ring again, I'd think about my high school buddies who'd been sent to Vietnam and all they must be enduring and I'd feel sick to my stomach. I hated seeing our country split apart. All this strife and conflict didn't sit well with me. I wanted to be outside running in the fields, where I could escape this feeling of worry and agitation. But these were perilous times and perilous times don't allow for chasing butterflies.

The fact that we were all working off our alternative service was a special distinction that didn't endear us to the hospital's straight-laced, horn-rimmed bureaucrats. In their eyes, we were dirty hippies who had failed in our duty as Americans to serve. Was helping patients get off their bed and onto gurneys integral to the country's welfare? Probably not. But the way I looked at it, I was "fulfilling two years of national service in some civilian work of social value." More importantly, I was not another cog in the inhuman war machine. I felt great about that.

While hospital management viewed us as a bunch of unpatriotic, pot-smoking cowards, fit only for menial labor, to the thousands of young people who'd transformed the city into a hotbed of free love, psychedelic music, and fringe culture, we were fighting the good fight of nonviolent protest. The hospital administration did like one thing about hiring a bunch of no-good, long-haired scalawags. They could pay us peanuts. Jason and I took it in stride. The important thing was that we weren't stuck behind a desk. I don't think I could have lasted a couple of hours before breaking into a full-body rash.

While I loved the fact that I was always moving, the job could be very stressful at times. Every time a code red emergency was announced over the address system, a giant knot would form in the pit of my stomach. A nurse would activate a STAT. That meant somebody's heart had gone bad. It was my job to rush the patient to the surgery room on a gurney. My legs were moving but I felt disconnected to them. I was in shock. Please make it, whoever you are, I told myself. Sometimes they made it. Sometimes they didn't. That's what you learn working in a hospital.

Occasionally, I had to roll a lifeless person through the long, white halls to the cold, metal slabs in the basement. None of us liked to do that. As I pushed the sheet-covered body on the gurney past the fluorescent lights overhead, I cast my eyes down at the head resting a couple of inches from my waistline. This could be my childhood friend Gerald returning from Vietnam. The thought was almost too much too handle. Thankfully, Gerald made it home without getting shot, which isn't to say he came back whole. Drug use was prevalent among soldiers over in Vietnam and, like many others who fought there, Gerald returned addicted. After he came back, an undercover cop caught him trying to buy drugs. He did some jail time. It made me sad when I heard what had happened to Gerald. Charlie and I had known him since he was little. We'd chased squirrels with BB guns together. We went fishing in ponds. He was always a real smart kid. He just got caught up in the war. Tough stuff.

At this time in my life, I was living in a place on Westland Avenue with Jason. The city was full of cheap places back then; a haven for the young hippie hordes who migrated there. Our apartment was near the Back Bay Fens, a large park with rolling lawns, athletic fields, and a rose garden. It was a classic example of the "poor postgrad" aesthetic of the time: two bedrooms, a bathroom, and a long, narrow hallway that led to a tiny living room/kitchenette. Jason and I made chicken scratch at the hospital—seventy-one dollars a week—but it was enough to muster up the ninety dollars for our share of the rent with enough left over for cigarettes, gin, and movie tickets.

We'd just gotten out of school and landed smack dab in one of the strongholds of the counterculture scene. Everybody was having a good time and that's what we wanted to do. Boston was a cool city, especially for two white suburban kids with hair down to their shoulders. We drank beer, we went out to clubs, we chased girls, and we listened to rock 'n' roll. It was great.

The alternative scene was still young and there was little money to be made outside the mainstream. We saw the Moody Blues and the

Rolling Stones, despite barely having two nickels to rub together. Free concerts blanketed the city. You could walk down to the public garden and see the Allman Brothers Band for nothing. Duane Allman was probably not that much different than Jason and me. He was a young guy with long hair who happened to be a good guitar player.

Standing there on the grass, you'd be surrounded by hundreds of long-haired, pot-smoking kids who shared a similar mind-set. Rejecting the status quo, rejecting a conventional life. We didn't have any answers. We didn't join a political cause. Our cause had always been running, replaced now with our patriotic duty to support the local economy, primarily Jack's Bar.

Jack's was a great little pub in Harvard Square in Cambridge with live music and free peanuts. On weekend nights, the place was bursting with energy. People were packed to the gills and there were peanut shells all over the floor. It was one of the best places in the city to see local artists from the exploding Boston music scene—a young, redhead spitfire named Bonnie Raitt, James Taylor's brother Livingston, folk guitar hero Spider John Koerner, and blues harp player James Montgomery. Jason and I went to Jack's to hear great music but also, truth be known, to meet girls. The amount of success we had, well, that was another story.

Around this time, Jason bought a Triumph BSA 650 from our high school friend Randy Cook. The BSA was a seriously cool ride. James Bond rode one in *Thunderball*; so did Hunter S. Thompson. Charlie was next to get his hands on this British beauty. I didn't see much of my brother in those days. He lived with his girlfriend down in Connecticut, where he worked at a drug and alcohol rehab facility. I'd catch up with him at holidays at our parents' house in Newington. Once in a while, Charlie would drive up to my place in Boston and appear at my door with a bundle of groceries. I knew my mom had told Charlie to check on me; she would want to make sure I was eating enough. After all, a man needed his ketchup for his brownies, his mayonnaise for his pizza, and his orange soda pop to wash it all down.

Owning a Triumph, like Jason and Charlie, was all I could think about. If Jeremy Drayton's dream in 1970 was to win the Boston Marathon and repeat at the Fukuoka Marathon, mine was to feel the rush of air and the power of the engine's roar as I rode my Triumph through the city streets. Then, out of the blue, Jason learned of a guy in the neighborhood who was selling his Triumph 650. I'd been saving up to buy a motorcycle for months but was still short. I had to face facts. It wasn't going to happen.

One day, after my shift ended at the hospital, Jason and I went to give the Triumph one last look. We stood in front of the motorcycle like a bunch of teenage gawkers. She was a terrific-looking thing. Without saying a word, Jason put a bunch of folded bills in my hand. He probably didn't know he was making me the happiest guy in the world. Then again, he was barely scraping by himself, so maybe he did.

Did we need high-performance bikes—those Triumphs could really move!—just for getting around town? If you asked my twenty-one-year-old self that, the answer would have been "absolutely." It also didn't matter that, mechanically speaking, we were clueless; things were always rattling or loosening up or vibrating strangely on our bikes. While these kind of issues would have probably have sent my mom into a tailspin of panic, they didn't concern me in the slightest.

Cruising around the city streets on our bikes, Jason and I thought we were Dennis Hopper and Peter Fonda in *Easy Rider*. In reality, the long hair and the leather jackets were the only real similarities between them and us. We were no more cosmic hippies than we were hardcore bikers. While we never jumped on the bandwagon of free love, acid, and tie-dye spirituality, Jason and I shared a steadfast love for personal freedom, as well as a steadfast distrust of authority.

At the same time, we were a bunch of former college athletes from the suburbs of Hartford. The only LSD I had ever tried was the kind Amby introduced to me in college: Long Slow Distance training. Neither of us traveled to Woodstock in August of 1969; I was delivering mail to people's houses in the Newington suburbs; Jason was working in a kitchen in West Yarmouth on the Cape. The "we're all in this together" feeling that hippie kids were looking for in the flower-power scene, Charlie, Jason, and I had always found in one another. The Three Musketeers! We felt a deep kinship with other runners. If you ran, you were one of us.

Except, of course, I was no longer running.

FIVE

Washed Out on
Westland Ave.

APRIL 21, 1975
NATICK, MASSACHUSETTS

A record-size field of 2,041 runners had entered the 26.2-mile race from Hopkinton to Copley Square in Boston but, in reality, only seven runners ever posed a serious threat. Now there I was, not even halfway along the course, and I'd left all but one of them in the dust. Tom Fleming, the Jersey brawler. Gone. Ron the Hill, the record holder. Gone. The Mexican, Mario Cuevas. Gone. And now, unbelievably, there was only one man still up front in the lead with me. Jerome Drayton. He must've been looking at me, thinking, Who's this guy running a sub-five-minute pace? Because there were only a few guys in the world who could keep up that kind of speed and he knew exactly who they were.

We matched each other stride for stride into Natick. We were not running the inclines and declines. We were charging them. This almost never happened: a side-by side duel in a marathon, starting this early in the race, and extending over miles. More incredible was the pace that we were running together. I didn't know what my splits were, nor did I care—I was running against Drayton, not the clock—but we were cruising along the rural roads at under five minutes per mile. That's pouring-it-on speed. It turned out we were two seconds behind Ron Hill's course record.

Here's the thing about the marathon: It only takes one man to out-run you and you've lost. Just ask the hundreds of runner-ups in this race. All of them, at some point along the 26.2 miles of road, had the same thought: I'm going to win the Boston Marathon. Maybe the thought only lasted a brief, intoxicating moment, but that's all it takes for hope to take hold. And hope is a dangerous thing to have as a marathon runner because all it takes is one man, at any time, at any mile, to wipe you out. He has ravaged your psyche, obliterated your spirit, crushed your will to win, but that's not the worst of it—because don't forget, your body is still on the course, and you still have the agonizing business of getting to the finish line, which could be several miles away. It's not like boxing, where one uppercut is all it takes to put you out of your misery. In the marathon, you have the chance to watch your dream get pummeled slowly, yard by excruciating yard, knowing there's nothing you can do about it. You're already maxed out. There's no recovering. No catching up to that competitor who left you for dead. The rest of the way is pain and heartbreak. Until it's over. But it's not really over because you'll be muttering to yourself for years afterward: I was going to win the Boston Marathon. Become champion of the greatest road race in history. How did it all go wrong?

Through Natick, Drayton and I ran, linked at the elbows, gauging each other on the fly. Do I make a move? Do I challenge him to run a faster pace? All the while knowing that it could blow up in my face. Once you lose the upper hand in a marathon, it's almost impossible to get it back.

Drayton wanted to annihilate me. He wanted to put a dagger in me. But if Drayton expected to leave me in the dust, it was not going to happen. I was too fit. Too feisty. Too fired up. I didn't care how relentless the onslaught, I refused to falter. I'd trained for this moment. I'd trained to win.

All that stuff about how running in the lead makes you vulnerable and puts you at risk is the truth. But Drayton and I shared the same mentality on this day: I'm not going to die out there in the middle of the pack. I'm not going to die running at a safe, controlled pace. No, if the course is going to kill me, it's going to kill me running in the lead, trying to take down its record.

Drayton and I went at each other through town after town: through the rolling hills of Ashland, past the old clock tower on Chestnut Street, into Framingham, past the industrial factories, past the Framingham train station and into Natick. You won't find roads like this at any other major marathon in the world. That's the beauty of Boston: As much as it's confined and restricted by its history, it's also literally confined and restricted by narrow country roads. Run the New York City Marathon or the Chicago Marathon and you'll find wide-open avenues with all kinds of room to maneuver. Boston is a tight, up-and-down pressure cooker the whole way.

We were hammering away at Hill's record, trying to beat the other one into submission. I liked this course. This was a "duke it out" course. It said, *Do you dare to run fast up this hill? Do you dare to chase me down this steep incline?* We were engaged in a bare-bones fight. A savage battle of wills. This wasn't just another marathon to me or Drayton. This was Boston. Since its first run in the spring of 1897, people have traveled far and wide, at times without a penny in their pocket, for their chance at glory. As I opened my stride and pumped my arms, I imagined Abebe Bikila, the Lion of Ethiopia, the greatest marathoner ever, pounding through these same streets.

In the tailwind, Drayton and I battled side by side in the lead, speaking not a word. The man in the dark sunglasses ran like a machine—methodical, brutal, unstoppable. His face betrayed no emotion. This was do or die. Kill or be killed. Old-fashioned gladiators dueling it out. The road literally pushed Drayton in on me, barring me from feeling, even for a second, that I was out there running alone, just running against time. No, I was running against Drayton. I could hear him breathing and I could hear his footsteps echo off the road and I thought I could even hear him wishing me to fail.

Drayton was doing everything in his power to make this happen. But he didn't know me at all. He didn't know about my breakthrough at the World Cross-Country Championships in Morocco. He didn't know how hard I'd been training, how many miles of Boston hardtop I'd covered in the past twelve months. He didn't know that I'd run 537 miles last month so I'd be ready when this time came. He saw a skinny blond hippie in a handmade T-shirt and oversize gardening gloves. He didn't see the Bikila-like lion roaring inside me.

FOUR YEARS EARLIER
BOSTON, MASSACHUSETTS

For two long-haired, Frisbee-playing bikers in search of groovy times, Boston was heaven. We weren't loose and freaky enough for San Francisco, with its be-ins and radical politics and nude acid parties. After all, we were regular, middle-class kids from outside Hartford who drank cheap beer and smoked Winstons. We were happy wasting a sunny afternoon in the Boston Commons, watching the beaded hippie girls dancing barefoot, or hanging out at Jack's Bar in Cambridge, where you could get free peanuts, listen to some down-and-dirty blues band, all the while safe in the knowledge that most of the bar knew Carl Yastrzemski's batting average.

It was a summer night in Boston in 1971. Jason and I were walking home from Jack's Bar in Cambridge. A couple of Irish kids with pasty faces, long hair, and Boston accents, fresh out of college, rooming together on Westland Avenue. The scent of Jack's Bar—mostly cigarettes and peanuts—still clung to our jeans as we walked through the city late at night, cracking wise the whole way.

"Those girls at the bar were so into us."

"Yeah, right up to the point that they left with their boyfriends."

"Ha ha. So close, man. So close!"

We walked a good ways down Mass. Avenue until we reached Westland Avenue. Something kept us from following it down to our dumpy little apartment though. How the idea came into being, or by whom, Jason or myself, is unclear. What is certain is that a decision was made to walk our slightly inebriated selves a couple blocks up to the Prudential Plaza and run across the finish line of the Boston Marathon. It was a fluky thing to do. Like stopping to serenade a girl from outside her window.

After a short walk up the street, we reached the plaza and stopped in the shadow of the massive Prudential Building. This is where the finish line of the Boston Marathon was every year, at least back when Prudential was still a main sponsor of the race.

Our plan for running the end was poorly conceived. Nothing like the elaborate ruse pulled off by the late, great George Plimpton when he was a Harvard student in the 1940s. Long story short: Plimpton had applied to the school's exclusive journalism club and was told the price of initiation was running the Boston Marathon. On race day, Plimpton blended in among the throngs of people gathered along Beacon Street to catch a glimpse of the runners as they came down the home stretch. The moment the leader came into view, Plimpton leaped onto the course behind him, wearing running shorts and sneakers. The startled runner used a big finishing kick to hold off the lanky kid with the stiff, goofy-looking gait. Moments later, in the press tent, Plimpton fessed up. At once, the winner lunged at him, but was held back before he could take off Plimpton's head.

When Plimpton made his infamous dash, he had the advantage of an actual finish line to cross. We couldn't find any marker on the street, so we had to eyeball the spot. Fortunately, only a few months earlier we'd driven our motorcycles to the finish line area, where we found a spot along the course to watch the runners' final push to glory.

A hundred yards from our imaginary finish line, Jason and I assumed the starting stance, which was really no starting stance at all. More like two guys in street clothes with their arms dangling at their sides. This would be my first "competitive" race since the winter of my senior year at Wesleyan when I raced a sub-9:00 two mile at the Coast Guard Academy. I had just accomplished my personal mission to break the nine-minute mark and I had been elated. Everything changed after that. I quit going to track practice. Gave up running. I had good reasons. At least, they were good reasons to me.

We sprinted down Ring Road and past the huge statue of Prometheus Unbound that stood in the reflecting pool in front of the Prudential Center. I glanced over at the Greek titan who'd stolen fire from Zeus's lightning. I wish I could say a steady stream of brilliant light shot from his outstretched finger, zapped me in stride, back into life, awaking me at once to the true destiny that awaited. But it would be a lie to say that Prometheus spoke to me in that moment. That Jason and I went back to our apartment and started planning our comebacks. Or that the next day I quit my dead-end job at the hospital, stopped going to bars, stopped smoking cigarettes, and started making something of my life. We had our selective service jobs to do, and that was it. There was nothing beyond that.

I heard the sound of my feet hitting the concrete as we sprinted across the imaginary finish line, falling to the ground, laughing our heads off. Chalk the whole incident up to two former runners who'd had a few drinks at the bar. We had no plan to run the real race, not that night, not ever.

God, we laughed hard that night.

Winter arrived. As those who've ever spent a winter in Boston know, the cold can be rough. Heavy snow is also pervasive. Like most locals, I was cooped up inside all day, either stuck in the crummy confines of the hospital or the cramped rooms of my tiny apartment. If I didn't find a way to burn off some of my nervous energy, I was going to explode.

For weeks I had walked right past the YMCA on Huntington Avenue, near where I lived. One day, I decided to go inside and get a membership. I had never been inside a YMCA in my life. There was a weight room and a tiny slanted track.

I was starting over from scratch. If I had any goal at that point it was to obtain a minimal level of fitness. I wanted to see if I could run a half mile around the track. Most times I wouldn't even use the track; instead I'd get on a rowing machine. The other guys there would be lifting weights or jumping rope hard in the mirror. But all I wanted was to feel a little strength return to my body. Guess that's all I could handle at that point.

When I came into the YMCA to run a few laps, I would see a few guys training for the Boston Marathon. They would blow by me on the track. Most of the time, I slipped in and out of the Y without ever being noticed. It didn't matter that the other runners saw me as a nobody, if they saw me at all. In the world of running, I *was* a nobody.

When any of them asked me if I was also training for the marathon, I would tell them the same thing: "No. I used to be a distance runner. Not anymore."

Run the marathon? Were they serious? I was lucky if I could make it five miles around this miserable little track without wheezing to death.

"I once roomed with a guy who won the Boston Marathon," I told them.

I could tell from their reaction they were impressed.

"What's he doing now?" they asked.

"I don't really know. I think he's still competing. He might also be a schoolteacher down in Connecticut."

I continued running sporadically at the YMCA, running laps around this slanted track that was so small I had to run twelve laps around to equal a mile. It was easy to lose my bearings running around the banked track, lap after lap, like a roulette ball. As I picked up my pace, I wasn't so much running as I was orbiting the track, twenty-four laps in a row, then thirty-six laps . . .

The other runners on the track, all training for the Boston Marathon, sprinted by me. I paid them no attention. Instead, I kept running at my slow, steady pace. I worked up to forty-eight laps. Then I climbed to sixty laps, which translated to five miles. Eventually, I was running close to a hundred laps around the tiny track, three or four times a week. On Saturdays, I'd do an extralong run to prepare me for the extralong night of drinking and smoking in the bars.

You could call my workouts at the Y an escape from the boredom of winter. But it was more than that. I needed to move. I was meant to move. Even at my lowest point as an athlete, the magnetic pull was still there. The pull was weakened in the presence of life's overwhelming burdens, but it hadn't disappeared altogether.

Even though I had improved my fitness on the track, I was still apprehensive about running outdoors. After all, doing exercise of any kind in public was highly unusual in those days. In the neighborhood where I grew up, I knew of two adults who kept themselves in great shape. Only two. Back then, you almost never saw a person going for a run or peddling a bicycle. The only people who did these things were kids. It's almost as if adults weren't allowed. If you did run in public, you felt uncomfortable. You felt strange. I know women who used to run in the woods out of shame, or fear of verbal attacks. But male or female, it was not a good time to be a runner on the road.

Month after month of the same routine—hitting the bars, smoking cigarettes, staying out late—started to take on a stale and funky odor. I was keyed up all the time, but it wasn't a good energy. It was a nervous energy. I used to rid myself of this chronic angst by running ten miles with Amby. Now I did it by smoking cigarettes. I traded one addiction (with side effects like increased physical strength, lower blood pressure, and a natural emotional high) for another addiction (decreased lung function, promotion of fatigue, and harm to every organ in your body). Nice swap.

In April, Jason and I decided to ride our bikes down to the Cape for some mindless fun in the sun. Jason had worked the summer before at the Chrysler Art Museum in Provincetown and made some friends while hanging out at the bars. These same friends now offered to put us up for the weekend. My reaction was: "Let's go. Let's ride as fast and as far as we can."

Once we arrived, we met up with Jason's contacts—a group of scruffy, party-hard, Allman Brothers–listening, Jack and Coke–drinking guys. By then, Jason was getting more into the Grateful Dead and starting to dabble in heavier, mind-expanding drugs, which was a part of this new scene. As much as I shared Jason's carefree spirit, I could never go that route.

Jason was an original—definitely a sixties-seventies type of guy. I remember once when we were living together, he came home with some LSD. I didn't like this. It scared me. I thought it was dangerous. I was working inside the hospital. I saw the hazards of taking drugs on a daily basis. Jason was working out in the parking lot, listening to the Doors. He didn't see all the sick, beat-up people.

Jason was always telling me, "Billy, you've got to be spontaneous." I preferred to run through a couple of million scenarios in my head. Also, my parents raised me to always think about the consequences of my action. Of course, in those days, I was thinking more about the consequences of my inaction.

I followed the wolf pack as they careened from bar to bar in search of babes for whom to buy tequila shots. For Jason and his new pals, chasing after girls was fun. For me, it was stressful. Like trying to catch a giant swallowtail butterfly without a net—in a tsunami.

I remember sitting in this smoky beach bar when an empty feeling came over me. I tapped my restless leg on the booze-sticky floor as I burned through another smoke, and silently watched girls pass by with their orange-skinned complexions, thick, black mascara'd eyes, and long shiny fingernails. The war had taken my life on a detour. I'd just arrived at the dead end. This can't be it, I thought to myself. There has to be something more to life than drinking, smoking, and staying out all night with my friends. I was once a pretty good New England runner. Now look at me.

I was going nowhere. I was tired of going nowhere. I was tired of being squashed down. I still didn't know where I was headed, but I felt deep in my bones that I wanted to be heading somewhere.

That Sunday, Jason and I decided to wake up early to get back home in time to see the Boston Marathon, which neither of us had ever been to before.

After driving a couple hours north on Interstate 93, we reached Boston, and were soon winding our way through the streets. There was nothing that could have prepared us for the scene unfolding before our eyes. It looked like every soul in the city was outdoors, partying and having a good time. It was raucous.

We parked our bikes in front of our apartment and walked up to the race course, only a few blocks away. The scents of spring mingled with the scents of outdoor vendors cooking hot dogs and pretzels. When we reached the course, we marveled at the scene. Hundreds of thousands of fans lined the road. I was amazed to see there was hardly a policeman in sight. It was a total free-for-all.

The roar of the crowd was deafening as the cavalcade of press and motorcycles and runners came bursting into view. The moment sent chills down my spine. I watched as the race leaders approached. All of a sudden, I saw Jeff Galloway come into view. He even had on his Wesleyan singlet that I used to race in, too. I heard the announcer say, "Here comes Jeff Galloway of Atlanta, Georgia!"

Wait a minute, I know that guy! He was my teammate! I almost swallowed my cigarette in a gasp of surprise. Maybe I never ran the two

mile as fast as Jeff in college, but I could hang with the guy on our longer training runs. And there he was, battling for a top-ten finish at the
Boston Marathon. My mind was spinning.

I was still recovering from seeing my old Wesleyan teammate run
by in seventh place when I heard the announcer say, "Here comes John
Vitale of the University of Connecticut." Vitale? I ran against him! I
beat him! What the heck? I felt like the last person to show up at a
party. Oh, so this is where everybody has been.

By today's standards, the Boston Marathon I witnessed that day
was small, but it dwarfed any local New England road race I'd ever
seen. I was accustomed to running in tiny college dual meets that had
almost no spectators. I found it enthralling to see a road race like this,
on the big stage, with the big lights. I was mesmerized by the spectacle
of runners battling along the city streets flanked by thousands of spectators. There was nothing like it.

I had seen the Boston Marathon up close, and while a part of me
instantly desired to race in it, I knew the idea was bonkers. I was in
lousy shape.

One night, Jason and I crossed over the Mass. Avenue Bridge into
Cambridge and walked over to Jack's Bar. I can't remember which band
took the stage that night, but I do remember people dancing. As usual,
I was drinking my gin and tonics and smoking. Yes, I was still smoking
my Winston cigarettes. What did it matter? I was through with racing.

Jason pointed out a girl he recognized from around town. She was a
nice-looking hippie girl in casual attire. She wore a floppy hat over her
pin-straight, shoulder-length brown hair.

I was not an outgoing guy when it came to women. When I imagined walking over to a girl in a bar and striking up a conversation, I was
victimized by heart palpitations. As for my dancing skills, they hadn't
improved any since high school, when I'd sit up in the bleachers waiting
for some buddy to come by and knock my clip-on tie to the ground.

But there I was and there she was and somehow I got the nerve to walk over to the girl in the floppy hat and introduced myself. She smiled and let her eyelids flutter open, revealing her striking eyes, one brown and one green. Somebody once described her as having a Liv Ullman look of good, clear sense, whereas I had the Woody Allen look of a wiry, neurotic daydreamer. She told me her name was Ellen and that she was a receptionist at the children's hospital next door to the Brigham. We hit it off right away.

Ellen lived in an old Victorian house in Jamaica Plain with a couple of roommates. I started going over to her place to visit her. A lot.

When I met Ellen, I was barely running. Whatever confidence I'd built up from my runs at the Y was demolished during my run-ins with the hospital administrator in charge of the escort messengers, who he viewed as nothing more than a pool of low-cost labor. He would speak down to me and the other six long-haired young men because we were conscientious objectors. One look at his face, at the contempt in his eyes that shone through his horn-rimmed glasses, and I knew what he thought of my refusal to go to war. But I wouldn't accept the prevailing mentality—fight at all costs. I preferred that other saying: Make love, not war.

Now that I had an actual girlfriend, I felt it my duty to put my belief into practice. This meant spending all my free time with Ellen on our distant cloud. I was happy to have a girlfriend and not be alone in the big city. I think Ellen felt the same way. My lack of ambition was not a pressing issue. Between spending all my time with Ellen, rushing around the hospital as an escort messenger, and running around the YMCA track, who had time? Not to mention, I was now helping Howard set up a union.

Howard was a fellow escort messenger. One day, he pulled me aside and told me serious efforts were under way to start a union at the hospital. "Would you like to participate?" he asked. My first thought was, Why not? The hospital's supporting staff, like the receptionists and nurses, were paid poorly, worked under miserable conditions, and had no benefits. Who could be against trying to make things a little better?

As I said, I'd always been more of a follower than a leader, so I let Howard take the reins. In retrospect, that might have been a mistake.

Howard told me that if we got enough people to vote to unionize, the hospital would have no choice but to accept the outcome. It was our job to convince our fellow workers that it was in their interest to unite in struggle, and so for the next couple of months, Howard and I went around to the different groups—the receptionists, the nurses, the aides—and tried to convince them to take a formal vote to join Local 1199. All the while, I was wondering why I was the only one other than Howard to participate in this effort.

It was a winter day in 1972. I walked out to the hospital parking lot after my shift to get on my bike and ride home. I bent down and picked up the broken chain lying on the snow. Somebody had stolen the one possession I owned in the world. It wasn't the money I was out that hurt so much, but the freedom that had been taken from me.

Jason walked over to where I'd parked my bike and saw me standing there like a guy who'd been sucker punched in the gut. He told me he'd help me find my bike, knowing I couldn't afford to replace it. That's how we were. We were always in it together.

The next couple of days we spent going around town, trying to find my bike. Jason and I scoured the city. No luck. Jason said the bike had likely been stripped for parts. I was always looking on the bright side, but it wasn't easy between no money, my dead-end job, and my lack of wheels. This was bad—not rock bottom, but bad. Finally, I broke down and purchased a ten-speed bicycle. A few days later that got stolen, too.

That was rock bottom.

Early the next morning, I rolled out of the bed. I threw on some gray sweatpants, dug out my old sneakers, and put them on. After lacing up my shoes, I walked out the front door, down the paint-chipped steps of the Victorian house, and over to Arlington Avenue.

I paused a moment on the side of the road and stared out at the horizon. All at once, I started running down the road. I moved at a slow, steady pace. I could hear my breath as I glided over the hardtop. I passed by the grass front yards and storeowners unlocking their front doors and people washing off their sidewalks. By then, I'd lost track of how many days I'd gone without running outdoors. Had it really been four years since I soared through the countryside with Amby? Had it really been that long since my running shoes had been caked in mud?

As I blasted down the road, I could feel the blood slowly returning to my veins. I was running again. My muscles were loosening with each step. I sailed along, giddy as a newborn pup.

I had no idea how long I'd been running by the time I saw Peter Bent Brigham Hospital come into view. I passed Jason on my way up the front entrance. He didn't react surprised at the sight of me arriving to work on foot. He just glanced over at me as I passed him in my ragged sweatpants with my hair sweaty and looking unkempt. He gave me a small nod and grin.

I was still about to walk inside the hospital to carry out another day at my dead-end job, but the seeds of change had been planted inside me. Small events were pushing me to take action. Each one was propelling me closer to the keys to my salvation, which looked a lot like waffle-soled training flats. And yet, I still wasn't ready to commit myself. Something was still holding me back.

SIX

The Writing on the Hospital Wall

APRIL 21, 1975
NATICK CENTER, MASSACHUSETTS

As we ran toward downtown Natick, a foot apart from each other, I did know this: Drayton could duke it out. How did I know this? He was built right. What does that mean? He was thin but strong. Real strong-looking. I could hear the easy rise and fall of his breathing. I knew that under his maple leaf singlet his heart was not thumping against his chest but, as Edgar Allan Poe wrote, "beating calmly as that of one who slumbers in innocence." On top of that, he was running sub-five-minute miles like it was a piece of cake. Not too many people in the world can do that. Not in 1975. Not if you haven't trained your whole life at high altitude. At that pace, you're cracking 2:11. That's roaring.

At no point did Drayton talk to me. That was fine. I liked that. It told me he was a serious runner. That's what I want. I didn't care that other runners found Drayton aloof and standoffish. I liked that Drayton was a different breed of cat. In a way, you want the challenge of going toe-to-toe with a guy like Drayton—fit and sharp, cunning and ruthless—because it heightened your own senses and got your blood going. It forced you to react and think at a faster rate than you normally would, and demanded your body and mind adapt to the challenge thrust before you.

I liked Tom Fleming, too, but he was the exact opposite of Drayton. He liked to mix it up with other runners—he could be brash and talkative on the course. I didn't mind that, either, because I knew Tom was a serious runner. I knew the miles he put in. I knew the punishment he inflicted on his body in training. I knew that he didn't lack for want. Unfortunately for Tom, sometimes his outsize personality got the best of him. It cost him. He used up too much energy. He'd go out too hard in these big races. He wouldn't be able to finish strong.

The more experienced marathoners will take advantage of a day like this—cool with a tailwind. It's only the inexperienced runners that don't. Or the runners who have no competitive fire. They're running the same course, but they're not running the same race. They're solving crossword puzzles in their head or thinking about their grandma or talking to people along the way or visually embracing spectators. They're in a world of heartwarming delight where smiling children hand out orange slices to runners, where friendly faces show up in all directions, where a sea of people move alongside them in runner solidarity.

In my world, I was running beside Jerome Drayton and he was as light and cheery as the Terminator—his eyes hidden behind dark sunglasses, reinforcing the sense that he was a cold-blooded killer. But Drayton didn't intimidate me. Not for a moment. I had to deal with him but, at the same time, he had to deal with me. And I was determined to stand my ground. You have to be like this. You can't let anybody throw you off. You have to be feisty. Respect your opponent, as I respected Drayton, but never fear them. This is a duel. I'm there to beat him. He's there to beat me. I can't think of anything more fun.

Now we were ten miles into the race, passing along the shores of Lake Cochituate, where Tarzan Brown, the orphaned Narragansett Indian who'd won the race in 1936 and 1939, suddenly waved on the other runners, jumped the guard rail, and plunged into the cool waters during a scorching hot race day. I breezed past the spot where Tarzan took his famous dip, without breaking stride. The first time the brash youth had entered the race in 1935, he threw his shoes into the crowd and ran the last thirteen miles barefoot. As I battled Drayton through the mid-reaches of the race, my Prefontaine racing shoes flicked swiftly over the road. My feet felt great in my new shoes. I could skip going barefoot like Tarzan.

Ten miles into the race, I felt my confidence rising. I was making headway and my body was telling me it was all systems go. If you're working real hard ten miles into the marathon, then it doesn't bode well for the next sixteen. It's not as if you're going to make a miraculous re-covery and suddenly feel great. We've all seen that pitcher who struggles in the early innings and almost gets stronger as the game goes on. Not in the marathon. This is the great weakening of your physical and psy-chological strength. That's the challenge. Most people are just trying to run the distance. "Can I finish the twenty-six miles?" Some people set limits like four or five hours. It's hard to get it down to the 2:10 to 2:15 range, but that's what people like Drayton and Fleming and myself were trying to do. Not so we could set a personal record, but because we knew that's how fast we'd need to run to win the race.

My mind, which tended to bounce, skip, and fly around in every direction, was now trained like a laser beam on the moment at hand. As the race wore on, I gave no heed to my inner dialogue, or the people and scenery that flanked the road—not even for a second. All my focus was on the road directly ahead of me. It was this effortless intensity and calm as I ran that separated me, not just from the casual weekend war-rior, but my other competitors. Where it came from, I'm not really sure.

It would have been easy, as I glided down the road, for random thoughts to enter my head—"Jeez, did I forget to turn off the coffee-pot?" Or, "I hope I can pay my rent this month"—but they didn't. In-stead, with every strike of my Prefontaine shoes on the pavement, I was tuned into what was happening to my body. The average marathon runner will tune out for a time, especially when the hard miles begin taking their toll. They will disassociate from the task they are performing, taking their minds to another place, focusing on anything but the pain they are feeling.

In his book *What I Talk About When I Talk About Running,* the great Japanese author Haruki Murakami, who's also an enthusiastic recreational runner, describes his method for successfully completing an ultra marathon. He talks about entering into a "metaphysical" state where he hardly knows who he is or what he's doing. He puts himself into a Zen-like trance, on the assumption it's better to transcend the physical and mental distress than to plug into it. But the worst thing you can do as a marathon racer is to deny, ignore, or repress what your body is telling you, every single moment throughout the race. Even if it's not what you want to hear.

While he's running, Murakami tells himself to think of rivers and clouds. In that moment, I tell myself to watch my form. Check my pace. Check my exertion level. Monitor the subtle in-and-outs of my breath. Listen to my body for the slightest hint of fatigue or injury.

Murakami talks about running in a cozy, homemade void. I love that feeling, going on a long run through the countryside, leaving my mind far behind. But I can't afford to think of nothing. Not there in the middle of the Boston Marathon. Not in the heat of battle against Drayton. If I want to win this race, I need total awareness.

Once the race was on, my ADHD mind somehow knew not to wander off on its own. It knew a momentary slip in concentration could do more than slow me down, or impede my performance, it could lead to a fatal mistake. It might be an early mistake, one I didn't even realize I was making at the time. Perhaps caught up in the thrill of the competition, I fall into the temptation to blast through the first few miles. If this early pace is just a tad too fast to maintain to the finish, the final miles will become a living nightmare.

Let's hope I didn't run those first few miles too fast.

I was coming up on the real nitty-gritty of the marathon. Everything else was just setting me up. This is the real challenge of the marathon—the last fifteen miles. I had run that first part carefully and it was very uplifting to feel my engine running trouble-free. I knew the center of Natick was up ahead; I had a sense of moving out of the wooded suburbs and of getting closer and closer to the bedlam of Boston. You really feel that as you run. And it's flat, so it's easy running, and you're making progress. The halfway mark was coming up, and that's a significant marker psychologically.

Drayton and I continued stride for stride into Natick Center, a wide-open downtown that captures the signature feel of a small-town New England celebration, much like Hopkinton does. We flew by an officer directing traffic in the center of the road, kids handing out cups of water, and fans crammed along the town green cupping their hands to their mouth to better project their passionate support. At that moment, I was running the marathon as if it were a cross-country race, as if time didn't matter, only position. I was running with a "go-for-the lead" attitude.

The crowds were clapping and rooting for us like Roman spectators at a gladiatorial match. Amid the throngs of cheering fans the spirit of Spartacus could be heard: "Oh, comrades! Warriors! Thracians! If we must fight, let us fight for ourselves! If we must slaughter, let us slaughter our oppressors! If we must die, let it be under the clear sky; by the bright waters; in noble, honorable battle."

THREE YEARS EARLIER
BOSTON, MASSACHUSETTS

I was running to work one day when I spotted my Triumph as it zipped by me. I could have given chase, I suppose, but I was never a speed guy. Besides, maybe the stranger on my bike had done me a favor. I wasn't back on my feet, but at least I was *back on my feet*. Okay, so it wasn't Prometheus and a bolt of lightning.

When I wasn't working at the hospital, or sporadically running outdoors, I was spending my time with Ellen, mostly over at her place in Jamaica Plain. I was almost never at my apartment on Westland Avenue. Jason knew I had a girlfriend, which was a good thing, because otherwise he might have thought his friend had been abducted by aliens. I don't know if Jason was mad at me for dropping out of his life like I did. He knew how badly I had wanted a girlfriend, so he likely forgave me. Also, he would have known that a jittery nicotine puffer like me could use the calming influence of a good woman.

And that's exactly what Ellen brought to my world: a sense of calm. Almost instantly, I left behind those nights spent going to pubs with Jason. Quiet dinners at Ellen's replaced loud music and booze at Jack's. Her sparsely decorated living room became my new favorite hangout; most nights we curled up on the couch and watched TV. After all the aimless drifting that I had done since graduation, I felt relieved to have stumbled into a stable relationship with a girl I could be myself around.

It was August now. We were at Ellen's, sitting on her frumpy couch, watching the Olympic marathon on her tiny TV set with the rabbit ears. It was the final day of events. By then, the athletic competition had been overshadowed by the massacre of eleven members of the Israeli Olympic squad by Palestinian terrorists. After such a shocking event, played out live on TV to a world audience, the rest of the sporting contests became an afterthought. And with good reason—people had died. Still, as a former college runner, I was curious to watch the marathon.

The smart money was on the Europeans or Japanese to take gold, while the Americans were considered inferior competition. As a matter of fact, the last time an American runner had won a gold medal in the marathon was way back in 1908 and not without controversy. An Italian named Dorando Pietri had been the first to cross the finish line, but he had collapsed down the final stretch and had been assisted to the finish by British officials. Eventually the Italian was disqualified and Johnny Hayes, a New York department store clerk, was awarded the gold medal.

Frank Shorter, a former track athlete from Yale, was considered America's best shot for a medal. He was a couple of years ahead of me in college, so I never raced him head-to-head. But Amby did. In those days, he beat Shorter handily—and, in fact, was only vaguely aware that there was some kid named Frank Shorter finishing somewhere behind him. He didn't register on my radar at all. Of course, I wasn't aware that Shorter had won the ten-thousand-meter title at the 1969 NCAA track championship during his senior year at Yale. Or that he had won the U.S. National Cross-Country Championships in 1970 and again in 1971. I didn't follow the sport in those days. I was following the peanuts as they hit the ground at Jack's Bar.

Last I had heard, Frank Shorter had gone to medical school and then later decided to attend law school. At any rate, I assumed that like most college runners he'd eventually quit the sport and had found a stable way to make a living. He could do that as a lawyer. I considered that vocation myself back in college, and I was nowhere as smart as Shorter.

What I didn't know was that a friend of his named Kenny Moore, who graduated from the University of Oregon and took fourth place in Munich, had convinced him to try the marathon. Grad school gave Frank the time to run and so he decided to go for it. Kenny Moore was to Frank what Amby had been to me—the guy who saw untapped potential and encouraged him to push himself and see what he could do. Only Frank had responded to Kenny's plea, while I'd ignored Amby's.

The race started in the Olympic Stadium, and was run over an out-and-back course. Shorter had taken the lead early and was demolishing everybody by several minutes. For the last sixteen miles he was just on a leisurely tour of Munich. I remember seeing Frank emerge from the dark of the tunnel onto the stadium track. He was alone in first. I couldn't believe what I was seeing. Nobody could. It was such a wonderful moment because you knew it was being beamed around the whole world, but also because of the way he ran that day—with absolute grace and ease and perfection. Nobody's ever looked fitter or better than him at an Olympic running event. It was a galvanizing moment for all runners. As a fellow American, you looked at the video and you saw the image of the perfect runner—in complete control of his game, while the rest of the world ate his dust. An absolutely sublime, dominating performance—like in 1960 when Abebe Bikila, a virtual unknown from Ethiopia, conquered the streets of Rome barefooted in world record time, becoming the first black African to win an Olympic gold medal.

Sensing a buzz in the air, ABC played up Frank's run over the next several hours. The network brought in Erich Segal—the Yale classics professor, *Love Story* author, marathon aficionado, blah, blah, blah—to provide color commentary. Toward the end of the race, Segal was going crazy, not because Frank was a quarter mile from Olympic glory, but because an imposter had entered the stadium seconds before him and was taking a victory lap. The crowd was cheering wildly for the imposter, not knowing the truth. Shorter recalls hearing the roar of the crowd as he entered the tunnel into the Olympic Stadium only to be greeted with absolute quiet when he emerged. "As I ran the final lap around the track, the crowd was silent and I'm thinking, Well, I'm an American, but give me a break." An outraged Segal was calling the imposter all these unspeakable names on the air and yelling out to Shorter, "It's a fraud, Frank!" It made for entertaining television.

That night at Ellen's, I was just one more American watching the highlights of Frank Shorter's victory in disbelief. Only a few days earlier, everybody had experienced a very different kind of disbelief, watching the tragedy of kidnapped and murdered Israeli athletes unfold. It was painful to watch such a despicable act of faceless terror. But thanks to Frank's perfect marathon run, we, as a nation, could now celebrate an act of individual achievement. It mattered that it came in the marathon, the event that perhaps more than any other symbolized one man's heroic triumph against a host of fierce challengers and in the face of daunting conditions. It was a hopeful, cathartic moment.

As fired up as I was to see a former U.S. college athlete like myself win Olympic gold, I didn't leap up out of my seat and charge out the door with the goal of competing in a marathon. But it did alter my perception. I suppose it was like how people once thought it was impossible to put a man on the moon and then one day they turn on their TV to see Neil Armstrong hopping on the lunar surface. Frank Shorter was, in that moment, Neil Armstrong walking on the moon. Suddenly, the possibilities for an American runner were endless. There was a way forward and it was suddenly okay to dream the impossible dream—even if you weren't Amby Burfoot.

It was early fall by now. Things were going well with Ellen and I was still spending all my time over at her place, so I decided it was time for me to leave Westland Avenue.

I arrived at the hospital, but instead of going right inside to join the other escort messengers I walked around back to the parking lot. I found Jason in the shack, listening to the local rock station and watching the clock go around.

"So Ellen and I are getting married," I said.

"Get atta here," said Jason. "Really?"

"Just kidding."

"You frickin' loon."

"I am moving in with her."

Jason said nothing for a few seconds, then smiled. "Right on."

Jason knew it was the logical next step. If he'd had a girlfriend, he might have done the same thing. And he had lots of friends who needed a place to live, so finding a roommate wouldn't be difficult. With that said, I could see from the look on his face that the news was a little traumatic. His best pal was going away. On some gut level, we both knew we were going in different directions.

Jason and I were developing different sets of friends. I wasn't interested in where he was going and he wasn't a good enough runner to run a hundred miles a week. I used to come back from a long run, soaked in sweat, and Jason would be sitting on the stoop of our building with a forty-ounce bottle of Black Label, hanging out with some of the other people in our building. It was nothing really that out of the ordinary. That's what young people did back then—they hung out and drank and smoked weed and listened to Led Zeppelin and the Rolling Stones and hooked up on rooftops and alleys.

The real truth of the matter was that I was the guy that was out of the ordinary. I was the guy that was about to head off in a direction that was less than typical. I would miss Jason, all the same.

By the winter of 1971, I'd grown more involved in the push to establish a union at the hospital, which more and more resembled the personal crusade of one man—Howard. But it was, in fact, a two-man operation: Howard at the top, in charge of overall strategy, and me, who went along with Howard's plan.

I wasn't concerned about my own pay. I was in selective service so I had already struck my sweet deal with the government in which I would be their servant for two years and in return they wouldn't put me in jail. I was more concerned with the nurse's aid, toiling in subhuman conditions for slightly more than a pouch of magic beans. Meanwhile, Jason and the other parking attendants stood around, smoking pot and listening to the radio, supposedly keeping a watchful eye on the chrome-slathered boats driven by our bosses: shiny, pollution-belching monsters like the Lincoln Continental, Chrysler Imperial, and Cadillac El Dorado.

One day, Howard decided to implement a new communication strategy, which involved writing pro-union slogans and hanging them up inside elevators and offices and storerooms. I knew the higher-ups would not view this exercising of our First Amendment rights in the same noble, positive light as we did. At the same time, horrible things went on every day in the hospital and nobody seemed to care, so putting up a couple of flyers wasn't going to be a big deal.

Howard and I were brought down to a windowless office where a couple of stern-looking men in suits were waiting to interrogate us. All that was missing was a lamp, turned up to its highest setting, to shine in my face. They put a piece of paper in front of us, which, as they explained, was a report from a leading handwriting expert, who had determined that the dastardly people who wrote those pro-union slogans in the elevators and the offices and the storerooms had the identical handwriting Howard and myself.

Howard immediately denied the charges. I don't think I helped his case, though, because I burst out laughing. "Yeah, I did it," I said. I could feel Howard's eyes on me; I don't think he was happy I had confessed to the crime so easily. After all, the only thing they had on us were the pro-union flyers, a conclusive handwriting match, and the fact that for the past twelve months we were the only two people actively going around trying to sign people up to join a union.

The hospital went into crisis mode. This was going to be treated as "the crime of the century"—only slightly less heinous than the kidnapping of the Lindbergh baby. Of course all they could really do was fire us. So that's what they did: They fired us.

Well, now Howard had them right where he wanted them. Building on the momentum of our unjust dismissal, and the ensuing outrage among the rank and file, he convinced thirty other workers at Brigham to march on the personnel office. We stormed down there and made our demands known: 1. We wanted the right to take a formal vote on forming a union; 2. Howard and I were to get out jobs back. To be honest, I dreaded the second part but I figured now wasn't the time to mention that to Howard, seeing as he was on a roll.

A man came in to see us. He was the head of Personnel. We had forced a face-to-face with the head honcho. Glancing over at Howard, his face brimming with confidence, the air of victory hung in the air.

The head of Personnel said: "The police are on their way." Well, I could see from Howard's reaction, him sprinting for the door, that we had ceded the upper hand.

I fled the scene along with Howard and the other thirty workers. I hadn't run that fast since I outlasted the Frenchman at the Coast Guard two-mile race. The cops hadn't caught me for squirrel hunting in Stanley Park and they weren't going to catch me now.

Following my near arrest, I stayed clear from the hospital. Let the heat die down. After a week, I walked into the hospital and they were circulating papers with a description of me. Holy cow, you'd think I was some arch-criminal! In truth, I was lucky I didn't get lost coming to work every morning. The papers said that if I was found to be anywhere on the premises I was to be apprehended and the police should be called in.

Did I think my small act of vandalism was going to be viewed as a vicious attack on the entire health care infrastructure of America? No. I never thought about getting fired. I wouldn't have wanted that, seeing that I still had six months left of alternative service. I just did something, in my own clumsily naïve way, that I believed would improve the place and make it better. But the powers that be didn't like that. So now my picture was circulating around the hospital with the following description: Young male, ragged clothes, long hair in a ponytail.

SEVEN

Power of the Emerald Necklace

APRIL 21, 1975
NATICK, MASSACHUSETTS

Drayton and I had broken away from the pack. We were rolling. Hammering away at each other. I must have looked pretty intense at the moment, going mano a mano with Drayton, who had ice water for blood. I was in racing mode, every one of my senses fully engaged in competition. The physical chess game was fun. I was assessing Drayton's condition and he was assessing mine, and this was all happening without so much as a glance in each other's direction. If I could get a read on him before he could get a read on me, I'd gain the upper hand. He was thinking the exact same thing. So who was going to make the first move? If he decided to burst ahead, should I retaliate with my own surge? Or would I think, No, that's just what he wants me to do. I'm going to hang back. Let him get tripped up in his own trap. A hundred subtle calculations were taking place in our heads, which would be hard enough in itself, without flying along at a sub-five-minute pace.

With the town of Wellesley just beyond our view, Drayton and I continued to match each other step for step. We had run the first ten miles at a blistering pace. There was a possibility that Fleming would be right: that our personal duel would be the undoing of both of us; taking so much out of each other that we had nothing left to fend off the other challengers. Just then, a woman standing along the route shouted, "Go,

Jerome! Go, Jerome!" Although his face showed no emotion behind his dark sunglasses, Drayton was apparently fired up by the show of support because he suddenly surged ahead.

I felt a jolt of anger shoot through me. If that unknown Boston spectator had dumped a bucket of cold water on my head, it would have been the same thing. Okay, I got that I was a nobody in my own hometown; I got that my bronze medal at the World Cross-Country meant nothing to anybody back here; I got that the press thought so little of me that I wasn't included among the race favorites. But this is the Boston Marathon—you root for the home team. You root for Clarence DeMar and for Tarzan Brown and Les Pawson and John "the Elder" Kelley and Johnny Kelley and Amby Burfoot. You root for the guy running with a giant BOSTON hand-written in marker across his shirt, not the guy with the fancy red Maple Leaf on his. That's plain wrong.

At once, I shot off down the road like a heat-seeking missile. As for that spectator, I don't know who she was—I'll probably never know who she was—but I'll tell you one thing: At that moment, she was Jerome Drayton's worst enemy.

The whole way, Drayton and I had been feeling each other out. But when that woman yelled "Go, Jerome!" all that careful calculating went out the window. The adrenaline kicked in. While I had years of the most extensive training under my belt, it was that comment that got me going. It was the shot in the arm that I needed. Okay, I'm ready to go now. Let's take the gloves off. Let's do this. I caught up to Drayton and roared past him.

Going through Natick, which is about 10.5 miles into the race, I had been trying to pull away, churning with a light but relentless gait. Now, I was going to see how the man in the dark sunglasses responded. Was he going to give chase? Usually when you surge, if someone's going to go with you, it's clear—they'll pull back even with you pretty quickly. Maintaining physical contact, and even pretty good visual contact, is very key in all this. Once there's a certain gap between two competitors—

and it's probably around seventy-five yards—you start to lose the sense of competing; you can't compete as well. The closer you are, the more you can compete with someone in a road race, in a marathon. So I was trying to open that gap on him, but it was impetuous. A dizzying blend of feelings came over me. Boldness and butterflies jostled with each other while sailing at a brisk clip—the exhilaration of playing with fire mixed with the possibility of getting burned.

I had made my move around eleven miles into a race that most serious runners will tell you started at mile 20. Drayton was probably thinking that the real race wasn't going to start until the Newton Hills. He was probably thinking, He'll come back to earth. But I had no intention of coming back to earth. I'm going from here, this is the move. I'm driving hard the rest of the way. Why shouldn't I? I had the cool weather, the tailwind. I had the shoes! Everything was working for me. Well, I had my answer. He let me go. Big mistake.

THREE YEARS EARLIER
BOSTON, MASSACHUSETTS

Dawn was breaking through the window of our apartment at 32 Oakview Terrace. The mild, cloudy weather lent the city a romantic touch. I looked at Ellen's side of the bed. Empty. Already left for work. I stood in front of the bathroom mirror. My thoughts turned to the hospital, my source of employment, until I was chased off the premises.

While I was happy to be spared from witnessing any more emergency room horror scenes, my life had been flung into doubt. I feared what the selective service board might do to me now. For a year and a half I had worked as an escort messenger, which meant I still owed the government another six months. What would they do to me if I couldn't find another alternative service job? Would they find one for me—in some harsh, barren region of the country, far from my family and friends? Or maybe they would just toss me in jail. Being locked up in a tiny cell would be the ultimate torture for a guy like me. Find me the most rambunctious golden retriever in the world. His need to run around outside was nothing compared to mine.

My first thought was to go around to the other hospitals in Boston. I figured one of them must have a need for an experienced escort messenger. Not so. Every place I tried turned me away. I remember going up to the Baptist Hospital on Mission Hill and having the door literally slammed in my face. Had I so enraged the higher-ups at Brigham Hospital that they had me blacklisted from every hospital on the Eastern Seaboard? It looked that way.

Unable to find an alternative service job, I had no choice but to try and secure any means of income. That wouldn't be easy. The country was in a recession. Jobs were hard to come by. When a position did open, the competition was fierce. The fact was, I had a degree in sociology from a good college and it was worth about as much as the loose change in my tattered jeans.

I was in a serious bind. On one hand, the government made it clear that they were going to get those six months I still owed them. Or else. They assigned me a case agent with whom I had to speak on a weekly basis to discuss the status of my job search. From time to time, as I lay awake in the dark, I concluded the government's real aim was not to find me a job, but rather to cause acute anxiety and as much humiliation as possible. Payback for not fighting in their messed-up war.

After weeks of fruitless search, I finally landed a job working behind the counter of Arby's Roast Beef on Huntington Ave. I knew before I started that one of the job requirements was to wear a white paper cap, but it wasn't until I actually affixed the little triangle hat to my head—announcing "It's a pleasure to serve you!"—that I felt the full weight of degradation descend on me. I quit after a few days.

I couldn't find work, and when I did find work I couldn't keep it. I knew this local guy named Kirk. He was a very big fan of the sport; a track fanatic. He had all these issues of *Track and Field News*, like forty of them. I borrowed them all. I would stay up and read through them until three in the morning. Flipping through the pages, I would read about people I knew from college. Amby Burfoot had become a world-class long-distance runner. Jeff Galloway had taken seventh place in the Boston Marathon. Frank Shorter had become an Olympic champion. And what was my great claim to fame? Completing a hundred laps around a crummy YMCA track?

I needed something to take my mind off the constant burdens in my head. I had already moved all my worldly possessions into our new apartment. That took a total of one afternoon. I couldn't stomach another pass through the classifieds. I stared out the window at the rolling lawns and shady trees not far in the distance. Our apartment was near the border of Jamaica Pond Park, which was part of the Emerald Necklace, a long string of parks running through the heart of the city.

Looking ahead at the distant scenery, I flashed back to when I was a kid and I'd dart through the woods with Charlie and Jason, leaping over shrubs and streams without the slightest care. All those times, desperate to rid myself of the nervous energy that plagued my body and mind, and feeling a sudden need to be away from people, I would go running alone through town. And the longer I ran, the more settled I became. How else to explain my rash decision to run twelve miles on my own when I was a kid, other than a precocious spirit that often moved me to act without a road map? The point is, I could always count on running to act like some kind of root medicine for my brain, drawing out the toxins, replacing it with a soothing calm.

There I stood, an aimless, jobless twenty-four-year-old, longing for that childlike sense of well-being, when the world felt perfect, limitless, radiant. Before I knew it, I had slid on my running shoes, tucked my unruly hair behind my ears, and bounded out the door. I set off running down Centre Road, past rows of run-down Victorian houses, a testament to the hard times plaguing the neighborhood.

New England fall days are at the whim of Mother Nature and this day she was in a great mood. There was no excuse not to go running outside. But I wasn't looking for reasons to stay indoors and do nothing; I was eager to escape my grim thoughts.

Before I could enter the park, first I had to cross a four-lane death trap called the Jamaicaway. Motorists, hyped up on Dunkin' Donuts coffee, zoomed by me as I formulated a plan for surviving my mad dash across the road. If I had ever doubted that a car could be an instrument of irrational rage, I was convinced now.

After surviving the perilous crossing of the parkway, I emerged into the wide-open vista of the park's gorgeous sixty-eight-acre pond. Once I reached the small dirt path at the edge of the pond, I started running along it. Quickly, I settled into a nice groove. There was no better feeling in the world to me than this high. A beautiful morning. The soft breeze at my back, the skylit water to my right, the morning sun falling through breaks in the clouds, landing on my forehead. It was like going sightseeing, but instead of traveling by bus or car, my two legs carried me forward. I lifted my eyes to see the blossoms blooming on the trees, shifted my gaze ahead at the unending blur of nature's colors, and then looked over at the Canada geese frolicking on the water's edge.

Circling around Jamaica Pond in Jamaica Plain, I felt like I was suddenly making a connection with an ancient part of my being that had existed throughout time. A primal emotion lying dormant in my bones was released. My earliest ancestors ran in search of food and to escape predators. I no longer run for survival like them, but perhaps the traces from the past lived on in my DNA. I believe this biological need to move is felt more intensely in some than others, but I believe it's within us all.

With every step I took along the dirt path, the worries that had been nagging my mind drifted away like the butterflies I once chased as a child. In that moment, it didn't matter that I had no idea what I was going to do with the rest of my life. Or how I was going to support myself. Or how I was going to pay the rent. All the usual troubles sailed on behind me.

For the next couple of months, I did nothing but run around the pond. At first it wasn't about distance or speed, but about finding satisfaction in the doing, in cultivating the spark. I wasn't frustrated to be starting all over. I was moving at a comfortable pace—or what I call "running within myself." I was not chasing or strategizing or competing. It was enough to be on my way. Enough to be back on a path.

I was in the very beginning stages of becoming a long-distance runner. I needed to lay a foundation of fitness before I could move on to the advanced training methods I had learned from Amby. Of course, today it's called "building your base."

Every morning, before I went out running, I set a course and an amount of time to run. I remember in those first few weeks going out and trying to run five miles at a quick pace, but I couldn't do it. I wasn't ready. A lot of runners make this mistake. They run too fast at the start. They forget the first step: building up the muscles in the heart so it can pump blood farther with less exertion. You can't take on the world with a weak heart. You need to cultivate its strength first. Did you know that the heart can grow twenty percent larger in size?

I started to keep a training log again so I could see my progress. Otherwise, it's too abstract. I gradually started to build my pace, strengthen my heart, increase my endurance. My movements became more efficient. My running form looked more natural. It brought me back to my former days of running, when I'd had some success in life. In a way, it brought me back to life, back to me, the real me, the one who was happy and carefree and in love with the world and its infinite possibilities. That's a feeling that you just can't get wheeling dead bodies to the morgue.

The loop around the pond made for easy, idyllic running. I wasn't aware of it at the time, but John "the Elder" Kelley had run the same loop, who knows how many hundreds of times, in the 1930s as he trained to become Boston Marathon champion in 1935. Who knows how many more trips he had to make around the tiny pond over the course of ten years to reclaim glory in 1945. Perhaps no fewer than his protégé Johnny Kelley had run in the 1950s in his personal quest to carry the mantle, which he did through the fifties, winning the Boston Marathon in 1957. I don't think Amby ever ran that loop, but in a way he did because just as a part of Kelley was in him when he ran, a part of my old college roommate was in me when I ran. That's the way it is with runners. That's the way it is with brothers.

Months of running the loop around Jamaica Pond gave me confidence to leave its safe confines and go out farther along the Emerald Necklace. Each time I ran, I felt that biological click go on. This never happened running around the indoor track of the YMCA. Here, in nature, all things were possible. I wondered to myself, Can I run up that hill that I see in the distance? Yeah, I think I can. I think I will. And with that, I'd veer off the path and start climbing to the crest. I was once again the Peter Pan adventurer of my youth! The fearless searcher! The wild blond rascal!

Day after day, I ran along the Emerald Necklace, slowly increasing my mileage over time. I went out seven miles one day, which meant seven miles back, and I'd think to myself, I'm going to keep going. I kept pushing myself to go farther out—nine miles, ten miles, eleven miles. Challenging myself to go farther still. I could feel my body and mind gaining strength with every mile. After a while, no distance felt impossible.

I got to the point where I was running once in the morning and once in the evening—like I'd seen Amby do. That's a lot in a way, but I had slowly built up to it. Some sports put heavy hours in, like swimming or gymnastics. With running, you don't. Even the top runners in the world don't. I never ran more than two hours a day.

In many ways, Ellen and I were a perfect match. She was of a practical, down-to-earth, friendly, and quiet nature. She always made sure I left the house with everything in my pocket, no matter what kind of rush I was in. Or she'd stick a hat on my head as I was heading out for a winter run. I'd come back, cold and spent, and Ellen would cook me a nice, warm meal. She possessed an earthy gentleness that endeared her to me. We were two young, lonely free spirits in the big city, finding refuge in each other. Ellen was my first real relationship, the first girl that I could say I truly loved.

We lived a very simple, low-key existence. Our apartment had once served as part of the servants' quarters of the building. Ellen had her job, so she was bringing home money, and the rent was almost nothing: one hundred and ten bucks a month. Our costs were low. We had no health care. We didn't have any kids. We had a cat. Sometimes I would meet Ellen as she was getting off the trolley, coming home from work. We would pick up dinner at the market. We didn't live too lavishly. Once in a while we'd go out to the movies. Or eat pizza over a friend's house.

My life was very basic and regimented, almost a militarylike situation. I'd wake up in the morning, maybe grab a cup of coffee, and in no time at all, I'd be running loop after loop around the leafy pond at a six- or six-and-a-half-minute pace. I'd run once in the morning and once again in the evening. I'd sleep ten hours a night, but wake up twice. The first time, around three a.m., to eat my fourth meal of the day and go to the bathroom. I'd stand at the refrigerator, chugging quarts of soda, milk, peach nectar mixed with ginger ale. I'd shovel food into my mouth. Oreo cookies, potato chips, pickles, Hostess Twinkies, macaroni and cheese, horseradish, tartar sauce, and mayonnaise, which I'd eat straight out of the jar with a big spoon. Sometimes I wondered if the real reason I ran so many miles every day was so I could eat like that, or if I ate like that so I could run so many miles.

I felt like I was making a comeback and it lifted me up to see the progress I was making. Ellen was not a runner herself, but I think she understood that going on long runs, twice every day, was something I needed to do for my peace of mind. She did occasionally inquire how the job search was going. But she never yelled at me for training all the time. Years later, she did tell *People* magazine: "When we were first going together and he would leave to run, I thought, 'He'd rather do that than be with me?'"

Ellen never told me that was how she felt. But, looking back, I can see there was an element of selfishness in following my passion for running. Maybe every quest, no matter how good and heroic it may be, starts off kind of selfishly. Ultimately, Ellen supported my reawakened interest in running and for that I was thankful. I think she recognized that I was trying to do something positive, which was to quit smoking and get into shape. It's hard to criticize somebody for that.

Of course, most people back then had an easy time criticizing me for spending as much time as I did running. "Why do it?" they would ask. "You're not making money at it." I didn't share the common viewpoint that an activity had little value if it didn't result in some financial gain. I championed the idea of doing things just for the sake of doing them, be it running outdoors or playing a song or painting a canvas or writing a love poem. I didn't want to live in a world where something as positive and uplifting as running in nature didn't have value. As a matter of fact, I refused to.

The past five years in America had been full of excitement, hope, and urgency but they hadn't allowed for many truly peaceful breaths. For some of us—those who had experienced the whirlwind of war, love, protest, purpose, revolt, joy, and madness in our early twenties—a desire to live a simple life swelled in our hearts. No more mass political movements, no more violent clashes with police, no more "fight the power." Tend to your own garden. Like the Beatles said, let it be. For all of us hoping to recline our minds on peaceful shores, running was the perfect activity. After all, could there be a less mentally taxing activity? It's one foot in front of the other.

For all the good feelings my running along the Emerald Necklace generated inside me, it provoked anger and ridicule from the motorist passing by me on the Jamaicaway. Once, I felt an empty beer can whiz by my head. A couple of rowdy guys in a pickup truck on their way to work. This was nothing new. Getting heckled on runs. You'd hear stuff like, "Who are you running from?" or "Where's the fire?" or "Hey, fruitcake! Nice underwear!" Football was a real sport; running was for freaks and fairies. How could such a peaceful action—running down the road, communing with nature—ruffle the feathers of so many?

Not everybody was hostile toward runners, but the majority of people who saw me running alone through the park, in the middle of the day, did look at me suspiciously. They couldn't help but wonder, Why are you running? Why aren't you out looking for a job? I think they took offense at the idea of somebody escaping from their real problems. But what's so wrong with escape? Escape can be a wonderful thing.

Of course, I don't think my running was only about escaping from the pressures of life. For three years, I'd been drifting through the world only half alive. Everything felt like a life-and-death situation, a state of constant emergency, and in the hospital, many times it was. I liked zooming around the hospital and interacting with patients all day. But in a larger sense, it was strange to be in a perpetual state of motion and yet feel like I wasn't going anywhere. In that way, running wasn't an escape from life; rather, it was an embrace of it. As I bounded along the park trail, I wasn't sailing around in chaos. I was charging forward with purpose.

Running through the heart of the city, I thought about my sudden change in fortune. What if I hadn't met Ellen that night at Jack's Bar? What if I hadn't moved to Jamaica Plain with her? I'd always felt overwhelmed living in the center of downtown Boston. I felt much calmer living on the outskirts of the city. And of course I was a stone's throw away from this gigantic oasis of green amid the urban landscape.

Also, how lucky was it that I ended up doing my alternative service in Boston? After all, I could easily have done it in Newington or Hartford or any number of places. But it was here in Boston that I experienced the Boston Marathon for the first time. It practically passed outside my window. What if Jason and I hadn't driven back to Boston early that Sunday and I hadn't witnessed the grand spectacle with my own eyes? What if I had not been caught up in the race's mythical web?

I was suddenly given this chance to get back to running. That is, I had all the time in the world to run. Not to mention, I was now living across from the perfect running spot. I would wake up, throw on some sweats, and literally be running the dirt path along the pond five minutes later. Even though it was only 1.5 miles around the pond, I never tired of running lap after lap in the middle of nature.

From mid-October on, I was averaging one hundred miles per week around the Emerald Necklace. I had never run this much in my life, not even during my senior year of college, when I was at my peak as a runner. I never came close to achieving the weekly distances I was now.

I had entered a brand-new world as a runner; it was an exhilarating place to be. In September, I set a new high mark: 124 miles for the week. Why stop now?

I was driven, but not like most twenty-four-year-olds living in Boston. What drove them was making money and having a nice house and a good career. I was driven to run. I was this penniless athlete aiming for an ideal. It was like Plato and the perfect city, you know?

What the war had taken away from me was my motivation to run. After all, who cared about running when I might have to leave my country and family and seek refuge with the kiwi birds in New Zealand? But what the war also took from me was my freedom. Suddenly, I was required to find a job that fulfilled my alternative service duty or face prison. This life I was forced to live offered no room for a steady running routine. In that way, I lost the freedom that came from liberating myself from my troubled mind. Running was my way of stepping outside myself, of tolerating the human condition. I no longer had the chance to be a kid at play. My soul diminished. My world collapsed. I fell apart.

Once I started running around Jamaica Pond, those positive feelings came rushing back. I had been dead in places without even knowing it. I felt alive again. I felt hope. I don't think I could have stopped running each day in the park even had I wanted to. First of all, there was the sweet rush of the runner's high. Those endorphins raced through my brain, repairing the damage done. The war had screwed me up. The filth and noise and congestion from the city had screwed me up. Smoking and drinking had screwed me up. Taking bodies to the morgue had screwed me up. Being treated like a peon by administrators had screwed me up. Running in the park was a powerful form of recovery.

Here's what you have to understand: For runners, progress is the root of pleasure. While progress in life can be hard to see, sometimes impossible, all I had to do was open up my ten-cent running diary and peer inside. My physical evolution was clearly laid out before my eyes—where I was when I started, where I was now. It was a way of grabbing the reins of life: I ran five miles yesterday, I ran seven miles today, and next week I will run ten miles. The more work I put in, the stronger I became. I felt good. I felt fit. Now I was really tapping into my human potential. No substance on the planet can rival a rush like that.

Now there was no turning back. The voice inside me that said I should focus on finding a job was drowned out by the much louder voice inside me that demanded that I feed my appetite to move. It told me that I had starved my soul for too long. Nursing that shrunken nub back to health was now my only concern.

The medicine that one needs to take to cure his or her shriveled soul depends on that person. Most people search their whole life looking for this medicine, sometimes in the most bizarre places. Sometimes they try to find it in another human being. But all one ever has to do is move. Moving is the medicine. Running, walking, jumping, hopping, skipping, dancing, twirling, swimming, hiking, biking—they all have the same inexplicably powerful effect on our being. I discovered the potent remedy of movement as a child. I was possessed by a frantic mind and prone to foolish behavior. Running was the shelter from the storm of chaotic emotions—impatience, hurt, loneliness, frustration. If I ever lost my true self, all I had to do was run long enough and far enough and there I'd find it.

That fall, I got a letter from selective service. It said that I'd fulfilled my obligation to the government. I was deemed a permanent conscientious objector. They'd finally let me go. At long last, I was free.

By now, I had no doubt as to my objective. I knew it before that moment but wasn't ready to admit it to myself. The undertaking was too daunting, too dangerous, too bold. But why else had I been training so hard all those months? The truth was, I had been preparing for battle. I knew what was next. The comeback was already on.

I was going to race the Boston Marathon.

EIGHT

Battle at Silver Lake

APRIL 21, 1975
WELLESLEY, MASSACHUSETTS

As I broke away from Drayton, I felt a mix of exhilaration and apprehension. To start racing hard at eleven miles, with fifteen miles ahead of me, I was taking a big leap into the unknown. I had reacted spontaneously to events as they unfolded. It wasn't that different than the artist who follows his creative impulses.

Look at the way Frank Shorter suddenly made his move in Munich in 1972. I don't know if he was planning to charge to the front at the nine-mile mark, and keep pushing the tempo with seventeen miles to go, but he did and blew away the field by over two minutes to become the first American gold medal winner in sixty-four years. Did my friend and fellow New Englander Joan Benoit Samuelson plan to surge ahead only three miles into the 1984 Olympic marathon while her competitors were playing it safe in the brutal heat, or was she just feeling feisty in that moment? She finished a minute and a half ahead of the overwhelming favorite, Grete Waitz, to take gold. They weren't worrying about breaking down when they made their move. Neither was I when I made mine against Drayton.

I felt good making this aggressive move; I saw a little gap and I was going to drive through it like a thoroughbred horse—fearless in flight. As for Drayton, I lost him quickly after I shot to the front. He soon became out of sight, out of mind.

For the first time, I found myself alone in the lead of a major race. In the World Cross-Country Championships, I had two other guys fighting for the lead with me. But suddenly there I was running out front by myself. It was a powerful feeling to be roaring along the road with a sense of no obstacles in my way. I was on my way toward the finish. I had nothing to lose.

As I made my way through an isolated area outside of Wellesley, I ran with the same relaxed, powerful strides that I used following Amby through the winding trails around campus, or, as he'd said, "always a half-stride behind, eyes nearly closed, right arm flapping and light hair bouncing rhythmically to the cadence of the run."

I could hear the rumble, like distant thunder, of the crowds in the distance. It could only mean one thing. The infamous Wellesley "scream tunnel" was getting close. In a moment, I would encounter thousands of Wellesley College women lining the streets, hollering their heads off, carrying signs saying, KISS ME, I'M A SENIOR or KISS ME, I'M A CHEMIST or HOW ABOUT A QUICKIE? or GIVE ME A HUG. I felt energized by the cheers of the female superfans growing closer and louder.

As I came into Wellesley at mile 11.5, the road narrowed and the growing crowds squeezed in around me. I felt momentum running through downtown, past all the Wellesley College girls, standing along the edge of the road, screaming and whooping and offering kisses.

I know Tommy Leonard, the larger-than-life bartender at the Eliot Lounge, the local hangout for us runners in the Greater Boston Track Club, particularly enjoyed running through the gauntlet of out-of-control female students: "These girls, I love when they come out. They're all good-looking chicks. I try to make dates. See you at the Eliot Lounge, but none of them show up—I'm oh for twenty-one." In contrast, at the 1992 Boston Marathon, Kenyan runner Ibrahim Hussein put his fingers in his ears to block the deafening roar of the coeds en route to victory.

As for me, the waves of screaming female coeds had no impact on me. It's not that the shouts of encouragement from the Wellesley women didn't provide me with a nice lift—it definitely did—but I wasn't there to make dates. The pope could have been there giving out blessings and I wouldn't have stopped. Such was my drive to win the race.

As I ran alone through Wellesley, the road got narrower while the crowds got bigger. And louder. And more intense. There was increasingly less room on the road for me to squeeze through, but I loved that in a way. I reacted to the energy of the crowd and it drove me on. If you talk to anyone who's ever run the Boston Marathon, they'll all say that: The support from the cheering crowd gives you a huge lift. So I had that on my side when I was taking off. I'd never enjoyed the special attention of running in the lead. I was the awkward little brother at the high school dance, the wallflower, the one who was too shy to ask the girls to dance. And my parents, while patient and loving, weren't the type to lavish praise on my brother and me—most of the time they had no clue where we'd run off. I was relishing the moment, eyes ahead, feet soaring, arms pumping, a tongue steeped in the sweetness of adulation, to quote Willy Shakespeare.

Moving past Wellesley campus, I headed deeper into the center of town. I sailed past the quaint brick-and-stucco–faced shops and rowdy masses, cruising over some nice subtle downgrades. Nobody called out my name. Nobody held up a sign that read GO, BILL. But it didn't matter that I wasn't a well-known runner. It didn't matter that I wasn't Frank Shorter. Once they spotted the Boston insignia on my chest—alerting them to the fact that a hometown kid was leading the Boston Marathon— they went crazy. I savored the sounds of their ecstatic cheers, the sense that they were on my side. Collectively, they were telling me, "You've got this." Fats and carbohydrates were fueling my body, but it was the people lining the road that powered me forward. Emboldened by my newfound fans, my legs glided along the road, with long, quick, fluid strides. I was tearing up the miles, hurtling them behind me, putting as much distance between myself and the other runners as I could. At this stage in the race, it was all or nothing.

I didn't know it at the time—I was moving too fast, too focused—but one of the spectators I passed here was "the Rookie," Alberto Salazar. He was standing along the road with his father, Ricardo, waiting for the lead pack to arrive.

This is how Alberto would recall in his memoir that moment. I rocketed past him: "There was skinny, spacey Bill, with his long hair flowing in back of him, the guy I'd eaten BLTs with at Friendly's ice-cream restaurants. He's wearing white tube socks that stretch up to midcalf and a pair of shoes sent out from Blue Ribbon Sports in Oregon, the forerunner of Nike. He's wearing a ratty T-shirt on which he's crayoned the letters 'GBTC.' Despite this motley getup, Bill is wailing. He's opened a four hundred-yard lead in the most prestigious marathon on earth, and I can see very clearly that nobody's going to catch him. 'I know that guy!' I shouted to my dad and brother. 'I run with that guy!' But mostly I'm shouting this amazing fact to myself, and at that moment, like a bolt, it comes to me: This is the marathon; this is what Coach Squires promises is waiting for me. At that moment, I resolved—at that moment, *I knew*—that I was going to grab that destiny with both hands. I knew with every fiber of my being that I was going to become the greatest marathon runner in the world."

All things are related in this sport, as they are in life. I didn't understand the allure of the Boston Marathon until the day I stood along the side of the famed course with Jason and witnessed the intensity and magnitude and beauty of the spectacle. I was struck with amazement seeing Jeff Galloway, my teammate from Wesleyan, and John Vitale, whom I ran against at the University of Connecticut, competing with the top runners for victory. I thought, Wait a minute, if they can do it, so can I. The same way Amby had heard the powerful calling as he watched his hero, Johnny Kelley, race by him, I had heard the powerful calling as I watched the familiar faces sweep past me. And now Alberto had heard the same calling watching me. Maybe the next great American marathon runner to hear the call, to grab that destiny with both hands, to embrace the challenge of the human spirit, is reading this story. Maybe it's you.

Two Years Earlier
Silver Lake Dodge 30K Road Race, Hopkinton, Massachusetts

It was a cold February morning. I stretched my legs beside the small town green. Standing guard over me and the other runners warming up in the center of town was a bronze World War I soldier statue, a monument to the one hundred and fifteen locals who fought in that war. The dominating presence of the statue let anybody entering Hopkinton know the high regard in which the townspeople held military service. On second thought, maybe I wouldn't tout my conscientious objector status at the general store.

Downtown Hopkinton was a postcard of tranquil winter in rural New England. Hard to believe that here, in this one-horse town, the Boston Marathon, the most famous footrace in history, kicked off every April. As I scanned the center of town, I tried to picture the sudden transformation on the big day—the downtown teeming with activity, food and craft vendors spread out across the grass, runners from all over the world unloading from buses until they numbered in the thousands, then assembling themselves on the starting line. I allowed myself a moment to imagine that I was one of those runners, crouched like a tiger, ready to take off on the 26.2-mile race to Boston. A 26.2-mile quest for running immortality. Thinking about it was enough to give me goose bumps.

I watched the other racers on the green, jogging back and forth to stay warm, making last-minute preparations. Almost all of them were from New England. Guys with regular jobs. Teachers, carpenters, real-estate brokers. Lots of former college track and cross-country athletes.

They would train months on end to the bewilderment, perhaps even frustration, of friends and families. They would suffer the dirty looks of motorists passing by them as they ran alone at dawn. And all week, at work, at home, doing the mundane routine of life, their minds would be consumed with the next grueling battle on the road. To be honest, they were a little on the crazy side. How else to describe guys who spent every weekend driving up to 150 miles of bad road to run a road race against a bunch of other adrenaline-junkie running mercenaries? How else to describe guys who chose to put their bodies and minds through the agony of a twenty-mile duel in below-freezing weather, no less in pursuit of some prize like a color TV or a mattress set?

As for me, I was a neophyte. I had no idea if I could survive such a daunting competition. I was winging it, even though racing twenty miles on foot in the brutal cold of winter was not something to wing. Same goes for any tough physical test—nobody says, "Everest? Yeah, I'm winging it." I knew the incredible physical effort and mental focus it took to cover fourteen miles in a training run—and now I was going to be fighting it out with these amped-up mooses at a distance of twenty miles. Seriously, was I crazy? But I had to race Silver Lake; it was my last and only hope of gauging whether or not I was prepared to run the Boston Marathon, only two months away.

I knew what Amby would tell me: Before trying to compete in my first marathon, I needed to run at least five shorter tune-up races to get my body back into the attitude of running that hard and fast. And he'd be right. Racing is the best simulation for racing.

The men I'd be going up against were experienced road runners who'd run several tune-up races to test their mental and physical fitness. They'd done lots of hard speed work to build up their endurance. I'd done almost no hard speed work around Jamaica Pond. For one, it wasn't my nature. Secondly, it was winter. Exertion in the snow and cold is not fun. I was stupid—naïve, if you're being kind—to think I was ready to compete in a marathon, let alone a twenty-mile race in the middle of winter. I just hoped all those laps on the pond had paid off.

The race I was about to run would cover the first twenty miles of the Boston Marathon course, but that would be where the similarities ended. The roads would not be lined with thousands of people cheering, clapping, and passing out cups of water. The only spectators gathered at the kickoff of the race were a few bored townspeople, and the friends of runners who'd come to lend moral support.

The scene at the Silver Lake Dodge was typical for a local road race. This was strictly for hardcore runners. No bells. No whistles. No officials. No fans. It was as close to pure competition as you could get. And, believe me, the racers relished these bare-bones, do-or-die affairs.

I was still warming up near the start line when I spotted a tall, lanky figure coming toward me. That stiff, almost robotic gait was unmistakable. It was my old roommate Amby Burfoot. I hadn't seen him since he graduated Wesleyan in '68. I was excited to see him.

"Bill, I hardly recognized you," said Amby.

"It's been a while," I said. "How have you been?"

"I've been good. Got a job teaching little rugrats down in Connecticut."

"That sounds like a good job."

"I also got married."

"Wow," I said. "That's great news!"

"I heard you were up in Boston," Amby said. "Doing your service." I was sure Amby'd heard stories of me riding around town on my motorcycle, smoking a lot of cigarettes, hitting bars, but he was far too polite to bring up my wastrel activities. Besides, I knew Amby's position when it came to telling other people what they should do: It's not up to him to get people to change, it's up to them. I hoped that he would see from the fact that I was racing in the Silver Lake that I was at least trying to change. Then again, from the slightly quizzical look on his face, he might have just been wondering about my running attire: ragged blue jeans and a tattered sweatshirt full of holes.

"You look . . ." Amby started. He paused a moment, as if trying to find the right word and then continued: "Kind of homeless."

We both burst out laughing.

"Bill, this is great! It's so wonderful to see you! I'm glad you've decided to do some jogging," said Amby in a gentle fashion. "I think I heard you had started smoking."

"I was," I said. "But I'm done with that now."

"You're trying to get back into shape. That's a good thing, Bill."

Amby had always encouraged me to stay fit in college—I can still hear him telling me to run five miles every day in the summer. Ha!—so I wasn't surprised that he'd expressed his support of my attempt to return to running. It was a bit odd, however, that he was talking to me like some overweight, middle-age guy who was new to the concept of exercise.

"Do you have a team to run for?" asked Amby.

"No," I said, surprised. "Do I need one?"

"Don't worry," Amby said. "Just put 'BAA' down on your entry form."

As I lined up beside the one hundred runners, I felt a rush of excitement. To be back at the start line of an actual race got the juices flowing. And to be going up against Amby Burfoot. My roommate, my teammate, my friend, my mentor. I hadn't expected that. Amby Burfoot. Boston Marathon champion. Undefeated for four years at Wesleyan. Fifth in the Fukuoka Marathon, missing the American marathon record by one second. He would be the highest-level runner I had ever raced against.

As I stood there waiting for the gun to sound, my raggedy sweatshirt and jeans offered little protection against the cold. I kept thinking about the distance I was about to run. Twenty miles. That was a long haul. Road races are almost never that long anymore.

The race was under way. I saw Amby vault to the front of the pack. Instinctually, I did what I'd done so many times before on training runs in college—I followed him.

In Ashland, a clear lead group emerged—Amby, myself, and two guys I didn't know. After we broke free from the rest of the field, we settled into a fast but steady pace. Although we were covering the same course used in the Boston Marathon, this had a very different feel to it. For one, it was February, not April. The cold was brutal. Also, there were no spectators, no ropes, no cops on motorcycles, no media trucks, no water stations.

Cars and trucks drove past us and they had no idea a race was going on. We were just a bunch of wackos running down the street in the damn cold.

It was a four-man race as we ran through Ashland and into Framingham. The pace was quick. Maybe too quick. But racing was different back then. Nobody was too concerned with his splits. Nobody was checking his digital watch. Most of us didn't even wear watches. Beating the competition was the be-all, end-all. Everybody wanted to win those tires, and we were willing to thrash one another on the roads to get them.

I knew from my training that I was in good shape, but I had no idea that I'd be able to do what I was doing now, running neck and neck with Amby in the lead. It gave me a powerful psychological boost, and the energy to stay with him mile after mile.

It was an advantage to be in a two-man duel at the front because all I had to do was concentrate on staying with Amby. I didn't have to think about the other runners. Whatever extended a few feet beyond us and a few feet behind us didn't exist to me. Sometimes a training run evolves into a race, and other times a race evolves into a personal battle of wills. That's what was happening here. I respected Amby. I respected what he'd accomplished. But in the heat of battle, all I could think about was trying to outlast him.

I was in my first high-mileage road race and loved that it demanded an intense, rough-and-tumble style of running. I wasn't like some of the runners today. They run solely for time. I could care less about my time. For me, it was always about the competition. It was about being in the hunt. Racing in the lead pack. That's tremendously exciting. Any runner who races will experience an incredible surge of adrenaline and exhilaration, but to be in the hunt for the win is a different deal. It's a totally different deal.

In the cold weather my feet froze, my face froze, and nothing worked at full capacity—my heart, my lungs, my muscles, my joints—and yet never in my life had I felt a high like I had at that very moment. My whole being was engaged in the task before me. Matching Amby stride for stride. I had been catapulted through a portal. In this new universe, all my senses were fully engaged in the here and now. I was connected to the road and to my breath and to my adversary—he was no longer my friend Amby—moving in perfect harmony beside me. An electrical current flowed from my mind to my heart to my fingers. This feeling was different than the running high I got from training hours in the park; it was more than a release of endorphins. I had tapped into a primeval fight-or-flight impulse. I was energized as hell.

Ten miles into the race and I was still attached to Amby's hip pocket. Amby glanced over at me in disbelief. He had not expected to see me bouncing alongside him with what he called my "goofy stride."

Here's what you need to understand: To all of a sudden be holding my own against Amby was an epiphany. I had never duked it out with him like this before. I could never stay with him back in college. We ran the two mile back then. I could have trained day and night and I'd never have been able to beat him at that distance. Even when I got my time under nine minutes in my senior year, I still would have been no match for Amby. I didn't have his speed. I didn't have his finishing kick. I didn't have the psychological wiring to run short distances. It wasn't what I was born to do. I knew I'd never be anything but ordinary at short distances. It's a big reason I quit running. It was like my mom always said: If the point isn't to be the best, why do it?

By now, I was relying on adrenaline—or whatever you want to call it—to maintain my position up at the front with Amby. I glanced over at him. He was running exactly like he had fifteen miles back—steady and methodical.

That's when things got weird. With each step I took, the gap between us steadily grew larger. First Amby was only a couple of yards ahead of me. I told myself, Stay in striking distance. But no matter how hard I ran, I kept falling farther and farther behind. Before I knew it, he was twenty yards ahead of me. Then thirty yards ahead. All at once, the invisible rope that connected us snapped and Amby took off into the distance.

What had just happened?

I'll tell you what: Amby had increased his pace, but in such a subtle fashion that I hadn't picked up on it at first. Didn't matter. There was nothing I could do at that point to save myself. I couldn't go any faster. I was maxed out. Amby still had another gear. He had marathon strength. He was fitter than I was. He had the edge and he knew it. I was done for.

It suddenly became clear to me. From the very start, Amby had been analyzing his progress, keeping close tabs on his exertion level, making sure he was maintaining the correct pace. I should have been doing the same, but instead my entire focus was on keeping stride for stride with Amby. Not the most sophisticated strategy in the world.

Meanwhile, Amby had been patiently watching me all those miles. Judging me. Measuring how he was feeling against how I was feeling. Assessing how long he could keep this pace up versus how long I could. Waiting for the right time to make his move. How had he gotten it so right? Could he tell by how hard I was breathing? Could he perceive the muscles in my neck straining slightly more? Could he have sensed a minuscule change in my gait?

Once I had dropped a couple of yards behind him, he knew he had me. I couldn't see what was happening as clearly. I thought I could hang on. But it didn't matter how hard I ran, he kept opening the gap farther and farther. There's something about being overtaken by a physically superior runner that can only be understood by experiencing it—the sense of inexorable doom, the overwhelming helplessness, the dreamlike state where you can't move any faster, you're doing your best, but it's not enough. I had simply run out of bullets. The worst part was Amby knew it before I did. He knew I was toast. I was his good friend, but he did what he was supposed to do. He left me behind. He went for the win.

Luckily, after losing sight of Amby, I had another runner come up on me, so we commenced to race. What was I going to do, walk off the course? My legs cramped over the last few miles. I gritted my teeth and fought on. Having somebody to race against helped me get to the finish. One of the weird dualities of the sport is that sometimes your fellow runner is a competitor, other times he's your helper.

In the end, the unknown runner beat me by seconds. The moment I crossed the finish line, we shook hands. The code of conduct among runners is powerful; it's what makes it a true gentlemen's sport.

Once inside the warm confines of the dealership showroom, I began to thaw out. My body was freezing cold and tired from running so hard. I was also cramping badly. I looked around for bagels, bananas, and hot chocolate. All I found was a small pitcher of water. I would've loved to slip off my iced-over blue jeans and throw on a pair of warm Gore-Tex pants. Unfortunately, the fabric wouldn't be invented for another three years. In my ratty jeans and sneakers, I was not exactly ready for my Nike ad.

Moments later, the owner of the Silver Lake Dodge dealership congratulated Amby on his victory and awarded him his grand prize: a set of four tires. This was the essence of New England road racing. You didn't run to become rich or famous. You ran to test your mettle. You ran to see if you had what it took. You ran to compete. Nothing more, nothing less.

Amby didn't have a car, so he offered the tires to the second-place winner. He also didn't have a car, so he offered them to the next guy in line, which was me. What was I going to do with four tires? Build an obstacle course? In the end, who knows how many broken-down runners they had to go through before they found somebody with a set of wheels.

Amby came over and I congratulated him on his victory. Over the last few miles, he had built a three-minute lead over the rest of us, and was still running at a five-minute-per-mile pace. His win was decisive. He had run a great race and I wanted him to know it. I wasn't surprised that he'd beaten me. He'd always beaten me in college. Besides, I was sky high, just knowing I had hung with Amby for as long as I had. Coming in third place in my first race back was more than I could have ever expected. Frankly, I was stunned. From the look on Amby's face, I could tell he was, too.

"Have you been doing much speed work?" he asked.

"No, I've just been running easy around the park," I said.

"That's amazing, Bill," he said. "Where you got the ability to run that fast for that long is a miracle." He looked me right in the eye. "You have a great gift."

Receiving such a compliment from Amby, who I respected more than anybody in this world, made my heart swell.

I had discovered I could run at longer distances. And not just run—I could be in the mix. After all, I had just stayed with Amby Burfoot for twenty miles. Just then, an older man approached us.

"Who are ya?" he said to me in a thick Scottish accent.

"This is Bill Rodgers," Amby interjected. "My roommate from college."

"Some guy just told me 'my guy from the BAA' took third place," said Jock in a calm—too calm—tone. "I take it you're my guy."

I looked back at him, slightly nervous.

"Well, in that case, nice job out there, young lad."

"Thank you," I said.

"I take it you plan to race in the Boston Marathon?"

I liked how he'd said that. Not "run in the Boston Marathon"—"race in the Boston Marathon."

"Yes," I replied.

"Well, how would you like to run for the BAA," he said with a glint of excitement in his eyes.

I looked over at Amby as if to confirm that the moment was real. "Absolutely," I said.

"That's what I like to hear!" said Jock, his face breaking into a big grin as he slapped me heartily on the back. "Come by my clinic over at the Boston Garden and we'll talk."

A few weeks later, I went over to the Garden. I got lost for an hour wandering through a labyrinth of dark hallways until I finally reached the door of Jock's clinic. I expected to be knocked out by some fancy place with carpet and enamel sinks. Instead, I found Jock in the bowels of the Garden, bustling around the tiny room in an old T-shirt, white duck trousers, and sneakers. One moment, he'd be taking a Bruins player from the rubdown table to the whirlpool, the next pulling a couple of brokers out of the steambath, all the while rushing back and forth to a constantly ringing phone to answer inquiries about the marathon. Some runner called, asking for a bib number. Jock suspected he was some kind of clown, and not a "real runner." He slammed the phone down.

While all this was going on, I stood staring in awe at the framed photographs of famous runners hanging on the walls. Suddenly, I heard Jock's booming voice: "Hey, you over there. What do you want?"

"I met you at the Silver Lake Dodge race a couple of weeks ago," I said sheepishly. "I got third, right behind Amby. You said that I could join your team, that I should come by and see you. You said—"

"I said 'come right over,' didn't I?" Jock said, a glaring smile now stretched across his face.

"What?"

"I said 'come right over,' not 'wait three weeks.' Get on a table here. I'll move one of my men. Mickey, get up there, willya? This fella here ran third at Silver Lake Dodge. Climb on, lad. Let's see what legs you have attached to ya. I've been bettin' people you'll be the next Johnny Kelley."

From that day on, I would occasionally stop by the Garden after a long run, at which time Jock would tell me to hop on the table and give me a rubdown, all the while regaling me with these amazing stories of the Boston Marathon. My appreciation of the race and the men who ran it over the years would grow with each visit.

As for the Silver Lake Dodge, my first real introduction to competitive road racing had taught me much. Whereas I was winging it the whole way, Amby had run a smart, deliberate race. He had been patient and methodical, mile after mile, quietly judging his strength against my strength. He had been careful not to strike too early. He was content to match me stride for stride for over an hour before making his move. I couldn't fathom ever being that patient—I was too impulsive, too reactive, too fiery.

Incredibly, Amby picked the perfect moment to test my resolve. He sensed it. If you think about it, that depth of awareness is amazing. But if you want to be a truly great road racer, you need to possess this talent. Incredible fitness is not enough. You need to be attuned to your surroundings. That means simultaneously mindful of the weather conditions, tapped into the emotional and physical state of your competition, and still hypertuned into your own body. It's hard to be that "in the moment" for more than a few seconds. Seeing up close how an experienced road racer like Amby could lock in to that mind-set for twenty miles was exhilarating.

On that cold winter day, running through small town after small town, I had unlocked another huge secret: I was a threat at long distances. After all, if I could run with Amby—the 1968 Boston Marathon winner—then I could run with anybody. I was excited to show everybody what I could do on the biggest stage in long-distance running. I wasn't thinking about winning the Boston Marathon. That was too much to dream. But what about a top-fifteen finish? Or even top-ten? Of course, to pull that off, I'd have to run a 2:20. Difficult, but not impossible. Not if I ran like I did here at Silver Lake. I was running close to a 2:20 pace, and Boston was practically the same course, only 6.2 miles longer.

The next day couldn't come quickly enough. And when it finally did, I knew exactly where I'd be. Blasting my way around Jamaica Pond. Gunning for the race of my life.

NINE

Nothing but Heartbreak

C oming out of Wellesley, I encountered a great downhill that continued for almost half a mile. There's no descent like this in any major marathon. Not in Stockholm or Amsterdam or Berlin or London or Tokyo. Ask me why Boston is the most exhilarating long-distance road race, I would point to spots like this—a half-mile, hundred-foot drop into Newton Lower Falls! I looked at the steep descent as a gift. With little exertion, I let gravity pull me down the steep stretch of road. I flowed like a river.

I've always thought of this as the perfect place to attack. Here's where you can throw in a hard surge and see how the competition responds. Test their will, their determination, their endurance against yours. But I had nobody to test myself against. I was alone. Just me and the lead vehicle. On this day, I had already thrown in my surge—when I broke away from Drayton around mile 11. Surging is an emotional thing. There's someone next to you and you're feeling very competitive. One runner will surge and the other will surge back. It's like when boxers slug it out for a bit, but this is noncontact. Frank Shorter was great at throwing in surges to break his opponents. He could sense if a guy was struggling and throw in a 4:30 mile and that would destroy him. Surging can be a nasty business. Necessary but nasty.

I don't know if other runners attacked this downhill section before me. I don't know about how Clarence DeMar or Johnny Kelley ran this part, but I made a point of running hard here a number of times, probably because I trained on the course. I knew I could really move down the hills. For some people, flying down a sharp, hundred-foot descent meant potential disaster, but for me it meant I could push the envelope. This was a chance to chew up some miles before hitting the infamous Newton Hills. It was easier running, it cost me fewer calories, and required less work. Of course, the descent could be a real problem for the legs and the arms, almost similar to body shots in boxing, especially on a warm day when the muscles were working extrahard. That's why I disagree with people who say Boston isn't a legitimate record course— the constant stream of uphills and downhills put tremendous fatigue on your legs. I think the extreme elevation changes, not to mention the variety of weather conditions, make Boston the most difficult marathon course in the world. This marathon demands the most of top runners— physically *and* mentally. No question about it. Nowhere else is race *strategy* such a critical matter.

After reaching the bottom of the half-mile drop into Newton Lower Falls, I ran over a patch of flat road before starting up the first hill of Newton, a tough half-mile ascent that takes you along a long overpass that crosses Route 128. The climb over the highway is gradual, but its length, almost three quarters of a mile, causes some runners to consume more energy than their bodies can afford, especially with the really big hills straight ahead. But running in the lead was exhilarating. I had a feeling like, Nothing can stop me. This is it. I'm doing it right now. I'm going for it. It was very intense. The lead vehicle, a hundred yards ahead of me, gave me something to aim for. I was getting closer and closer. And no one was coming up on my heels.

The whole way I was keeping tabs on my effort level. I felt I was running at the right pace. I was extending myself, but it wasn't killing me to maintain my speed. Once I crested the hill, I let the wind push me down a nice downhill past the hospital. It was a great place to catch my breath. I was coming up on eighteen miles and felt the sense of "this is all that's left. I've already run a lot of the Boston marathon. I'm close to home." The more you have that sense, the easier it is to race.

In 1909, a *Boston Globe* scribe wrote, "The long hard slopes in the distance have proved to be the undoing of many ambitious lads." And it's true. Nobody gets to go through the Newton Hills without their body paying the toll fee. It's the classic line, "Anyone can run twenty miles. But can you go twenty-six?" Those hills make it especially true at Boston.

As I passed through Newton Hills, Jock Semple popped his head out of the back of the moving lead vehicle. He was wearing a fedora. He was very fired up. On marathon day, Jock went wild! The old competitive marathon blood heated up in him.

For years, Jock would come up alongside runners, wired as can be, hang out of the press bus, and scream out words of encouragement in his thick Scottish accent. In 1957, he leaped from the still-moving press bus at the Newton Lowers Falls to give Johnny Kelley a water-soaked sponge and oranges on his way to victory. In 1968, he caught up to Amby Burfoot as he was cresting Heartbreak Hill in the heat. "Give it hell down the hills!" he yelled to Amby, who was desperately trying to hold his lead. Amby later wrote, "Semple's blustery words renewed me."

"Do you want me to take your gloves?" Jock shouted to me from the bus.

I shook my head no.

During all those miles I had run alone that winter, I ran with my mittens and would take them off and put them in my pockets, and then put them back on when my hands got cold. I suppose I was used to wearing something on my hands. Also, my brother Charlie had bought them for me, and I wasn't about to give them away to Jock.

Focusing on the lead vehicle kept me running steady and determined mile after mile. I was charging from the front. The crowd was on my side. They were cheering so loud for me. Everyone gets cheered at

Boston, but the cheers aren't like that for eight hundredth place. People are looking for the winners. So it was a very powerful feeling, just a surge of energy.

I would be uninterested in a little race, way out in the country with no spectators. I may as well have been on a training run. It meant nothing to me. I needed to hear the crowd and be slugging it out with a rival as we matched each other footstep for footstep down the course. The more cheers, the better. I always responded to that. To some people it means nothing. Not me. It got me even more hyped up. I felt unbeatable.

As I run, I'm hyperattuned to my body so that I can hear what my powerful reptilian brain—which thinks in terms of physical survival—is telling me. The marathon race is a grueling test. I don't have the luxury to listen to my normal brain, scattered with thoughts and memories and wishes and perceptions. I need to be free of the clutter and chaos of my ADHD mind, but I also can't shut off my brain. How else will I know if I'm running too fast or too slow, if my muscles are exerting too much effort or not enough, if I'm breathing too deep or too shallow, if my arms are in the right position, if my gait is efficient?

I was running five-minute miles, pushing my body to the limit. It would be easy to check out for a mile or two, lose track of the essential real-time information being transmitted to me about my physical condition, to momentarily forget about strategy or the whereabouts of my competitors. But I know I'd be putting myself in danger the moment I crossed that line. I might miss warnings of impending trouble. I might make a critical error that could cost me the race. I might run at less than full capacity. That's unacceptable. If you have any chance of winning the Boston Marathon, you need to maximize your potential, not just some of the time, but all of the time. Not just every mile, but every stride.

I blasted down the road, I wasn't checking out the smiling, exhilarated faces in the crowds. I wasn't marveling at the raucous sideshow.

No mantras. No metaphysical states. Just me running down the road in a state of calm, intense focus, my feet striking the ground at a steady tempo, my mind cleared of distracting chatter, where everything comes down to the race and dealing with the race.

I was acutely aware of how far I had come and how far I had to go. I didn't have a watch, but I had been so tapped into my pace, mile after mile, that I had a good idea of my current time. Not that I cared. At that moment, my mind was plunged deep into its mission—going for the win. It would have taken a Kenyan runner to beat me. I was fired up. Pure fun.

Two Years Earlier
Boston, Massachusetts

The day after my twenty-mile assault on the Boston Marathon course in the Silver Lake race, I ran thirteen miles around Jamaica Pond. Actually, "ran" isn't the right word. "Very slowly trotted" is more like it. My legs ached. My muscles felt like steel cables. But nothing, not even electrified fences, was going to keep me from working out in the park. When you feel your soul starting to take flight, you don't trample on it. No. You see where it's going to take you.

The Silver Lake road race had revealed unexpected pleasures: the thrill of running in the lead, the excitement of being in contention, the exhilaration of dueling at high speed. I loved all of it. The pure rush of excitement I felt racing took me back to my childhood days chasing butterflies in the fields with big brother Charlie and Jason. Back before the war, the draft, the government obligations, the physical deterioration, the smoking in bars, the empty and lost and trapped feelings. Being in contention for the win, after three long years away from running, encouraged me to set my sights even higher. I hungered to explore the reaches of my potential. I committed myself to a single pursuit: the

Boston Marathon. It was a chance to embark on a new adventure. I couldn't wait.

My first long-distance road race did more than spark a new passion, it also taught me some important lessons. I learned that while it was good to be an ambitious runner, acting on emotion alone spelled ruin on the roads. That quick bursts of adrenaline at the start might carry you for a few miles, but it zapped precious energy, opening you up to fatigue, the archenemy of all distance runners. Sooner or later, you will wilt. I observed firsthand that the methodical runner who uses every tool in his bag of tricks to lure his opponents into error wins the race. His body performs as efficiently at the end of the race as it did at the beginning. With his calm demeanor, his steady pace, and his relentless obedience to his plan, he can dismantle the more disorganized and impulsive runners. Like me.

I knew that if I wanted to compete against the world's best runners at the Boston Marathon, I needed to intensify my training over the next two months. For most runners, "intensify" means running harder and faster in workouts. I had a different definition. For me, it meant running twice a day, about twenty miles total, but at a slow and easy pace, around seven minutes per mile. I didn't do speed work, which at the time was considered an essential part of any elite marathon runner's training routine.

I had a good reason for going against the grain. I had watched my college roommate use this unorthodox method of training to win the 1968 Boston Marathon and become a top international runner in the late sixties. I also learned from Amby about where he learned this secret training discipline: his mentor, Johnny Kelley, winner at Boston in 1957 and the greatest marathon runner of his era.

The combined success of these two New Englanders dwarfed all other U.S. marathon runners over a period of seventy years. I was a believer. I'd just gone head to head with Amby and crumbled in the face of a calm, steady, almost boring juggernaut of destruction. What I didn't realize at the time was that by incorporating their wisdom into my training routine, I was carrying on a sacred tradition. I was becoming the next link in the epic New England running legacy.

I could have used Amby to help coach me for the big race, but he was a schoolteacher in Connecticut. He had a family to support. I didn't have Coach O'Rourke to push me. I didn't have my brother, Charlie, to keep me in line. I didn't have my Wesleyan teammates to encourage me. If I was going to meet this challenge, I was going to have to meet it alone. At the same time, I knew what would happen if I didn't try. I'd never know what kind of runner I could be. I wanted to prove to myself I could be great.

When it came to preparing for the marathon, I fell back on what I remembered from watching Amby at Wesleyan. He worked out every day and never made an excuse to get out of training. So on Tuesday, even though my legs still ached, I ran twelve miles in the early afternoon and three miles later in the day. On Wednesday, the weather was warm and I ran eleven miles in the afternoon but had to turn in early because my jock strap broke.

That night, I wrote in my training log: "The hard training begins tomorrow." The next day I ran thirteen miles around Jamaica Pond in the afternoon and six miles after dinner. I was still one mile short of my goal to run twenty miles per day. Around midnight I got out of bed, leaving Ellen asleep beside me, quietly put on my shoes, walked out the front door, and ran through the neighborhood, lit only by streetlamps. I completed one mile, took off my shoes, snuck back into bed, and fell asleep. Twenty miles for the day. Now I was satisfied.

No matter how cold or snowy it was outside, I stuck to the same routine—one shorter run, one longer run. For example, later that week, I ran four miles in street clothes and then in the afternoon I ran the final thirteen miles of the Boston Marathon course. By the end of seven days, I had run a total of 127 miles. That number reached 394.5 for the month of February. I was in a military of my own making.

I found out about two road races that were within driving distance. Together they represented my last chance to test myself in a race situation before the Boston Marathon. My performance in these smaller tune-up events wouldn't determine how I'd fare in the marathon, but I hoped it would give me an inkling as to whether I was ready for the enormity of the task ahead.

I went down to New Bedford, Massachusetts, for the first race—the New England 30K Championship. I nearly pulled off the victory, but a guy named Rick Bayko beat me by thirteen seconds. I didn't like losing—at all—but I was pleased with myself for having run the 18.6 miles in 1:24:1. My good time proved to me that I'd made solid progress in the month since I'd raced at Silver Lake. On April 1, in Cambridge, I ran a twelve-mile handicap and won it in 59:17. My confidence was sky high.

Two days before the marathon, Amby arrived in Boston. On Saturday, we went on an easy three-mile training run together around Jamaica Pond. It was a fine spring day and I was happy to be spending time with my old friend. I felt some lingering effects from a chest cold I was getting over. I did consider that it might affect my breathing and overall strength during the big race, but I didn't believe it was anything serious to worry about. We went on another run the following day. Again, it was warm and mild. This time we ran four miles through Boston Common. As we glided across the green, I looked up at the blossoming magnolia trees. Life was good. Then I heard Amby speak.

"It's going to be hot tomorrow, so don't go out too fast. Be patient. Let your body adjust to the heat," he said.

"Sure," I said, half listening to him, half watching the magnolias.

"What's your goal?" Amby asked.

"I'd like to run a 2:20. Maybe 2:25," I said.

Amby glanced over at me, then said nothing for a moment. Finally, he said: "Add at least five minutes to that."

Add five minutes? I thought. How can I duel with the top runners if I'm behind them on the course? I'd been training for months and months, poured tons of sweat and sacrifice into this. If I was going to race, I was going to compete. A little heat was not going to slow me down. The remnants of a chest cold were not going to slow me down. Nothing short of Jock Semple was going to get in my way.

That night, I wrote in my training log: "I'm aiming for a 2:20 but it's probably more realistic to think of a 2:25. We shall see."

I woke up on marathon day, grabbed a cup of yogurt from the refrigerator, and ate it for breakfast. That was odd. I never ate yogurt. Whose yogurt was it anyway? Was it Ellen's yogurt? I was out the door and on my way to Hopkinton to run my first Boston Marathon. No pancakes. No bacon. No carb loading. Nope. One cup of yogurt.

Ellen dropped me off in downtown Hopkinton a few hours before the race started at noon. It was a comfortable morning. Not too hot. I went inside the high school gymnasium to wait with the other runners, at least those whom Jock Semple deemed worthy of admission. If the hard-nosed, irascible Scot didn't deem you a serious runner—and he alone determined the criteria for "serious"—you weren't getting inside, no ifs, ands, or buts. Jock made the doorman at Studio 54 look like a pushover.

As I waited in the high school gymnasium, I looked around at the other runners milling around. I'd never really seen runners before who weren't from New England. Here, I saw runners from all over the world. Many of them had run here before. Most had competed in top international events. A few had even competed in the Olympics. For the most part, runners of the same country gathered together. The Finns hung with the Finns. The Japanese hung with the Japanese. So on and so forth.

Serious American contenders like Tom Fleming and Jon Anderson, who unbeknownst to me was also a conscientious objector, walked by me as if I were invisible. I overheard a couple of writers making their picks. In their eyes, I was less than a long shot—I didn't even exist. One of the reporters commented that until somebody beat the record time set by the sport's king—Olympic gold medalist Frank Shorter—he couldn't call himself the best.

On the other side of me, I heard a group of top runners sarcastically joke about having to pay their own way to run in the most famous marathon in the world and how there was no prize money for the winner. I was just happy the entry fee to race was only two dollars. Today, it's $150.

I wish Charlie were here to keep me company, I thought to myself as I stretched my quads. Did he even know I was running today? I don't even think I told him. I know I didn't tell anybody else. Not my parents or my sisters. Not Jason. Who knows where he was? Probably hanging out on some beach, listening to the Grateful Dead. Charlie was probably helping some messed-up kid detox from heroin. Or if he had the day off, he was relaxing at home with his girlfriend. My dad was probably giving a lecture or grading papers or writing a research paper. My mom—I have no idea what she was doing, but I'm sure it didn't involve sitting still for more than two seconds. I knew that neither my mom nor dad would be watching the marathon on TV. They had no interest in the sport. Not a lot of people did.

I approached the starting line, filled with high hopes of delivering my best performance yet. The bumpy old road was jammed with runners. Jock had given me a high number, 38, allowing me to stake out a spot near the front of the field.

I stared straight ahead at the narrow street and the sharp ninety-degree turn just two hundred yards ahead. I didn't particularly like this. Everybody tensed, ready to shoot off like a rocket. What would happen when every rocket was shot off at the same time down a narrow chute? It was a nerve-racking couple of seconds, like waiting for the ground beneath your feet to slip away.

The gun went off. Too late now. I was part of the sprinting stampede and I either kept powering forward or risked being trampled. I reached the end of the straightaway and veered hard right. My eyes widened a little. I had no idea we'd be running down a small mountainside.

I charged down the descent, surrounded by runners, all bigger than me, jockeying for position. Once I reached the bottom of the hill, and realized all my limbs were still attached, I made a quick sigh of relief. Everybody spread out and I was able to lock into a fast pace near the front of the pack. I was running hard, determined to stay up with the top runners. I was ready to do battle. Bring on Captain Hook!

Here, with one mile behind me and twenty-five more to go, I realized something was wrong. My lungs weren't functioning at full strength. Bad sign. More alarming still, my body was having problems cooling down in the heat.

The heat! It came out of nowhere. In my journal, just three days earlier, I noted the conditions during my thirteen-mile run around Jamaica Pond: "cold," "in the 30s," "typical New England Bullshit Weather." I forgot the other characteristic of typical New England Bullshit Weather: Temps could fluctuate on you at a moment's notice, and without any warning. When I got up, you have to remember, it was around seven in the morning. I walked outside. It felt like an ideal day to run the marathon. Like the TV weatherman always said, "A nice beach day."

Then I arrived at Hopkinton and I was inside this building for three hours. I didn't know it was slowly warming up outside. Suddenly, I went outside, jogged over to the start, and *bang!* The gun went off and I started running. Next thing you know, the temperature was climbing toward eighty.

Mile after mile, I felt the full force of the sun burning my skin. I had no way to block out the scorching rays. The roads were wide open through here, sky-wise: There was not a lot of tree cover. I looked over at my shadow moving along beside me—how nice of it to provide shade to the road while I melted like an ice-cream cone in the blazing heat.

At that point in the race, it was becoming extremely difficult to stay on pace with the leaders. My body was working much harder than it should've been. I shouldn't have been feeling any fatigue, but I was. I was at war with my body. I still had the remnants of that cold, and the heat magnified my symptoms. The heat magnified my feelings, too. I had entered the heart of darkness. That's what the race had become for me—a dark jungle. A nice beach day! Ha! A "nice beach day" is a terrible day for a distance runner. An experienced runner like Amby or Jeff Galloway would know this; they were experienced. I was out there flying by the seat of my pants.

I had no back-up plan. I should have had a back-up plan. I was going to run hard no matter what. I should have considered, "This is going to be a hot day. How will that affect me?" I thought back to the day before, running with Amby in the park, and him warning me about not going out too fast in the heat. Now I was paying the price for failing to take his advice seriously. The marathon can be a cruel sport, no question about it. I was about to learn exactly how cruel over the next twenty-four miles.

The feeling of running in the heat over a long period was something new. Finally, around mile six, I pulled up. I couldn't believe it. I had never stopped during a race in my life. I didn't stop once at Silver Lake and that was twenty miles. I raced straight to the end. I was feeling bad, but I told myself to persevere. Keep going. Keep moving.

Every so often, a grueling effort can win you a marathon but in most cases it's the very thing that will cause you to lose it. It may sound counterintuitive, but truly sustained focus is a by-product of a relaxed mind. The harder I tried to make my body do what I wanted it do, and force my mind to concentrate, the more physical and mental tension I created. This produced the exact opposite of what was intended, knocking me further off balance while exacerbating the feeling of fatigue and cramping. I was learning an agonizing lesson: You can't force yourself into a perfect rhythm and flow; it only comes when you stand out of its way and let it appear on its own.

As I ran past the Framingham train station, at the 6.5-mile mark, I could hear the spectators cheering me on from the side of the course. It did nothing to motivate me. I was too busy fighting against the heat and losing miserably. This was crazy! It felt like the absolute dog days of summer!

I didn't sense any other runners near me as I continued to run headlong into the eye of the storm. This was the first time that I had suffered dehydration during a race, and it was not fun. I thought to myself, Maybe if I stop and walk for a little bit, I will start to cool down. So that's what I did. But it was too late. I was doomed.

When you start to hit the wall so early, that wears on you mentally: to know how much farther you have to go and that you're already beat up. It's like being on a sinking ship. It's very depressing because there's the feeling of "something is totally wrong here. What the heck did I do wrong?" That's the feeling I had.

Each mile, the struggle to put one foot in front of the other intensified. I was no longer running for victory. More like a small, defenseless animal. I felt like I was in a boxing match, being punched all over my body. I started to get side stitches. Awful, painful side stitches. They forced me to start doing the marathon shuffle: I took weak little steps but without surrendering to a full walk.

Around mile 8 or 10—who knew where I was at that point—my legs began to cramp. My hamstrings began to twitch. I should have consumed more water early on, I thought to myself. Of course, I don't think they had official water stops on the course that day. If they did, they were very limited. For a long time, Boston was a real shoe-string-budget affair. All the races were. Kids on the side of the road offered me orange slices. I remember gesturing to them with my hands, saying, "Water! Water!" Craziness.

Things were different during the early years of the Boston Marathon. You could have a handler who could follow alongside you as you ran. They had people going along on bikes with special drinks they had prepared for their runner. Some of them were bizarre concoctions, like arsenic and tea; things to stimulate or jolt the athlete back to alertness. I know what you're thinking: I'll stick with Gatorade. But sports drinks hadn't come to Boston even by 1973.

As a participant in the world's most famous marathon, you couldn't expect more than a few official water stops, which would be conveniently obscured along the route. Perhaps the BAA officials were concerned that the demands of pulling off a sub-2:15 time on the hilly New England terrain weren't nearly insane enough. Following his 1977 win, Jerome Drayton would have the audacity to complain that competitors should get adequate water while they ran a marathon. The response of race administrators was, "Look, this is the way we've always done things. And we're the Mecca of marathons. So if you don't like it, don't come." As a matter of fact, in 1927, race officials, looking for a way to keep costs down, decided to eliminate water stops altogether. With temperatures hitting the eighties, many runners collapsed from heat exhaustion and had to be helped off the course.

At this juncture in my first Boston Marathon, I had a pretty good idea how those competitors must have felt in 1927. My mind had shifted into the off position, too hot and weary to think. I was taking water from anybody offering it. Mile after mile. Stop, drink, stop, drink, stop, drink. But it didn't matter how much water I drank, it did nothing to quench my thirst. I was telling myself, This is miserable. This is miserable.

Oh, how I had let the easy downhill start seduce me. I had flown down that first descent like a banshee on fire. Done in by the same reckless aggression that had caused me to occasionally run afoul of the law when I was a kid, pick a fight with my neighbor Gerald, and accidentally burn down a train car.

In Natick, scores of runners began passing me, particularly older runners. That was a surprise. Never happened to me. I always ran at the front with Amby or whoever I was up in the lead with. I was already knocked down, beat up, getting cramps in my legs, and then everyone started passing me: that was destructive, debilitating, depressing. It was not fun at all, because I didn't know why this was happening to me. I thought I was going to run a good race, like at Silver Lake Dodge.

By the time I reached the Newton Hills, I had stopped along the course around thirty times from ripping cramps. It felt like somebody had strapped burning charcoal embers to my sides. My brain was a boiling pile of goop. This is ridiculous, I thought. What was the point of going on? My body was beat to a pulp. I didn't want to spend the next several days in the hospital being fed intravenously. What if they took me to Brigham where wanted posters with my likeness probably still hung on the walls?

Of course, in my dehydrated state, there was another possibility: I could keel over and die right there on the side of the road. Or I could try to trudge up the next hill, tear an Achilles tendon or a calf muscle, and then keel over and die. When I finally finished counting the myriad ways I could so easily be picked off, I made a decision: I was going to drop out. But not before I made it up Heartbreak Hill.

I dragged my pummeled body up the steep incline, one agonizing step at a time. My long, skeletal legs were shot. I was having problems with my hamstrings and calves. I had cramps all over my body. I had a cramp in my neck! I moved slowly. No gas in the tank. I was a dead man marathon shuffling.

I staggered to a stop at the crest of Heartbreak Hill and bent over with my hands on my wobbly knees. At least I had made it to the top under my own power. At least I had something to show for 21.5 miles of hard effort. This was my "victory."

I straightened up and gazed out at the city skyline below me. I knew that my apartment was not far from where I stood. Like it or not, at that moment, I was in full view of the spectators lining the streets below. Some of them started to shout up words of encouragement to me: "Keep going!" "Hang in there!" "You can make it!" I was too beat up to respond. I could've used an IV of fluids. Of course, they didn't have medical attention back then. Just words of encouragement.

Somebody handed me a can of soda and I instantly guzzled it, craving the sugar. The soda had a bad effect on my stomach. I felt sick. Of course, I hadn't eaten anything all day except that cup of yogurt. I started limping home, fried to a crisp. What a terrible sport this is! I thought to myself. What was I thinking?

Once I got home, I began licking my wounds. I couldn't decide what hurt more: the cramps that lasted for the next six hours, the worst sunburn of my life, or my pride in thinking I could compete against the world's top runners.

Gradually, my appetite came back and I went about replenishing my severely dehydrated body. Now came the fun part. Trying to figure out what I did wrong.

My training had gone well, I thought, but once the race got under way, I had made all the mistakes a beginner could possibly make. I didn't adjust my strategy to the weather conditions. I didn't drink enough water beforehand. I ran too fast at the start. I held firm to my unsustainable pace. I didn't feel my way through the early stages. I didn't pay attention to my competitors to see how they were reacting to the heat. I had been too cocky, too naïve, too full of myself after good showings at a few local races. I had wanted too much, too soon. I was thinking about top ten when I should have been looking to just finish. I was shooting for a time of 2:15 to 2:20. Man, was I wrong. In that kind of heat? Lunacy. The winning time was 2:16, for crying out loud!

It hadn't occurred to me to hold back my energy in the early stages; that I didn't have to be right up there with the leaders from the start. I was a cross-country and track runner; I was used to racing up at the front, you know? Usually I could do that. That's how I ran Silver Lake. Like a cross-country race. And it had worked. But it was forty degrees cooler out. My body could handle it. This hit me like a ton of bricks.

I thought about all the summers I took off from running when I was younger because I had rather have been at the beach. Because I disliked training in the hot sun. It didn't agree with my pale Irish blood. "Train over the summer," Amby used to tell me, but I never listened. Here, withered up on the couch, I wished I had.

The marathon had humbled me. I was so devastated by how poorly I had raced that I began to question whether I could ever succeed at such a long distance, and against such high-level competition. I tried to resume my training, but it was hard. I felt angry and confused. Over the next several weeks, my running was sporadic. By the end of the month, I had stopped running completely.

I had quit running before. Was I about to do it again?

TEN

Boston, You're My Home

Once I blew past Drayton, I never again bothered to look behind me to see where he was. My eyes were fixed straight ahead. I had made my move and it was a clear break. I had gotten away. Maybe he thought I was going to kill myself at that pace and come crashing back to earth on the hills. As a matter of fact, I know that's what he thought. My good friend Tom Fleming believed the same thing. There was no way I could last the distance.

You have to understand: Nobody today tries to run away with the Boston Marathon as early as I had that April day in 1975. It doesn't happen. There are too many good runners these days. Everybody's more careful. They aren't breaking away until at least mile 19 or 20—that's where the race starts getting more competitive and emotional. The crowds are bigger, the runners are more tired, but the fitter ones will go for it. By that I mean they will throw in a surge. Change up the pace for a hundred yards, or three hundred yards, and test the strength of the competition.

Even my own brother, my most loyal supporter, thought I had lost my marbles.

Charlie pulled up to me on the press bus, stuck his head out, and shouted: "Billy, slow down! Are you nuts?"

The verdict was still out on that one. With that said, this was my third time running the Boston Marathon. I felt I knew how much more I could handle. This was Drayton's first Boston. He may have been worrying about the hills up ahead. I trained on those hills. I felt I would be ready for them when the time came. I could see from Charlie's pained expression that he was not nearly as sure about this.

I understood the look of concern on Charlie's face. He had watched me succumb to the merciless nature of the marathon for two straight years. He had seen his little bro suffer the agony of trying to run on legs that felt as if they were filled with cement, and the heartbreak of ending up a twisted wreck on the side of the road. But this was a different kind of day. Finally, I was running a marathon where I felt strong, relaxed, in command. It was a huge lift to be gliding along without a trace of fatigue. The doors felt wide open. I could run as fast as I wanted to.

I was sailing along, easily in front. I had tens of thousands of people roaring me on with every stride. They spurred me on to keep a pace that would have broken most runners. Every inch along the course was lined with people going nuts, and I was knocking out sub-five-minute miles as I flowed between the rowdy hordes. It was like a Fenway Park crowd during the seventh game of the World Series, only spread out along a twenty-six-mile country road. Their deafening screams of support drowned out the sound of my footsteps and any doubts in my mind. That intensity was pushing me into places I had never dared go before as a runner.

I felt like it was my crowd. They were on my side, particularly when I broke away from Drayton. And in a strange way, I was on their side. For instance, I didn't know that Tommy Leonard, the man who always had a big smile and a cool drink waiting for me at the Eliot Lounge halfway through my long training runs, was having a hard time miles behind me on the course that day. Recalled Tommy: "Billy's fighting to prove how good he is and I'm way back in the pack. I'm ready to drop out and just then I hear the crowd roar—Billy's just pulled into the lead. I'm telling you, he gave off mystical vibrations. I got so high I ran my best marathon ever. Three hours and seventeen minutes."

I liked this feeling of breaking away early and running on my own. In later races, I would break free from the pack, but never as early as I did on this day. Usually, I would take off around sixteen or seventeen miles. That's where I always made my move in New York City. I would start racing hard over the Queensboro Bridge, come off the expanse, and keep surging hard for another mile or two. I hoped to drop the field with this burst. Sometimes I did.

Everything was going well as I turned the corner onto Commonwealth Ave. For all us runners, whether you think about it or not, if you're still running good at eighteen miles, you're going to have a solid race. But if you've struggled to get to that point, the last six miles are going to be hell.

I hit the first of the three hills on Commonwealth Ave., which a lot of people say is like the first punch in the runner's face, but I was thinking, This is not that tough a hill. I was running steady with my eyes focused like a laser on the lead vehicle just ahead of me on the road. It became the center of my universe; everything outside of my narrow field of vision faded from existence.

My parents always told me, "Bill, you can't go through life with blinders on." And they were right. But if running straight ahead, free from the worries of the past or the consequences of the future, was a great liability in my life, it was a great gift as my smooth strides ate up the miles to downtown Boston.

Was it coincidence that my habit of focusing on what was directly in front of me, and nothing else, gave me the power to run 26.2 miles like few others in the world could? After all, I've never been able to look too far down the road, not like my brother, Charlie. I think this is typical of somebody with ADHD. Since I was a boy, I had lived a life that was spur of the moment. There were times, plenty of times, I paid the price for not thinking beyond the now. Sometimes I was so focused on what was directly in front of me, I missed the brick wall up ahead. But the same rules that applied to life didn't apply to running a marathon—if you were strong and fit enough, there were no brick walls ahead to fear and thus no need to put on the brakes. If you were strong and fit enough, there was only an open road for you to soar down. That's what it felt like running alone in the lead—like I was soaring and there was nothing to stand in my way.

By the time I rounded the sharp corner at the Newton Fire Station, located around mile 18 and just before the first of the four dreaded Newton Hills, I was struck with a horrible realization: I had blown it. I had run too fast over the first three quarters of the race, and now I was going to get wiped out on the demanding hills. I flashed back to the disaster I had experienced last year—and the year before that—on the final ascent into the city. The leg cramps. The dehydration. Was this going to be an instant replay?

I didn't know how hard I had pushed it, getting away from Drayton, but I knew I'd been flying like a bat out of hell up to this point. In fact, I was running thirty-eight seconds under Ron Hill's course record pace.

If I was a racecar driver, at that moment I could look at the gauge and see if I was, indeed, running at an unsustainable pace, or what's called "redlining." But my only gauge was my brain; it was the only thing that could tell me right then if I was working too hard at eighteen miles or still running within myself. What if Charlie had been right? What if I had let my compulsion to take on Drayton eclipse my rational thinking, leading me to make a panic move that was about to send me on a suicide mission through the hills?

The first of the Newton Hills suddenly rose before me. This was it. My moment of truth.

TWO YEARS EARLIER
NATICK, MASSACHUSETTS

I got licked in my first marathon. It didn't take long to recuperate from the acute dehydration; recovering from the deep wounds to my self-esteem would be an entirely different story. Maybe I wasn't cut out for the marathon. Maybe I couldn't handle the competition at Boston. Maybe I had just fooled myself into thinking I could be a great distance runner.

I didn't want to believe that, of course. I knew I had to get right back in the cockpit. So the day after the marathon, I ran three miles at dusk. I was also checking to see if I'd incurred any injuries. The body felt okay, all things considered. But the body wasn't the issue.

After what had happened to me, I was gun-shy about running in the heat again. You need to recover completely from this chest cold, I told myself. It's 82 degrees out. Rest today. You'll begin training tomorrow. I was breaking Amby's number one rule: Never make excuses to get out of training.

I woke up the next day and broke the promise I had made to myself to get back on the road. Instead, I opened up my log entry and wrote: "Rested. No running. Running scares me." What did I do instead? Probably hung around the house, watching TV, eating Oreos and drinking Pepsi.

Friday. For a third straight day, I didn't train. Saturday. I finally forced myself to go on a fifteen-mile run in the park. I felt weak. When will I finally be rid of this demonic chest cold? I thought Sunday. I did another fifteen-mile run. I wrote in my log: "Getting hot out!! In the middle 80's! I find it very hard to run. No vim and vigor."

I was losing the willpower to put in the heavy mileage. As a marathon runner, if you're not getting stronger every day, you're getting weaker. This is day-in-day out business. I was in a dangerous place because once you stop putting in the work, you're done.

I'd heard stories about guys taking antidepressants and it making it easier for them to train. I'm the first to admit that training alone can be tough. Sometimes the hardest part is the boredom. Other times it's the pressure you put on yourself. I remember this kid named Gerry Lindgren who broke all kinds of records in high school. He was the best in the country for his age. I still consider him one of the finest distance runners in American history. But Lindgren pushed himself hard in college, running more miles than his young frame could handle. Part of it was that he loved to run, but he was also feeling the pressure to live up to expectations. In his mind, he had to keep breaking records, defeating tougher challengers, winning bigger races. It all became too much. He started developing ulcers and he never returned to the level he had attained in high school. He burned out before he ever came close to reaching his physical peak, which would have been in his twenties. I always wonder how great Lindgren could have been had he not fallen victim to fear and anxiety. In my heart, I believe he could have been a gold medal champion like Frank Shorter.

I was lucky that unlike Lindgren I never had to live up to past greatness. I could progress at my own pace. I never thought of myself as anything but a novice, exploring a new and challenging event. Still, the marathon had knocked me down. My miles per week kept dropping—seventy-seven for the second week in April, which dropped down the next week to fifty-four miles, then the next week to twenty-two miles. Then finally, in May, I stopped running altogether. You know all those good feelings I talked about getting from running—the tranquility, the peace of mind, the lifting of the spirit? I suddenly found them missing.

Running scares me, I thought. But that wasn't true. It was running *in the heat* that scared me. If I could train in warmer weather then I could acclimate myself to the heat, I thought to myself. Isn't that why Frank Shorter had moved from England to Florida? Same with Jeff Galloway? Hadn't they formed some postcollegiate running club down there? But Florida was too hot. I needed somewhere with warm, moderate temperatures. That night, I told Ellen that I thought we should move to California. Just like that. Let's go to California. Her response? Okay. Let's do it.

Maybe she was as excited as I was to make a fresh start. I think she was. It's not like we had a long, deep discussion about the implications of what it would mean for us to just pick up and move to the other side of the country. It's not like either of us had been to California before. What I knew about the place came from movies and TV shows. As a matter of fact, neither of us had ever been outside New England. Here was our chance to see the world that lay beyond Brookline.

We were winging it completely; a classic young person's exploration. We had no plan for our new lives in California. All we had were a few maps I'd found before we embarked. All I knew was that I wanted to live somewhere in Northern California. I carried a foggy notion—maybe one I'd come across in *Track & Field News*—about that region being home to a small running scene since the 1960s. Good training weather. I didn't feel I had an alternative. If I was going to conquer the marathon, first I needed to conquer the heat. That's what I told myself, anyway. What I really had to do was get back my passion for running. I needed to get back my verve.

Ellen quit her job at the hospital. I don't think it was a big deal. She never indicated she was leaving any long-term friends or career aspirations. I think she was excited and, of course, it helped that she got her parents on board. She was a classic only child. Very close to her mom and dad. They were kind and supportive parents and I got along well with them. Her mom was a strict Catholic, which meant that Ellen and I couldn't live together even though, of course, we did. When her parents came to Boston to visit her, I would hide out at a friend's place until they were gone. Those were the times we lived in.

Her parents must have been worried about Ellen getting safely to her destination 2,500 miles away so they bought us a Dodge Van. She and I loaded up the van with everything we owned in this world, which wasn't much, grabbed our pet cat, and drove off.

Driving through the country with the windows open, I shook my head in disbelief at the beauty of the vast, rolling stretches of the Great Plains. At night, we slept inside the van in our sleeping bags. Once in a while we stopped at a motel to wash up and so Ellen could call home. We were roughing it. Was it romantic? In the sense that two young, adventurous souls driving across the country is romantic, yes. It was that whole Jack Kerouac thing. *On the Road*, right? But it wasn't romantic like a honeymoon. Maybe it was like *our* honeymoon.

When we reached the Rockies, I was still staring out upon the vast landscape with a dumbstruck grin on my face. We stopped at Yosemite, walked under the giant redwood trees, and looked upon the unspoiled beauty with amazement. We stood at the brink of the Grand Canyon and gazed speechlessly into its sublime depths. I thought to myself, How can a country of such natural beauty be home to such ugly divisions?

Somewhere along the journey we settled on a final destination—San Jose, California. We might as well have thrown a dart at the state map.

As we drove through San Jose, I felt like a deer that had accidentally wandered into the center of bustling downtown; the sight of cars and people everywhere spooked me. This isn't good, I thought. This won't work out. We had no contacts, no job leads, and very little money between us.

California is vast and we felt like a little speck of dust. I went there because I felt I needed a warm-weather place to train, but it didn't take long to realize that wasn't enough. I know Ellen felt the same way—her heart belonged back home. After only a couple of days, we came to the conclusion that the best thing to do was to head back east.

On the drive back, we stopped in Wyoming; I went fishing in a stream and caught a trout. I would've loved to cook the fish but, of course, we hadn't thought to bring any camping gear. Our next stop was Lake

Tahoe. We parked at a campsite in time to see the radiant sunset over the magnificent lake, which was massive in size and startlingly clear. It's hard to put into words the stunning beauty of the landscape. As somebody who grew up in New England, the awesome vastness of the mountains took my breath away.

In the middle of the night, I was getting out of the van to use the bathroom and our cat went flying out the door. She wanted out in the worse way. We searched everywhere for her, but it was pitch black and Tahoe is a big area. We were heartsick. We thought we had lost her for good. We felt stupid. Plain stupid. If Ellen and I were going to have our first moment of strife, this would have been a good time. I was a big proponent of avoiding conflict. So was Ellen. In fact, I can't recall either of us ever yelling at the other. We just weren't like that. For better or worse.

A couple of hours later, we were lying in the van when we heard a faint meowing outside. The cat had found its way back on its own, no worse for wear.

As we continued our journey through the country, I tried to think of another warm-weather training locale where we could live. Then a lightbulb went on in my head. Virginia! It's a beautiful place with green valleys and rolling hills. It just sounded nice. We arrived in Virginia, but I remember we didn't stay long. I think we both sensed we were putting off the inevitable. Ellen missed her family back in Worcester, and I missed mine. We both kind of looked at each other—let's go home.

When we loaded up the van and left for California, I was thinking this was about my running, but it ended up being about more than that. Ellen and I had gone on this great adventure into the wider world—a trip through Mother Nature's land that was both powerful and enlightening. I got to appreciate the soaring beauty of the West. If there was something else our trip showed me, it was that you should be where you're happy. I was happy in New England with my family and friends. In the end, I said to myself, I ran there before, I guess I can run there again.

We ended up moving to Vernon, Connecticut, a suburb outside Hartford. We rented a tiny house, moved in all our stuff, and I started looking for work. I took a job working at a Carvel's ice cream shop, a little family-owned place in Vernon. A short time after I started, this loud, piggish kid came in—he was the son of the owner, I think—and began ordering me around as if he were the heir to the Prussian throne and I was one of his lowly subjects. For some reason, I didn't feel I was reaching my potential here. I remember thinking, You know, this isn't where I'm going. I'm going someplace different. I'm not staying here. I calmly put down the scooper, removed my apron, and walked out the door.

It was a strange time for me as a runner. I didn't have anything to aim for. It's not like I was aiming for New York City that fall. Also, I had suffered my first major setback. The thing was, it took me by surprise. Up to that point, I had experienced the high of constant progress. I started from scratch, doing a few miles around the YMCA track. After I moved to Jamaica Plain, I started running twice a day and over 100 miles a week. In my first race back, the Silver Lake, I placed third. I ran strong in the last tune-ups before Boston, coming in second at the New Bedford 30K and winning a twelve-mile race in Cambridge. Seeing my progress had always motivated me to push myself further. So what happens when you don't make progress? What happens when you actually take a step back?

I couldn't see that one race was just that—one race. Or that every marathon runner experiences setbacks—even the Frank Shorters of the sport. It was a horrible feeling not knowing for sure that I'd be able to prevent another disaster in the marathon. That's what I didn't understand yet about the sport: You never know.

Eventually, I set off on some short runs from our house. Hot-weather training—the boring suburban way. I knew that motivation would be in short supply as long as I was condemned to the dull monotony of the Connecticut roads. I found myself wishing I was back home, circling Jamaica Pond, the wind fanning my cheeks as my eyes took in all that surrounded me. The park had a magic quality about it that gave me the power to run for miles and miles; it brought out the free-spirited kid in me.

Somehow I always ended up going where my instincts led me.

So after driving to the other side of the country, Ellen and I ended up right back where we began: in a small apartment in Jamaica Plain. It felt right. We were close to our families, and that gave us a feeling of safety and warmth.

On August 5, after three months of empty entries in my running log, I finally put pen to paper. I set a new goal. Get back up to running one hundred miles a week. I wondered: Was this too much, too soon? I hadn't trained seriously since dropping out of Boston.

I had to get back to a steady routine. Runners need routine. They need consistency. It helped to be back running around Jamaica Pond. This is where I'd found success before. Where I went from being a smoker to a runner. Where I went from nothing to finishing third in the Silver Lake twenty-miles, only three minutes behind Amby Burfoot, Boston Marathon champion. They were all good feelings.

I took it slow the first week back. For one thing, the daily temperature hovered in the nineties. Hot as a fart, as I noted in my training log on August 9 after running down and back from Government Center. I managed a total of sixty-nine miles for the week. Not much, but a start.

Although I felt I was in poor shape, I decided, for the fun of it, I would compete in a 10K race that Tuesday in Salem, Massachusetts. Probably because my occasional training partner, Mike Burke, was running in it.

It was my first 10K ever. My first long-distance road race since the Boston Marathon. I hadn't forgotten that debacle. But something weird happened: I ran great. Really great. In fact, I could have broken the course record but, near the end of the race, I decided instead to run across the finish line holding hands with Mike to insure a tie for first. That way he could split the prize with me.

The next surprising result came four days later when I won the twenty-sixth annual Haverhill 10.3-mile road race. Winning a couple of races spurred me on to train harder. By mid-August, I was meeting my goal of running at least one hundred miles a week. The heat and humidity were brutal, but nothing was going to slow this comeback now. When I got a side ache going up a hill, I kept pushing on.

On the first Sunday in September, I showed up to Brockton High School to run a one-hour race on the track only to discover I'd gotten the day wrong. This would knock me off my training schedule. I was angry. "Dog dung!" I wrote in my running log. "Only 6-day running week!" I should have run seven.

At the same time I was getting my fitness back, an amazing thing happened. After a year of looking for work, I was hired as an attendant at the Fernald School in Belmont, Massachusetts, the country's oldest state institution for mentally challenged people. When I first got to Fernald, I handled basic duties around the building, like mopping floors, making beds, and tending to the patients.

The first time on ward duty was intimidating. While the people I was looking after were grown men, they acted like little children, throwing yelling tantrums, banging on their heads, tossing their food on the floor. Right away, I was faced with making a choice: reject them or help them. I realized my natural instinct was to try and make things better for them.

But not everything I learned about myself on the job was positive. I had to recognize my own failings of compassion. There were times when petty resentment overcame true understanding. I once let a guy lie in his soiled bed for a day because I was sure he had done it on purpose. My supervisor made me ashamed; it wasn't my job to punish them, for any reason.

After only sixty days on the job, I was placed in charge of my own ward. It was my responsibility to look after seven moderately mentally challenged men, ranging in age from eighteen to fifty-five. My job was to try to teach them basic living skills, like using utensils, brushing their teeth, and folding their clothes.

I found my new job to be hard but satisfying. For one thing, I enjoyed working one-on-one with the patients, which I couldn't do in my drudge job at Brigham. Every day I worked with them, I seemed to learn a new lesson about life. For instance, they did not measure happiness by the people in their lives, which was nobody, or the things they owned, which was nothing. Instead, they found incredible joy in the smallest thing.

I'll never forget one patient named Joe. I discovered he loved Tootsie Rolls. Tootsie Roll Joe made me think about the simple thing in life that made me happy—running. That incredible sensation of moving freely outside with the wind at your back was something Tootsie Roll Joe would never know. All these years I had taken for granted that I was a runner, it's what I did, it's what I was good at. But maybe it needed to be more than that. Maybe I was supposed to do more with this talent I was given than just be a fairly successful local road racer.

Over time, I became very attached to Joe and other men in my ward. Sometimes I'd take five or six of them out of the building and onto the grounds. I did this even though it was frowned upon, but I didn't care. I thought it was good for them to get outside. I thought back to my mom and how she cared for so many people, working for years as a nurse's aid at Newington Hospital. It didn't surprise me that my brother, who worked at a drug treatment center, and I would follow in her footsteps. She showed us that taking care of others had great value while making lots of money should never be our priority.

But this was a real challenge, trying to care for people with no control of their lives. One day, a thirty-something-year-old patient in my ward disappeared for a few days. When they found him, he had removed all of his teeth. After that, he would call out, "My teeth, my teeth." While some of the patients, like him, were clearly too mentally disabled to get through to, I felt if I tried hard enough maybe I could reach a couple of them.

One of the men I hoped I could reach was named Gene. He was an autistic young man who stared at the walls all day, speaking in monosyllables. One night, I brought him outside into the courtyard. I was hoping to spark something inside him or maybe just connect on some level. I pointed up to the bright orb in the night sky. "Gene, moon," I said. He didn't respond. Night after night, I took Gene outside and repeated the same action for him. "Gene, moon," I said, directing his eyes high up into the night sky.

I knew that Gene would likely never improve enough to leave the institution. Being aware of this sad reality forced me to see that I was fortunate to come and go as I pleased.

I tried not to dwell on the grim circumstances of how these people ended up in this place, but I couldn't help but think about how their families had left them off here and, in some cases, wiped their hands clean of them. What if I had been born mentally challenged? Would my parents have swept me out of sight as if I never existed in the first place? Would I be one of the forgotten people here, abandoned by society, living in filthy confinement, fed meals not fit for human consumption? Would I be gazing all day at the wall, dead to the world, while Charlie and Jason rode freely down the highway on their motorcycles? Or Amby dashed through the woods behind Johnny Kelley? I wanted to believe that such a thing could never have happened, but the fact that it was happening to these people meant that it could happen to anybody.

Never again would I see going out and training hard for miles as a chore but as a privilege. I thought back to how I had felt humiliated after dropping out of the Boston Marathon; now I saw that I was lucky to even be out there, giving it my all, no matter the final outcome. And instead of feeling demoralized, I should have felt blessed that the very next day I could put on my sneakers, head down to the park, and run freely around the pond. What had I really lost? A race. That's all. Nothing was stopping me from going back out and trying again. Nothing but my own fears and insecurities. What did I really have to fear? Failure? How about the fact that I had the chance to fail or succeed on my own. I had the opportunity to try. That's something the people who ended up in this institution would never get in their whole life. The people here never had a chance. I remember one kid in my ward who was blind and severely mentally challenged. He couldn't go out and go do a simple thing like go for a run. His life was so limited. My life didn't seem limited to me at all. I knew my talent for running long distances came with lots of fun; maybe it also came with the responsibility to use it to its fullest.

One night, as I stood alone in the courtyard with Gene, the answer was as clear as the stars that twinkled high above our heads. Gene slowly lifted his arm and pointed his finger into the sky. "Moon," he said.

Now, six months later, I was reinvigorated in my personal quest to succeed at the Boston Marathon. My schedule at Fernald was perfect in that I was able to get in a long run in the morning before work, and another long run at night after work. I enjoyed splitting my time between running countless loops around Jamaica Pond—building up my mileage base—and supervising my ward of seven patients at Fernald School. I was happy to be back where family and friends were, to have finally put that disastrous marathon behind me, and to have the stability of an actual paycheck. I was living the best kind of life for a runner—simple.

It was going on three years now that I had been training by myself. Not always a bad thing. I set my own schedule. I got to run around Jamaica Pond when I wanted, as many times as I wanted, and at the pace of my choosing. I didn't have to worry about some workout partner canceling, showing up late, or flaking out altogether. But it could be tough at times to be fighting the good fight all alone.

Well, this was all about to change.

ELEVEN

San Blas

APRIL 21, 1975
NEWTON HILLS, MASSACHUSETTS

I had reached the Newton Hills, which I've called the most significant stretch of course in the racing world. The Fukuoka course in Japan had some major spots, but to me, nothing identified the challenge and beauty of marathoning more than this section of the Boston Marathon. When I said that I was thinking about Johnny Kelley and Tarzan Brown battling through the hills in 1936 with Brown shockingly surging past Kelley on the final climb, "breaking his heart." Boston wouldn't be Boston without the hills.

I charged up the first ascent in the Killer Chain. I was about to discover whether or not I had run smart up until now. Had I done a good job of pacing myself and reserved enough energy for the tough inclines looming before me? Or had I failed to keep my stride in check over the first eighteen miles, started out too fast, overextended my muscles, underhydrated my body?

Twice before, I had run out of gas on the steeps. Twice before, I had dropped out on the side of the road. Twice before, I had run with reckless abandon, thumbing my nose at the heat. Twice before, Mother Nature got the last laugh. Twice before, I thought I had the training under my belt to finish strong. Twice before, I was dead wrong.

Here's the thing: Both times I didn't realize I was in trouble until it was too late. All the little mistakes you make—not just during the early part of the race, but sometimes before ever walking out the door (you didn't eat a big enough breakfast), or the night before (nerves kept you from getting much sleep), or weeks earlier (you decided to taper down your training miles too early; you didn't prepare for running in the heat; you brushed off that minor discomfort in your big toe)—accumulate out of sight into one giant ball of hurt.

It's only when you are at your most vulnerable, when your body is running low on fuel, perhaps at mile twenty, just where Heartbreak Hill begins, this giant ball of hurt strikes as hard and as swift as a meteor. (As Olympic marathoner John Farrington once said: "Marathoning is like cutting yourself unexpectedly. You dip into the pain so gradually that the damage is done before you are aware of it. Unfortunately, when awareness comes, it is excruciating.") Suddenly, three miles from the finish line, your body is wracked with cramps, your legs are locked up, and you're mumbling to yourself, *can I make it to the finish line?*

I climbed the second of the Newton Hills—it felt much like the first hill, just closer to the finish line. As I churned along with nineteen miles already on my legs, the ever-enlarging crowds pressed into the road. A sub five-minute pace won't set any NASCAR records, but I was moving.

For a long time, my eyes bore down on the back of the lead vehicle, always ten feet ahead of me. If I was a stalking tiger, the big heavy vehicle was my prey. Sometimes I would challenge myself to catch it. I nearly did a few times. That's a powerful feeling—to almost be outrunning the lead vehicle.

As I ran along the course, the only thing scarcer than water stations was crowd control. There was absolutely nothing to keep back the boisterous masses, which included a good number of people that had been drinking since the crack of dawn. Had I not been running with such single-minded purpose, the precariousness of my situation might have dawned on me. How little it would it take for a crazed fan to step into my path, wallop me in the midsection, and deny me victory.

Think it couldn't happen? In 1905, Fred Lorz had to leap past a horse at mile 20 and then hurdle over a bike at the finish line, catching his foot and crashing through the tape for victory. In 1922, leader Clarence DeMar jumped out of the way of a car that had accidentally veered onto the course. In a burst of rage, he sent his fist through the open window, but his punch missed the driver and hit the passenger beside him. Fearing payback, he looked over his shoulder as he continued on to the first of his seven championships. In 1978, as Jack Fultz sped down the hill onto Commonwealth Avenue, he was pinned between a big bus and the thick crowds pressing into the road. In 1981, Patti Catalano was working her way through congested Cleveland Circle when she was sideswiped by a police horse. A year later, during Dick Beardsley's famous Duel in the Sun against "the Rookie" Alberto Salazar, a drunken spectator ran out and slugged him in the gut, knocking the wind out of him. Further along the route, Beardsley managed to tear himself away from another blitzed fan who'd taken hold of his shirt only to be nearly run over by the press bus.

Despite the history of bizarre confrontations, I ran toward the next mile, sweeping over the ground with long smooth strides, oblivious to any potential threats. As I charged straight into the teeth of the impassioned hordes of spectators, I was too zeroed in on winning the race to feel any fear. Besides, I didn't feel like I was snaking through an angry mob on the verge of stoning me. More like a conquering knight returning home to his people.

The feeling in those days was that any country had a shot at winning—and that question mark created great excitement. Would it be a runner from Italy, Spain, Finland, Colombia, Japan, Korea, Great Britain? Seeing me in the lead—a hometown kid—elicited a powerful emotional response from the crowd. As the miles wore on, their support for me was a tangible thing that hung in the air. Their cheers continually charged me up like a battery, inspiring me to push even harder, to succeed even more.

I think this is true for everyone who runs Boston. The crowd's support lifts them up. You have to remember: These aren't your average running fans. They are as loyal as they come, showing up year after year, rain or shine. They know the marathon, they understand its tradition, they admire the runners, and they sure know how to party. It's like loving the Red Sox. They've been around a hundred years, and so has the Boston Marathon. It's a lifetime relationship.

As I ran sweat flew off the back of my long blond hair. I felt the rush of air on my face. My feet hardly touched the pockmarked road. I knew the big hill was still ahead. There's always a certain amount of anxiety as you approach Heartbreak. I don't care who it is. You've run twenty miles by then—even the Kenyans have got to be feeling that. But I had a great advantage. I had run the course before, I had trained on it for months, and I had the ideal conditions to run. The wind was just blowing me along.

I was coming up now on Heartbreak, where I had been murdered every time before. There was no question I had great respect for the final ascent. But there comes a time where you don't want to respect Heartbreak Hill, you want to conquer it.

For me, that time was now.

TWO YEARS EARLIER
BOSTON, MASSACHUSETTS

My training had gone well in August and September, and I was getting back to the shape I had been in prior to Boston. Then, over the final week of September, I managed to run 142 miles. My enthusiasm was noted in my log entry: "A new ta-rah-rah personal record in miles per week!" Now it was time to test out my progress by running as many local road races as possible.

On September 15, I entered a five-mile cross-country meet against Tufts and Boston State. Without meaning to, the night before I got semiblitzed at Jason's twenty-sixth birthday party and didn't hit the sack until three a.m. I took first place anyway, covering the five-mile course in 25:22. A week later I traveled up to Manchester, New Hampshire, for a 15K. It was a great day to race, beautiful fall weather. The one thing about road races at the time was that they were loose and fairly disorganized. Screwing up the distance was a typical occurrence. So while we were supposed to run a 15K, which worked out to 9.32, the course we ran ended up being 9.7 miles. Not that it mattered: I beat the field with a time of 47:09.

Road races were very nuts and bolts affairs. No traffic control. No clocks. No spectators along the roads. If you placed in the top three, you'd get a medal at the finish. The fee to enter each race was tiny; the Boston Marathon was a whole five dollars. At the finish there might be hot dogs. There was almost no media coverage. Maybe a local newspaper guy. I do remember seeing an article about my victory in the National Championships at Gloucester in a magazine called *Yankee Runner*. So not exactly front page of the *Boston Globe* sports section.

At the same time, Ellen started to come to some of my races with me. It's very exciting to be at a road race, not to mention I was winning. Maybe it was also a way to spend more time with me. After all, I was working full-time at Fernald and going on six- to ten-mile runs before and after work. She also started running a little herself, and would occasionally join me for a jog around Jamaica Pond. I was happy for Ellen that she was getting into running. I knew that she wanted to quit smoking, and I had experienced firsthand that the best way to kick a bad habit was to replace it with a positive habit, like running.

Unfortunately, in those days, road racing was a male-dominated sport. It's not like it is today—you didn't see lots of couples or families showing up to races. I didn't know any running couples, and to see a woman runner was shocking. Some would think: Oh, good grief, there's a woman runner. My attitude was: Good going!

By competing in these New England road races every weekend, I started meeting people like myself—that is, runners who shared my passion for training and competition. One of the people I ended up meeting was Bob Sevene, or Sev, as he was known by his friends. Sev had been one of the top collegiate eight hundred-meter runners before going off to fight in Vietnam in 1967. He served five years as an army captain, during which he survived a three hundred-foot fall from a maimed helicopter into a dry rice paddy. After a young surgeon was able to pop all of Sev's broken ribs back into place, he spent six days in a coma and another nine weeks in a full body cast. Five months later Sev was back jogging. That tells you something about his toughness. It says even more about his love for running.

The war nearly cost him his life, and caused him to miss the 1968 Olympic trials, for which he qualified in the eight hundred-meter race, and yet Sev never blamed society or the war for what happened to him. Had he lost the use of his legs, that would have been a different story. Because Sev was like me. He was happiest when he was running. He had to be around it or he felt lost.

I have such vivid memories of running through Waltham with Sev. You want to talk about hills? It was one hill after another. We usually ran along Trapelo Road, which is where the Fernald School was located. I was working a three-to-eleven shift and using my lunch break to go out on training runs with Sev. We used to motor up around Hardy Pond Road—which is now all old hotels—and out past Route 95 and behind the Cambridge Reservoir. You couldn't even run along those roads today because of all the high-tech industry. Kodak and Raytheon are back there. Back then, it was deserted. We owned those roads.

Running is a very emotional activity for me. For example, Bob was a hawkish Vietnam vet and I was a conscientious objector and when we ran we would get into these passionate political debates. As the conversation intensified, so would our pace. All of a sudden, without noticing it, we both would be flying, running sub-5:30 miles, and then we'd just laugh and look at each other like, "Holy crap, what are we doing?"

One of the reasons Sev liked running with me so much was because

I could pick up his mood on any given night. If he wanted to go, I would go. If he was tired, I would just come back to where he was and match his slower stride. One night, we were both feeling good and flying along for miles. As we turned onto this dirt trail that crosses Route 9, I turned to Sev and said, "You know, I'm a little bit tired."

"What do you mean?" asked Sev.

"Well, I ran seventeen miles this morning," I said.

"I freaking fell over," recalls Sev. "He had been hammering out 5:20-minute miles alongside me like they were nothing. He was the one person I met in my life who was made to run. When I say that, I mean Billy loved to fly and did it with the lightest, most natural stride ever, as if running was as natural to him as breathing.

"Of course, I think people had a tendency to read Billy as flaky. But he's brilliant. And I'll tell you what—that brilliance goes into running. Billy could tell you at any time on the roads what pace you were going and he'd be right on the nose. He learned that from year after year running around Jamaica Pond, where it's measured, and just understanding pace exactly. The same holds true for downhill running—he practiced that like crazy because he knew how important it was at Boston. This was real early in his career."

On October 14, I entered the National Championship in Glouces-ter, Massachusetts. While most of the competitors were at the New England level, Dick Buerkle was a future Olympian who'd go on to set the world record for the indoor one-mile race. Recently, Sev told me about a conversation he had with one of the favorites, Tom Fleming, in the locker room before the race. He was changing into his race gear when Tom came strutting in full of Jersey confidence.

"Hey Sev, anyone I should be aware of in this race?" asked Tom.

"Tommy, watch this kid Will Rodgers."

At that point in my career, people were using the name Will, not Bill, and of course Tommy Fleming started laughing because of the famous cowboy Will Rodgers.

Sev said, "I'm not shitting you, Tommy. Wait till you see this guy. He's the greatest thing I've ever seen."

"Tom, needless to say, got his ass kicked," recalls Sev. "We all did."

Here's how it happened: The day was cool, ideal for setting a fast time, but for a change, when the gun sounded, I didn't take off like a pissed-off stallion. I fought the usual surge of adrenaline and the impulse to challenge my competition to a street brawl. Instead, I stuck with the rest of the pack and ran at a moderate pace. Amby would have been proud.

Dick Buerkle and I were battling each other neck and neck the whole way. Then about a mile from the finish line, I saw clouds of smoke billowing in the air. Suddenly, we were racing over fire hoses that had been laid across the street. The fireman spilled into the street. They thought somehow they were going to stop Buerkle and me in our tracks. But Jock Semple was ahead of us in the lead vehicle—and nobody stopped Jock. He barreled through the phalanx of fireman, yelling at them in his thick Scottish accent to get off the course. The guy was out of his mind—and the language he was using? Let's just say it was colorful.

I ran through the chaotic street, hurdling over water lines, rushing through billowing clouds of white smoke, dodging the entire Gloucester Fire Department as they battled with a crazy Scotsman. When I sprinted across the finish line, Dick Buerkle was still twenty-three seconds behind. It was a good win. I hadn't used up my reserves too early and, as a result, I had plenty over the last mile—when the scene resembled a war zone—to hold off my dangerous pursuer. In other words, I had actually employed strategy. That's what it took to beat a serious talent like Dick Buerkle.

After I returned home from my victory that night, I ran another 4.5 miles around Jamaica Pond. Later I pulled out my training log and wrote: "My one ta-da national championship zootie-kazootie! Won a 10-speed bike." That was the most valuable item you could possibly win in those days. Top of the line. The next week I entered an eleven-miler in Gardner, Massachusetts, and took first place. "Taroo! I won a table!" I wrote excitedly in my log. I was pumped.

By now, I had committed myself to ramping up for the Boston Marathon. I even wrote it down in my log. Monday. That's when it starts. I meant it, too. When I ran only eleven miles around Jamaica Plain that Wednesday, I wrote: "Only ran once today. I am pissed!" I thought back to my attitude after I had dropped out of the Boston Marathon, when I wrote in my training log about lacking vim and vigor. Well, that wasn't a problem anymore. I had lots of vim and vigor.

The next day, I entered my second marathon, albeit a much smaller one than Boston: the Bay State Marathon. My first marathon had knocked me down, but I was still very much drawn to the distance, maybe because each marathon represented this great leap into the unknown. Nothing, not all the training in the world, can fully prepare you for what you might encounter in those 26.2 miles. Most people stay clear of situations that they can't control or anticipate the outcome. Not me. I got a rush from charging into the wild frontier. I was okay crashing to the ground because afterward I could think about where things had gone wrong and adjust for my next attempt. It's like the Rolling Stones said: You can't always get what you want, but if you try sometime, you just might find you get what you need. That's really true in marathoning. Even if you bomb out, you learn from things and you can improve the next time.

On the day of the Bay State Marathon it was a windless day in the forties. Later on, I noted in my log that I ran a five-lap race—the first three laps at an easy pace and the last two laps at hard pace. My breathing was excellent, but I had aches in my legs and back for the last eight miles. Was it the shock of the road? I asked myself. Were my crappy shoes too thin? I didn't think I ran fast. My time was 2:28. At that time, in 1973, Frank Shorter was a 2:10 marathoner. He was 2:12 when he won the Olympics in '72. I wasn't even in the scene with him. I was no threat to him. I was no threat to anybody. Still, I was happy to win another first place prize. Maybe it would be a set of chairs to go with my new table.

Since my high school days, I've wanted to win every race I entered. When I got into the marathon, I got excited. This is for me. This is my distance. Not the two mile. The two mile was too short. I needed ten thousand meters and up. That's where I could turn the tables on all those speedsters who outkicked me at the shorter distances. Here, I could hold my own. Here, I could go toe-to-toe with the top runners in the world. That was fun to be able to do that. To have a shot at winning is very exciting and I went into every race thinking, I do have a shot.

One day while out running the hills of Waltham, Sev told me about a brand-new track club, which he had helped establish, for postgraduate runners who wanted to prolong their athletic careers. It was a bold idea for the time. You have to understand the anxiety and isolation that an amateur runner in 1973 experienced the moment he tossed his graduation cap into the air. You had almost no options beyond college, no way to train or race with a team, nobody to coach you, nothing in the way of structure or support. Jack McDonald, a Boston College senior and four-minute miler, deserves the credit for not just seeing the need for a post-collegiate club but having the audacity do something about it.

On August 21, 1973, McDonald brought together seven other local running junkies in a locker room at Boston College. Attending the meeting, in addition to McDonald and Sev, were Don Ricciato, Dave Elliott, Dickie Mahoney, and Kirk Pfrangle. Over the next hours, and many beer cans tossed back and forth, they started calling every coach they knew, hoping one would agree to train a bunch of running bums in his spare time—and for no money. After being rejected by several coaches, it looked like they weren't going to find a willing mentor. But as their hope dwindled, as well as their beer reserves, somebody stepped up to the plate. His name was Bill Squires.

Jason Kehoe, Charlie, and Bill Rodgers sitting on steps in Newington, Connecticut. (Rodgers Family)

the athletic department

99 W. 10th, Suite 104
Eugene, Oregon 97401
(503) 343-5010

April 9, 1975

Mr. Bill Rogers
Jamaica Plain, Mass. 02130

Dear Bill:

First of all congratulations on a fine race in Rabat. You
have really improved this last year and hopefully will
continue to until the olympic games.

The reason I'm writing is because Jeff Galloway told me
you were interested in training in our shoes. I'm sending you a pair of Boston 73's and a training shoe. Any
comments would be greatly appreciated. Just feel free
to drop me a line and let me know what you think.

Wishing you continued success for 75.

Sincerely,

Steve Prefontaine
wl

On April 9, 1975—less than two weeks before the Boston Marathon—running superstar Steve Prefontaine sent unemployed Bill a pair of shoes to race in, along with this personal letter.

(Charlie Rodgers)

Jerome Drayton from Canada and Bill duel in the early miles of the Boston Marathon. (Jeff Johnson)

Drayton falls back in Wellesley.
(*The Boston Globe*)

Racing through the Newton Hills, around 19 miles.
(*The Boston Globe*)

Heartbreak Hill dead ahead!
(*The Boston Globe*)

At 24 miles, tearing through Beacon Street. (Pat O'Donnell)

Turning to the finish line, 200 meters to go. (*The Boston Globe*)

50 meters from the finish. (*The Boston Globe*)

The finish line is in sight.
(Charlie Rodgers)

Flying along in his new Nikes,
courtesy of Steve Prefontaine.
(Charlie Rodgers)

The finish line! Cannot believe it! Proudly wearing the Boston singlet with his
running club emblazoned on it. (*The Boston Globe*)

Victory at the finish line. Holding the "racing gloves" given to Bill by his brother Charlie at the start to keep his hands warm.
(Charlie Rodgers)

Police guide Bill away from the finish line, through the huge crowds.
(Bill Rodgers Personal Collection)

Longtime race director for the BAA and former Boston Marathon runner Jock Semple (to right) helps Bill to the awards stand. (*The Boston Globe*)

Mayor Kevin White places victory laurel wreath on Bill's head. (*The Boston Globe*)

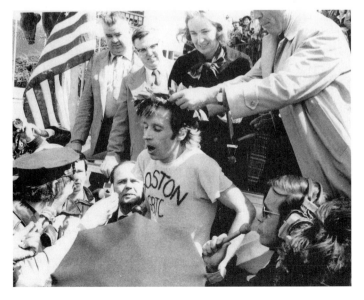

Bill reaches out to Charlie at the awards ceremony.
(*The Boston Globe*)

A Boston legacy—
Bill Rodgers, Amby Burfoot,
John "Young" Kelley, and
John "The Elder" Kelley.
(Andy Yelenak)

Jason, Charlie, and Bill at Bill Rodgers Running
Center in Faneuil Hall, all grown up.
(Charlie Rodgers)

One final piece of business had to be resolved—a name for the club. After "Codfishers" was crossed off the list and "Boston Beaners" was rejected, they agreed to a more straightforward name: Greater Boston Track Club.

While all that was going on, I continued traveling to road races on the weekend. I drove down to Manchester, Connecticut, for the Manchester Road Race, a 4.25-mile race held every Thanksgiving Day morning. Its status as one of the oldest road races of its kind—it started in 1927 with just twelve runners—lent it credibility and popularity with hardcore runners. It represented old-school New England road racing, and I knew it held a special place in the heart of Johnny Kelley, who had won the race six times, and Amby, who had won it nine times. I also had a special fondness for Manchester because it was the first road race I had ever run. For some reason, Coach O'Rourke thought I should give road racing a shot and so I got my first taste of long-distance competition—taking the high school division in a time of 25:18.

Unfortunately, once the 1973 edition of the Manchester Road Race began, I did not duplicate my success from eight years earlier. It was a perfect day to run, but I got a side ache in the first mile and my strides felt off the rest of the way. My lungs hurt during and after the race. I was disappointed to finish fifth. I was happy, however, that if I couldn't get the win, Amby did. Nobody wanted victory at Manchester more than he, and his win added to his amazing consecutive win streak, which peaked at seven in 1977. After the race, I surmised what went wrong: I was getting over a head cold and should have rested in the days before the race. In my mind, days off weren't an option.

A little side note about the race: I remember a group of women runners protesting their exclusion by the Amateur Athletic Union (AAU), which barred men and women from competing together. We all need a place to put our aspirations, and I had found mine in road racing. I got a rush from competing. It gave me an incredible feeling of accomplishment and drove me to put forth even greater effort in my training. I didn't like the fact that others were denied the same rewards.

The small group of women lined up at the starting line behind us, and ran the course anyway, even if their times weren't recorded. It worked. The next year they were officially allowed to race. What does this show? The crusty, male-only institutions of the sport were finding it harder and harder to stem the tide of enthusiasm for running that Frank Shorter's Olympic marathon victory had put in motion. The passage of Title IX, in 1972, which opened the door for young women athletes to continue their passion in college and beyond, also energized more women to compete in long-distance races. At the same time, trailblazers like Jacqueline Hansen, the 1973 Boston Marathon champion, and Miki Gorman, who in the mid-1970s became the first and only woman to win the New York City and Boston Marathons twice, were helping women to be taken seriously. The doors were slowly opening for more people to get involved in running. As far as I was concerned, the doors needed to be blown to pieces.

Most people couldn't understand why I used to ride my beat-up car up and down the East Coast to races. They couldn't fathom why I was running 120 miles a week to win a toaster or a jar of honey. But I felt more alive being part of the New England road racing scene, even as basic and limited as it was. I'd finally connected with people who shared the same passion. We could feel the excitement in the air. We were part of a sport that was taking off.

I built my world around running. It became everything to me. This is the ultimate energy-lifting, morale-boosting activity. Sure, there are days where my body felt like blah, or I stunk it up in a race, but, on the whole, running raised my spirits. It allowed me to quiet my mind and go inward, where I gained insights into myself and the world. Very powerful stuff!

Up until that point in my life, I'd found it hard to follow through on anything, even when opportunity was right in front of me. I had all the energy and none of the drive. Now I was following through on my running, training twice a day, every day. I even ran on New Year's Eve. It was only an easy four-mile run on the hills, but it showed my resolve and commitment to conquer the Boston Marathon in the spring. I wrote a final entry in my training log: "Yea & Hurrah! 73 was a good year! 3 toots and a whistle for 74!!"

It was March of 1974. In the year since wilting in the heat at Boston, I had competed in over fifteen road races around New England—and won most of them. But here's what you have to understand: It was great to win races; I got cool prizes and my confidence was boosted. I made new friends. But more importantly, I saw each race as a small part of an evolutionary journey toward a higher goal. I used each road race as another step toward the Boston Marathon on April 15.

Training sessions can give you some idea of whether you're ready to compete in a heavyweight battle like Boston, but tune-up races are where you discover where you really stand. Are you fit enough? Are you tough enough? Are you mentally strong enough? Can you handle that little injury that pops up on mile 12? Can you handle it when some foreign champion starts pushing the pace on mile 20? Can you hang with him when he's clocking nothing but sub-five-minute miles? Because if you can't do all that, you don't stand a chance of winning. Keep your eye on the big race, I told myself. On the race that counts.

Confidence is everything in the marathon. You can't run scared or you'll be eaten alive by the competition. Winning road races built me up. My victory at the National Championship in Gloucester gave me a huge psychological lift. I had defeated some very good runners there. Then I got a call from the local New England representative of the AAU and he suggested that I run at San Blas, Puerto Rico, and represent the United States. The thought of competing in my first international race sent shivers down my spine.

I remember that trip very well. On the plane ride down, I was reacquainted with my deathly fear of flying. Once I arrived in San Blas, I met up with my teammate Tom Fleming. Brash and outgoing, he spoke in a rapid-fire Jersey accent. He liked to make good-natured wisecracks. The gaudy uniforms of another country, for instance, would certainly draw a sharp one-liner. But while Tom was loose and cavalier off the course, he was a ferocious competitor on it. He was one of those guys who trained, trained, trained.

Tom and I stayed in a little guesthouse on the edge of town, surrounded by goats and chickens and fields of corn. Today, runners would be put up in luxury hotels. The simple accommodations offered a beauty all their own.

I remember Tom and me waking up at four in the morning to roosters crowing. We walked down the dusty street and stopped at a little café for breakfast. We used our per diem to get these very greasy eggs with bacon cooked in with them. They were delicious. Later, I met up with my old friend John Vitale, an old college rival from the University of Connecticut. We embarked on a five-mile run through the steep, narrow streets of the village. Afterward, Tom and I went for a boat trip and I stole a live sea creature—an urchin. Later, I attended a festival named after St. Blaise, the patron saint of throat sufferers. At the festival, we enjoyed singing, dancing, and carnival rides. In the evening, we attended a Spanish Rotary dinner. Here, I met some of the foreign runners, including Lasse Virén of Finland, Ron Hill and Don Faircloth of Great Britain, and Henry Rono of Kenya. Virén, who had recently won Olympic gold in the ten thousand- and five thousand-meter events at the 1972 Munich games, was the best distance runner in the world. I also bumped into Amby Burfoot. Once again, I was following in his footsteps.

On Friday, I went out and ran most of the mountainous course, about ten miles in the heat. Looking back, I was crazy to exert my effort like that two days before the race. I was also finding it hard to adjust from the winter air of Boston to the warmth and humidity of Puerto Rico. Practically overnight, I went from running through a blizzard to running in sweltering heat. I never considered that the sudden shift in conditions would have such a strong effect on me. Another lesson learned.

Back at the guesthouse, Tommy was telling me about his experience training in Finland.

"You hear what I'm saying, Bill?"

"What's that?"

"I'm talking about the Finish runners," said Tommy. "They're training full-time."

"How do they do that?" I asked.

"How do you think?" said Tom. "The government sets these guys up with some job that doesn't even exist."

"Lasse Virén?"

"Lasse Virén is supposedly a policeman. He's about as much a policeman as you and I are."

"Huh," I said.

"Virén isn't out their fighting crime on the mean streets of Finland. He's training for the Olympics. He's running a hundred fifty miles a week."

"One hundred fifty miles. Are you serious?"

"He doesn't have to hold down some crappy job like us. He can train to his heart's content. Day or night."

"If Virén's running one hundred fifty miles a week . . ."

"We should be doing one hundred sixty," interjected Tommy. "We're waking up at the crack of dawn. Slipping and sliding all over the road in the pitch dark. Freezing our butts off. What are the Finns and Russians doing?"

"What?"

"They're here! In Puerto Rico! Or some other warm-weather climate. They've been sent down here by their countries. Set up with training facilities. All their expenses have been taken care of. All they have to concentrate on is getting fitter and stronger."

"We need that kind of support."

"From who? The AAU? It's a joke. Joe Namath makes four hundred thousand dollars. We can't make a penny. He's got endorsement deals. What do we have?

"Zilch."

"A tiny per diem and a jersey with our name on it. Good luck, pal. Even the land Virén built his house on was given to him by the Finnish people. I'm telling you, he's treated like a rock star in his homeland. We're treated like freak show oddities."

"Lasse Virén. The Big V."

"Is that your nickname for him?"

"You like it?" I asked.

"The Big V is going down!"

I laughed. "I'm not too sure about that."

You couldn't find two guys with more different personalities. Tom was clearly a bull in a China closet, or whatever the expression was. He probably felt the marathon should have been a fifty-two-miler, rather than a twenty-six-miler. Tom was one of those guys whom the energy just emanated from whenever he came into the room; wherever he was, you felt the electrons zapping out from him. As for me, Amby used to joke that he wasn't sure if I was awake or asleep most of the time. But on some level, runners are runners. From that trip on, we became life-long friends.

The race started at four in the afternoon. It was about 85 degrees with high humidity. We were bused out to the starting line, a dusty road in the middle of the hilly countryside. We were way out in the middle of nowhere. Tom had run this race before, so he was less overwhelmed than me. It was exciting to be there, wearing the American uniforms, representing the United States.

San Blas was a wild and sometimes harrowing race that ran through narrow streets and mountain passes and then back again. Thousands of screaming fans flanked the tight, winding lanes, cheering us on. As we raced down the steep descent into the town, I could see the church spires at the finish line far in the distance. All the way down this long, long hill, we heard the roars of the thick crowds that lined the course. It reminded me of Boston, minus the Red Sox caps and pasty drunks.

San Blas was the most grueling race I'd ever run. I went out trying to compete with the Finns. I stayed with them for about seven miles, but then they started to pull away. The pounding on the rough and bumpy terrain caused bad blisters to form on the soles of my feet. I also got painful side aches in the heat. I estimated that the blisters and side aches had cost me at least a minute. I faded. A few runners started to pass me on the course. The Finns took the top three spots. Tom was the top American finisher, in fifth place. I hung on for seventh place, the next highest American.

An hour later I was lying in bed with a wet washcloth on my head, thinking about the lessons I'd learned racing for the first time against a bunch of international long-distance assassins. One: I needed to put in more miles. Big V miles. Two: A full-time marathoner has a major advantage over a part-time one. It was only a matter of time before the city of Boston made me an honorary policeman. Or not.

After all the official postrace celebrations and award ceremonies, Tom and I partied with the other runners at a local bar. Hours earlier we were trying to decimate one another along sharp-curved mountain roads, baking to death, and now we were enjoying ourselves with beer and cocktails, telling jokes and sharing laughter. The rum and Cokes flowed all night, which helped bridge the language gap between our respective countries. Ron Hill was dancing around, wearing a big grin on his sunburned British face. I spotted Lasse Virén take a big swig of rum from the bottle. There was a real macho "I can party as hard as you can" attitude to this sport. No fistfights, but a certain intensity lay beneath the raucous times. Maybe because a certain intensity was required as a distance runner—you trained hard, you raced hard, you celebrated hard.

TWELVE

Racing for Blenders

The runners who ran Boston many times—Tarzan Brown and John "the Elder" Kelley, and Young Johnny Kelley and Amby Burfoot and Tom Fleming and Alberto Salazar and Joan Benoit Samuelson—understood how the intensity of the race grows throughout the course, climaxing along Heartbreak Hill, six miles from the finish. The crowds that lined the six hundred-meter ascent cheered so loudly when the leaders approached you could hear them a mile and a half away. The crowd really let loose a wall of sound as runners crested the top of the torturous hill. This is where you get down into the nittygritty. The race is usually down to two or three runners. It was here in 1979 where I really had to duke it out with Toshihiko Seko of Japan, who was running his first Boston Marathon. "If you didn't have Heartbreak Hill," he would later say, "you would have an easy course here." True, and if wishes were horses, beggars would ride.

But in 1975 I was four years away from my duel with Seko on Heartbreak Hill. Right then, I didn't have another runner pushing me. I only had the sense of going for it, and wild-eyed Jock cheering me on with his Scottish accent that you couldn't understand. Here was the father figure to Young Johnny Kelley rooting me on, himself a top competitor forty years earlier. He wasn't just some bureaucrat or a number pusher. Today, there are more race officials and coaches who really know the marathon, but in those days it was different. Few people understood the marathon. Jock did. He knew the punishment runners put themselves through to run the race—the cramps, the blisters, the dehydration—and the significance of conquering the ultimate test of stamina and endurance. It's crazy that Jock had fired up his protégé Johnny Kelley around this same spot along the course in 1957 on his way to victory, and that the same encouraging voice had lifted my roommate Amby Burfoot over Heartbreak Hill in 1968, and now his booming voice was bolstering my courage through the most critical part of the journey.

Huge crowds screamed and yelled on both sides of the narrow strip of road I sliced through. To acknowledge them would have been a dangerous waste of energy. This was no time to be distracted. I needed only to let my mind wander for a moment to invite disaster. I focused my eyes straight ahead. Just because I wouldn't disengage from the battle, not even momentarily, to smile and wave to the cheering crowds didn't mean I wasn't emotionally feeding off them.

When I reached the base of Heartbreak, I caught sight of my shoelace flopping around. I stopped and bent down on one knee to tie it. I glanced up calmly to see Jock Semple barreling toward me like his hair was on fire. "Whatya doin', lad?" he screamed. "Don't stop! Don't stop!"

It looked like Jock's big Scottish head was about to explode. I didn't share his sense of panic. Just the opposite. I felt calm. In control. I knew I had time to stop and tie my shoes. This was as good a place to do it as any. And, of course, this wasn't just any pair of shoes, but "lucky" shoes sent to me by Steve Prefontaine, the magical distance runner who put Nike on the map.

But what if Drayton or Fleming or Ron Hill caught up to me? Okay, first of all, I felt I was far enough ahead of them that stopping for a minute to tie my shoes would not put my lead in jeopardy. But let's assume the worst-case scenario—I look back and there's Drayton charging toward me. Why panic about that? I had plenty left. I could match anybody's pace. If he came up on me then I would put it into another gear. We would have a fun race over the last six miles.

Nobody wants to give up a lead. The point is that stressing about losing your position at the front won't make you run any better; in fact, it will make you run worse and the fear itself may actually cause the thing you fear to happen. On the other hand, if the concern had never entered your mind, it would never have manifested itself in a reality.

Some runners won't stop for anything. They run with blinders on. I remember Amby running with this kind of singular purpose even on our casual training runs together through the trails around Wesleyan campus. He was baffled how I could take in the scenery, how I could stop to pick up items I spotted on the side of the road. But I didn't think there was anything strange about this—observing the world around me was a large part of what made running so fun. There were no rules. You could run faster or slower or stop altogether to examine a strange, glittering object poking out of a babbling brook.

Of course, some will say that's all well and good so long as you're talking about a training run. After all, the stakes are nonexistent. But a serious competition is different; it requires a serious, intense, grit-your-teeth attitude. But running maniacally is a good way to burn yourself out. I think we run best when we are calm and relaxed; at least, that's what I've found. I focus better when I'm calm and relaxed. I have a better idea of what strategy to employ; I can hear what my body is telling me; I can hear what my opponent is telling me. Because marathon racing is so brutally competitive, so physically intense, so mentally challenging, it's imperative to keep your head. You need to maintain a clear picture of what's happening in the here and now.

I'm not sure the leader of the Boston Marathon has ever stopped to tie his shoes, let alone six miles from the finish line. But stopping to tie my shoes gave me a chance to collect myself. Then, a little farther along the ascent, I stopped for water. The crowd lost their mind.

"What are you doing?" they yelled out. "Keep going! Keep going!"

Meanwhile, up ahead on the lead vehicle, Jock Semple was having a small coronary. I didn't see what the big deal was. I hadn't taken a lot of water earlier in the day. Now I needed the water. I stopped because I was never skilled at getting a good swallow while running, and also I recalled my high school track days when I felt great after stopping for a cold drink of water partway through a workout.

I ran a little farther up the hill and then stopped again to drink another cup of water. By now, Jock was pulling out whatever hair he had left. I swear you could hear his near-hysterical voice over the cheers of thousands: "Git goin', lad. Yeev got a chance to break the record!"

Here was Jock giving me the word that I was on pace to break Ron Hill's course record. I just kind of let that go in one ear and out the other. I didn't care. For me it was all about first place. I was fired up. I was racing the lead vehicle. I knew I was running better than I had ever run before in my life. I felt moderately strong when I won the Philadelphia Marathon the previous year, but not like this. I was floating along without any wasted motion, my mind focused on the rhythm of my smooth stride. No hamstring cramps, not even the slightest of muscle twitches. No blisters. No sores. No fatigue. Everything was just—perfect. Nothing would stop me now. That's the way I felt.

The road was narrow and the cheering crowds were up close and personal as I charged up the granddaddy of all the Newton Hills. The fans formed a funnel, guiding me into the heart of downtown Boston. Running through that narrow stretch was very intense—like the Tour de France for marathoners. I loved that! It was frenzied, but that was part of the excitement. I didn't know what was going to happen. I wasn't thinking about what was going to happen. I was just racing.

In the end, I had stopped four times for water and once to secure an untied shoe along the stretch of Newton Hills even though I was leading the Boston Marathon, even though I was on a record pace, even though I had a crazed mob of fans imploring me to keep running, even though I was only six miles away from realizing my dream.

At the end of the day, it didn't matter what Amby thought or Charlie or Jock or all those thousands of people lining the street. I was going to decide when it was time to stop, not anybody else. Because, first of all, you can always stop. You can always decide here is where I need to take in the scenery, here is where I need to take a deep breath, here is where I need a cool sip of water, here is where I need to tie my shoes. And secondly, you know better what you need than all the people in the world combined. Let them call you crazy. They will anyway. Run your own race. I'll repeat that: Run your own race. Trust me, you will find much more success in life if you do. And you'll have a lot more fun along the way.

ONE YEAR EARLIER
BOSTON, MASSACHUSETTS

It was the start of 1974. As they had for decades, iron-fisted governing bodies and backward-thinking race organizers controlled the sport of marathoning. Meanwhile, track guys dominated the races themselves. I was not a fast track guy. I was a road runner. More to the point, I was last in a long line of New England road runners. The tradition went all the way back to the early 1900s, to men like Clarence DeMar, Les Pawson, and Tarzan Brown. DeMar, who won seven Boston Marathons from 1911 through 1930, passed the torch to John "the Elder" Kelley, who passed it to Young Johnny Kelley, who passed it to Amby Burfoot. I was hoping to be the next to carry the flame.

How could you not run through the city streets with your head held high, knowing you were a direct descendent of such great men? Throw a million empty beer cans at my head as I run along the road in my gym shorts. Yell out the worst, most obscene words you can think of. Hassle me with your hulking vehicles. Denigrate my passion. This the thing I love more than anything in the world. Tell me it's worthless and idiotic.

Tell me I'm wasting my time. Point out that there's no money in it. Tell me I'd be better off looking for a job. Tell me that my focus should be on making enough so that I could afford to buy a nice home, drive a big car, and take a vacation to Club Med once a year. Do all this. I'm still going to run ten miles before work. Better yet, I'm going to run another six miles when I get home.

That spring, I enrolled as a graduate student in special education. I had told my Greater Boston Track Club teammate Don Ricciato, who then worked at Boston College and is now director of the BC College Campus School, about how much I had enjoyed working with the mentally challenged people at the Fernald School. He encouraged me to enroll in the special education program at Boston College and used his contacts to set me up with the right people, for which I thank him. My dad spent his life teaching—it made sense that I would follow in his footsteps.

Even though I was never a great student, I felt like I'd be able to fit in my studies while I aimed for the Boston Marathon. For one thing, I lived close to campus, meaning I could train before and after classes. During school vacation, I was able put in two-hundred-mile weeks. At the tail end of the program, I became a student teacher. Everything was going well. Powerful changes were taking place in my life—on and off the road. I felt a sense of direction; I liked that feeling. I was getting somewhere.

It was the morning of my second Boston Marathon. Charlie, our house guest, and I woke up early, got into my banged-up Volkswagen Beetle, and headed to Hopkinton for the start of the race. For nineteen miles, I ran boldly with the lead pack but once again, Heartbreak Hill ate me up and spit me out. My old demons did me in. I had started out too fast, determined to break away with the front-runners without thinking whether I could sustain that speed for 26.2 miles. I wanted to show my competitors that I meant business, that I had the strength—and the mental will—to go as hard as they wanted. It didn't matter to me that the lead pack was on a smoking 2:11 pace for the first ten miles. If they wanted to run five-minute miles, I was game. I thought nothing of keeping tabs on my pace to make sure I was executing my tactical plan. At that point, my only tactic was outrunning the three guys next to me.

The truth is, I lost the race the moment I lost hold of my emotions, and that was probably the first or second mile. I got too excited, and that opened the door for my opponents to throw me off my game. Neil Cusack was snorting like a buffalo the whole way and it drove me nuts. No way was I going to let him or Tom Fleming drop me. I beat Fleming at the National Championships in Gloucester, I thought, I can beat him here.

Finally, around the eighteen-mile mark, I slowed to a 2:15 marathon pace, or 5:10 per mile. It was too late. I had sealed my fate in the early miles when I exerted more energy than I could afford. At mile 20 I ran out of gas. Dehydration set in. My legs seized up. And here comes Heartbreak Hill. I couldn't have timed it more perfectly.

By the time Charlie caught sight of me coming up Heartbreak Hill, I was in fourth place. But he didn't know the awful truth—I had been hit with a terrific hamstring cramp. I gritted my teeth and tried to push through, but my legs were seizing up on me. I tried massaging out the cramp. I tried walking. Nothing worked. I finally pulled off to the side of the road at the top of Heartbreak Hill. Same spot I dropped out the first time around. I must have stood there alone with my thoughts for two minutes. My mind recalled what this Irish marathoner had said to me, how the race can turn into a "crucifixion." What do I do now? Should I try to finish? Was that even possible at this point?

Just then John Vitale came up alongside me. He encouraged me to get back into the race. You have no idea how hard is to set off again once you've stopped like that. I decided if there was a chance I could still finish, I had to take it. I started moving again and, mercy, mercy me, the cramps backed off and let go altogether. I finished fourteenth with a time of 2:19:34. In those days, if you could crack 2:20, you were considered to be a national-level marathoner. So I was glad I had stayed in the race until the end. The marathon is hard. You take your achievements where you can get them.

In retrospect, I should have pulled back and run at a more cautious pace. That's how Amby would have done it. Steady and methodical. Calm and composed. That's how you win a marathon. My way spelled certain doom. Reckless. Stubborn.

I had set my personal best time in the marathon, but I knew I could run faster. Runners are very seldom satisfied. They are always looking down the road. 2:19:34. That might win you a set of tires somewhere, but it wasn't going to earn you the laurel wreath at Boston. I vowed to improve, come back next year, and win.

How much faster would I have to run to become Boston Marathon champion? That year's winner, Irishman Neil Cusack, had crossed the finish line in 2:13:39. Tom Fleming, devastated after coming in runner-up for a second straight year, finished in 2:14:25. That meant in the next year I had to bring my time down by at least six minutes. But how? I suppose I could have told Ellen to pack up the cat, we're heading back to California. No, I couldn't blame the heat this time. My strength wasn't the problem, either. I was putting in 130 miles a week, wearing out the path around Jamaica Pond. I needed to make a change. That much I knew.

On a summer night in 1972, Tommy Leonard was working behind the bar of the Brothers Four in Falmouth, Massachusetts, a majestic little seaside village on the southwest of Cape Cod. Tommy all but ignored his patrons, too captivated by the action happening on the TV screen above the bar: Frank Shorter demolishing the field to win the Olympic marathon in Munich. Like every other running fan in the country at that moment, he promptly lost his mind with excitement. He made a promise that he'd host a road race in Falmouth so epic that even Frank Shorter, the newly crowned king of American running, would show up to compete.

Tommy was not your average bartender. He was the eternal optimist. People were eager to be in his presence because he always left you with a smile. He opened the Eliot Lounge within shouting distance from the Boston Marathon finish line. Tommy Leonard stories had you rolling on the floor. He ran his high school track championship, hungover, still wearing his tuxedo pants from the senior prom the night before. One day, while bartending at the Eliot, he served White Russians to a police horse. He also used to always have a beer waiting for Red Sox pitcher "Spaceman" Bill Lee, who would walk over from the ballpark in his cleats during rain delays. He offered free beer to anybody who finished the 1973 Boston Marathon and brought in their bib number.

We'd occasionally see Tommy working out on the BC track. He'd enthusiastically invite us to come by the Eliot after our workouts, where he always had a pitcher of beer at the ready for us. Tommy decorated the Eliot as a shrine to runners, with photos of marathon greats mounted around the bar. Each Boston Marathon, he hung foreign flags to represent the nations that had sent a runner to race. The Eliot soon became our unofficial clubhouse. Tommy became an unofficial member of our track club. More than that, he became our guiding spirit. I called him the Guru. What can I say? Some gurus enjoy Guinness more than others.

Tommy's first attempt at putting on a world-class road race in Falmouth in 1973 was by no means a disaster—he managed to get 125 runners to show up and race in the rain, and threw a wild postrace party that saw Johnny Kelley doing the jitterbug with his wife. But Tommy knew to really get the event off the ground he had to persuade me and the other GBTC runners—Randy Thomas, Bobby Hodge, Vin Fleming—to run in it. The promise of a big party whetted our appetites, but to close the deal, Tommy pulled out one of his classic marketing ploys: He told us that there'd be girls in bikinis along the route handing out Gatorade. I fell for that one.

Tommy also told us that Marty Liquori, the best miler in America at that time, was going to be competing, only this time he wasn't fibbing. Tommy had convinced Liquori's brother Steve, a Boston College student and regular at the Eliot, to recruit Marty, who was up at a camp in Poughkeepsie, New York.

On that humid August weekend, our small running tribe descended on this sleepy village to race 7.1 miles, or more accurately, from one pub down the road to another pub. Around noon, I joined the other 445 racers at the start area—outside one of Tommy's favorite bars, the Captain Kidd at Woods Hole.

The gun sounded. Marty and I set the pace. A few GBTC runners tried to give chase but we broke away. It quickly turned into a two-man race. We matched each other stride for stride past spectacular views of the ocean and long stretches of pristine beaches. The breathtaking beauty of the seven-mile route along Surf Drive continued as Liquori and I came around Nobska Point Lighthouse, overlooking Vineyard Sound. I'm not even sure Tommy Leonard realized that he had set up a course that was as close to nirvana as you could get for a road runner. Then again, maybe he did.

As we headed into two miles of gentle hills through the woods, I glided smoothly at a five-minute-per-mile pace. Liquori realized he was in for the fight of his life. I poured on the speed over the next three miles. Finally, Marty couldn't take any more. He dropped back. By the time I cruised along the sand-swept road into Falmouth Harbor, I had a huge lead over the rest of the field. As I churned down the home stretch to the Brothers Four, people on the media truck, expecting to see Liquori in the front, yelled out, "Who are you?"

I yelled back, "Bill Rodgers."

Of course, it came out as "Will Rodgers."

"Like the American humorist?" the reporters asked Tommy Leonard at the raucous party that followed. "Yep. One and the same," he said, dancing by them with a full beer.

The next day in the *Boston Globe,* the headline read: "Will Rodgers Beats Marty Liquori."

Marty thought he would show up and whip everybody's pants, but I had been doing all this mileage and there was no way I was going to let a miler, even a great miler like Liquori, beat me over seven miles. He had the speed, but I had the strength. In the end, I was right. I had taken down a running superstar by almost a minute and a half. I wrote in my training log that night, "Zapped M. Liquori! O What Glory!" What's more, I won a blender to go along with the other kitchen equipment I had picked up through my previous road race conquest.

After the race, I learned the cops had towed my little Volkswagen Beetle. Nice, right? It gives you an idea of how popular we were with the local residents. It was going to cost me twenty dollars to retrieve my car—a substantial amount for a guy living on Oreos and cold pizza. An irate Tommy wouldn't stand for this; he sent George Robbat, the owner of the Brothers Four, to the local police station to pay the fine for me.

In Tommy's mind, the champion of his great road race deserved to be treated like a prince. In fact, he felt that's how all runners should be treated. Unfortunately, that wasn't the case in Falmouth or anywhere else for that matter in 1974; we were just a big nuisance. The good news was that publicity from my victory over Liquori—Olympic-level runner gets beaten by unknown local—kick-started the Falmouth Road Race. It kept cranking up from there until eventually it became one of the biggest road races in America.

I focused my attention on the next marathon: the New York City. The stakes were high. The winner got a trip to Greece, to compete in the Athens Marathon over the original course, from Marathon to Athens. Tom Fleming had set the course record with a time of 2:21:54. I had just broken 2:20 at Boston and that was with stopping on Heartbreak Hill. I went in confident I could take first.

At the time, the New York City Marathon was a small race with only 527 entrants. The course didn't go through all five boroughs like it does today, but rather was confined to five loops around Central Park.

I remember it was a sweltering fall day. I tried to race away from the field and I did, opening up a three-minute gap through the first twenty miles. Then my old nemesis—the heat—struck me down. I started to develop severe hamstring cramps. I tried to get rid of them, rub them out, but it was no use. My body was too dehydrated. I pulled off to the side of the road.

I remember somebody came over to me and gave me water. He helped me to stretch my legs. I got back in the race, but by then I had way too much ground to make up. I jogged in and finished in fifth place in a time of 2:35:59, almost ten minutes behind winner Norb Sander. I believe the term is "getting your butt kicked." It was a major step backward.

I knew I hadn't run a smart race. I'd gone out too aggressively in the hot weather. I hadn't drunk enough water early on. I'd deluded myself into thinking I had the stamina to charge ahead to the front and stay there over the long haul. Basically, I'd made all my usual errors.

After the race, I had cramps all over my body. I limped back to the VW Beetle with Ellen and slowly lowered myself into the passenger seat. As we drove back to Boston, all I could think about was quitting the marathon. I said to Ellen, "I'm not cut out to be a marathoner." Maybe I should drop down to ten thousand meters, I thought to myself. Maybe that's all I could handle.

THIRTEEN

Will-Ha

April 21, 1975
Newton Hills, Massachusetts

I felt if I could make it to the top of Heartbreak Hill, nothing could stop me after that. It didn't cross my mind that I might again be struck with a paralyzing hamstring cramp as I mounted the steep incline. As I continued my battle against gravity, I focused my thoughts instead on the press truck ahead of me: You don't think I can catch you? I can catch you.

My high school coach Frank O'Rourke had taught me to conserve my energy going up hills. Wait until I reached the top and then push it hard coming down the hill. The first time I ignored Coach O'Rourke was when he told me to cut my hair. This would be the second time.

I was so pumped up at that moment that I stepped up my pace, which caused the thick crowds that flanked my narrow path to cheer even louder. I kept thinking, If I gun it to the top of the hill, I have this race sewn up. I surged up Heartbreak Hill. Coming over the crest, I saw the Boston skyline, defined by the Prudential Building, looming in the horizon. I felt a tremendous high. I knew that going downhill, nobody could catch me.

I took the left turn that takes you down into Cleveland Circle. This is among the best places on the Boston Marathon course. The crowds are raucous and overflowing and filled with Boston College students who've been partying since the sun came up. More downhill! All that downhill was a gift—a gift I was going to use to cut loose and really devastate the competition.

I zipped past Cleveland Circle, never dreaming that I'd open a running center here two years later. I was a broke student on food stamps. The running boom hadn't hit yet. But as I tore through the roaring crowds, I could feel the thunder gathering; the running explosion was going to rock the city.

Past Cleveland Circle, I found myself facing another long downhill. This is another great part of the course where you can really move and pick up momentum. The crowds were thick and several people deep and there was just enough space for me to squeeze through. I was feeding off the fervor of the spectators, parting inches from my face. I sensed the finish line was not far away.

I was getting into the tough physical part of the marathon. You're hitting twenty-four miles, and the feeling that you normally have at this stage is, "Whew . . . this is a long event!" You may have been running on emotion in the earlier part of the race, but now suddenly this distance catches up to you. This is a terrible event, you think to yourself. How can I be this tired? On a hot and humid day, you sort of shrunk back at this point. But today the sweet, cool winds were on my side.

I was heading into mile 26, coming through Coolidge Corner on Beacon Street, flying along the downhills on cruise control. It was exhilarating to be in the lead this late into the Boston Marathon. But I wasn't thinking about winning, or imagining how it would feel to wear the laurel wreath crown upon my head. I was just flying down the street, the sound of the breeze whooshing past my ears. An invisible force had taken over. Who knew where this positive energy had come from. Who cared? I was going along for the ride.

I remember when Amby Burfoot ran down Beacon Street in the lead in 1968, he was basically in a state of panic. He feared he would be passed any second by a former marine named Bill Clark, who had been dogging him for twenty-one miles. If that wasn't enough, Amby also had to contend with a hot day and an inexcusable lack of water stations along the course. But my old roommate went there to win, not just for himself, but for his beloved mentor, Johnny Kelley. He held the dream of winning the Boston Marathon deep inside him, and used his will to overcome the fatigue of the body and to keep pushing. No matter what happens, you have to keep pushing.

Just like Amby, as I ran the last miles down Beacon Street, I started worrying about somebody coming up on me—in my case, Jerome Drayton. The scary thing was, the silent, methodical running machine with the dark sunglasses could be breathing down my neck and I'd have no idea because of the huge crowds converging into the street right behind me. The same thing happened to Amby in 1968. It's a helpless feeling, not knowing what's going on behind you, if your challenger is gaining on you, if he's a few feet behind you. The invisible force had abandoned me.

I couldn't shake the vision of Drayton sneaking up on me from the side. I was losing it. Just then, out of nowhere, I saw a figure pull up even with me. But it wasn't Drayton. It was my best friend, Jason Kehoe, riding up beside me on a bike. I hadn't seen him in ages. He was shouting "Go, Billy, Go!" I glanced over at him in shock. How did he get through the thousands of screaming fans? How did he get past the cops, the race officials, Jock Semple?!

Seeing my old friend lifted me up like you can't imagine. In that brief moment, I looked at him as if to say, "I'm going to do it, Jason," to which he gave me a look that said, "Yeah, Billy. You are going to do this."

My mind flashed back to high school, to when Jason and Charlie cheered me on from the sideline as I tried to win my two-mile races. I felt a wave of calm overtake my body. I was suddenly able to shut out the noise, the crowds, the doubts, the fears. I ran the rest of the race like I was on a training run with Amby through the wooded trails outside campus; I ran like I was chasing butterflies through the fields with Jason and Charlie.

Jason had appeared on his bike out of nowhere, and then he was gone in a poof. Of course, had I bothered to look behind me, I would have seen a couple of overzealous police officers running Jason off the road. He was probably still yelling "Go, Billy!" as they wrestled him to the ground.

ONE YEAR EARLIER
BOSTON, MASSACHUSETTS

During one of our long training runs through Waltham, I told Sev about how I faltered at the New York City Marathon, and how I felt maybe I wasn't cut out for the grueling distance. He said he thought I would benefit from working with Coach Squires. "The guy is brilliant," Sev told me as we coasted along the road, our elbows and footsteps just inches from each other. "I mean, he's kind of strange. We call him 'Wack.' But I've seen what he can do. There isn't a guy that has trained under Squires that isn't worlds better now."

Sev invited me to come down to the Greater Boston Track Club's next workout at Boston College. What did I have to lose? It might be fun.

I showed up at the track and Sev introduced me to Squires. Speaking like the crazy guy at the end of a seedy Irish bar in South Boston, he said to me: "You need my coaching and you need a group to teach you how to run, unless you want to go off with the gun and do your little bullshit thing that'll get you in the Boston Marathon fifth at best. You need to be with my group on Tuesdays, because that's a speed thing, and that's what you don't have, pal."

From that day on, I was on the track twice a week with Squires. I wasn't the only distance runner to show up for Squires's workouts. There was Bobby Hodge, Randy Thomas, Vin Fleming, Dickie Mahoney. They were all local guys, running bums like me. They ran every day, no matter the weather or how they felt physically. Their running log was their bible, and once they committed themselves to logging a certain number of miles for the week, nothing was going to stand in their way. Mahoney was a mailman running 150 miles a week while delivering mail. That's the way it was. We did whatever it took.

The other guys in the group—Hodge, Thomas, Fleming—had all been serious talents in college. I don't know what they thought of me when I showed up—a skinny, quiet kid with shaggy blond hair and faded brown corduroy sweatpants. Probably not much.

Coach Squires was one of the first to incorporate speed work into distance runners' training. Before that, marathon runners were referred to as "plodders"—the old-style guys of the thirties and forties looked like they were just going so slow. I wasn't a plodder, but I didn't do enough speed training. I had the other pieces of the puzzle worked out—the daily high-mileage runs. What Squires added to my repertoire was the ninety percent–effort track workout. He had me and the others doing mile or mile and a half pickups at the world-class marathon pace of five minutes per mile. Nobody had their athletes doing long speed intervals like that in 1974. Number two, Squires believed these flow intervals should be run at a moderate pace, where it was hard and comfortable at the same time—where everybody else did them full-out. Eventually, I was running 5:20 a mile in practice and just floating along.

Coach Squires was a man so far ahead of his time I'm not even sure he always realized what the heck he was doing. He devised unusual workouts for us. One I remember in particular he called the simulator —as in simulating a race. He started us out with a quick one mile or two miles on the track and then we'd go out on the Boston Marathon route and run the hills, then we'd finish on the track with another hard effort. A hard start, a hard finish.

Squires made us run from Boston College out to Wellesley and back along the Boston Marathon course. The purpose of these hill workouts was not to break us, but to build us up. As Squires explained once: "A workout is an effort where you can control your speed. That means you can control your form. They always have more in their gun when they leave. I'm not into these practice runners, the Cinderfellas, who want a Purple Heart for their workout. I always say, 'Let's see what we do on Saturday in the race.'" If somebody did try to be a hero during a training run, Squires would give him a lengthy earful, much of it incomprehensible.

Squires knew that by having us train on the actual Boston Marathon course we would gain an edge. "We did it so many times," said Squires, "you could do it in your sleep." Preparation was key. Know the course, know your opponent, know yourself, your real power, get in touch with it. Only then were you ready to go into battle.

I liked Squires. He was quirky but wired—kind of like me. I fed off his intensity. We all did. He was one of the guys in a sense, living the runner's life, still running in races himself. Sometimes you couldn't make out what had just come out of his mouth—he spoke his own loopy language—but it didn't matter. What came through loud and clear was his passion. He wanted us to be great, believed we could be great, and got us all believing we could be great. But he required you to listen to him and not question his training program for you, not even if you watched him scribble it on a paper napkin at the Eliot Lounge. He demanded that kind of total belief in him. And he got it from us.

No matter what Squires put us through during practice, he kept it fun. He might direct his whip-smart sarcasm at you, especially if he thought you were stepping out of line, running too hard for his taste or not running hard enough, but he never got mad at anyone. He wasn't a drill sergeant. He didn't need to be with us. We were as hungry a bunch of runners as you could find. No need to crack the whip. We were aiming high. What Squires did was get us to think bigger than we'd ever thought before.

That Squires was willing to coach a bunch of out-of-shape guys clinging on to their college glory days—and do it for no pay—spoke to his ability to see potential in people where others saw none. This attitude was shaped by his own improbable journey from a working-class South Boston kid with a serious heart defect to a three-time all-American at

Notre Dame. After serving in the army, where he was part of a unit known for its runners, he came back to Massachusetts. For a second, he considered moving to California to work in the sales department of Wilson Sporting Goods. Then one day, while on a run at Wakefield High School, the high school runners begged him to coach their team. In his mind, it was practically his duty to turn these "pathetic crap-burns," as he called them, into real runners. And he did just that.

Relying on his own unproven training methods, his stubbornly independent philosophies on life, and his razor-sharp instincts, he led Wakefield to a state championship in his first year. A few years later, he was hired as the track coach at Boston State College, where, over the next eighteen years, he'd produce sixteen all-Americans—a very impressive feat. Say what you wanted about Squires's unorthodox coaching style, it garnered results.

I think of Squires as more than just a coach, but a kind of wizard. He couldn't wait to try out his wild concoction of training methods on us. While his daring brew involved a mix of strength training, high mileage, and speed work, the key ingredient to Squires's workouts defied explanation. It was as if Coach sprinkled pixie dust over our sneakers before each of our group runs and said, Awake! His spell caused us to magically kick it into another gear during our workouts and got us to perform at our highest possible level.

Squires, always bursting with energy and ideas, kept us fired up from the start of the workout to the end, when we were drenched with sweat and looking around at each other, wondering how in the world we'd just run as fast and as long as we had. But more than energizing us, Squires served as a spiritual antidote to all the harsh judgments made about us runners in those days. People would ask me why I ran so much, as if it were some form of mental illness. I was told I was too old to still be running; it was deemed an inconsequential activity and thus not an appropriate use of time for a grown man.

In the face of such prevailing attitudes, many of us quit running after college. As a consequence, many of us lost a big part of who we were, and what our hearts desired most. It wasn't until joining the Greater Boston Track Club that we got back that feeling we had lost. We were suddenly reminded how running, perhaps more than any other sport, is a celebration of life. It makes your world a brighter place. It gives you this lift, a confidence to stand tall and feel good. Better than good. Boundless.

We had let society shame us into giving up the one activity that gave us the most happiness since we were kids. Now that we were running on a team again, to many of us, it felt like we were living a second childhood. Squires was the man leading the charge, encouraging us to shout it out loud to the world, I'm a runner. I can do this. I can have this great thing in my life, and I can find satisfaction in achieving whatever it is I set out to do, no matter how many miles it takes to get there. I don't have to be afraid to pursue my passion even if it seems silly or pointless to others. After all, the point of life is to enjoy it to the fullest, not merely survive. This was our radical battle cry as runners against those people who sought to marginalize us. Choose to live life to the fullest. Choose to run. Over time, our call would prove irresistible.

We were pushing one another as teammates like the Kenyans are doing these days. We were lucky. Boston had been a center of track for years, from the fifties on. So there was a history here. I think it had to do with all the colleges around the area—a source of young runners—and the Boston Marathon. Those of us who didn't have the speed or coordination to be sprinters moved on to the longer races and later to marathons. There was a certain unstoppability about it.

The Japanese and Finns and Germans and Soviets had what we didn't—state support, training camps, high-paid coaches, and scientific training programs. In our own country, we were outcasts; a fringe group of hard-nosed, fun-loving individuals doing something that we enjoyed, for God knows what reason, because after you come up with the romantic clichés about loving running, the rest of it is all just hard, bone-grinding work, day after day. And I think, frankly, the people who

ended up running 150 miles a week were the people who started winning things and realized that winning, even if there was no cash prize,
was its own reward. So, we kept doing it for rewards of a not very traditional nature. We were clearly iconoclastic, rugged souls of some sort.

Tommy Fleming and I would talk every day on the phone about our
training. Tommy would want to know what I did. If I told him I ran
twenty-two miles, the next day Tommy would run twenty-three. So we
fed into each other's competitiveness that way. As Tommy once said:
"When I ran with Billy, he would use terms like 'crush,' 'kill,' and 'destroy.' I had never heard a runner talk like that. Which will give you
some insight into the fact that what you see on the surface is not what
is inside that man as a competitor."

Anyone who ever trained with me will tell you the same thing. You
would never in a million years predict that I would win the Boston
Marathon. I was just another guy who was part of the fun-run group.
An average, everyday runner. When I wasn't running, I was a friendly,
low-key guy. Some even used the term "spacey."

I remember training with a friend of mine and four other runners,
doing mile repeats on the road. My friend would always finish with a
terrific burst of speed. When I asked why he was running so hard, he
said, "You've got to win the workout." I had never heard that before. He
went to Michigan State. He was a track guy. The track world is very
competitive. Road racing is more "take your time, you've got a long way
to go." When Amby and Johnny Kelley ran together through the trails,
or when Amby and I ran together around campus, it was never about
winning the workout. When things were going well, I would just
be floating along the road without any effort.

Despite working for free, Squires was very committed to us. We never
had any real arguments. I was glad to do the workouts he suggested—the
pickups, the intervals, the hill work. I listened to Billy but sometimes I
took what he said or did with a grain of salt. Squires thought if you were
running more than ninety miles a week you were wasting shoe leather.

He used to tell the other GBTC runners: "You don't need to do all that loopy stuff Bill does, running a hundred fifty miles in the woods, staring at the bluebirds." But I liked running in the woods with the bluebirds. Squires was wrong. I did need all that loopy stuff. It was in my blood, just as it was in Amby's and a long line of New Englanders before us—Tarzan Brown, John "the Elder" Kelley, Johnny Kelley, and even Henry Thoreau, walking hours around Walden Pond.

It was nothing personal against Squires. I was a road runner. My training method was based on what Amby had taught me at Wesleyan. I wasn't going to change my high-mileage running routine. I was a very "I'm going to do it my way" person. With that said, I was excited to know that I could take a break from running a million laps by myself around Jamaica Pond to meet up with a group of good guys who could hang with me on runs, even push me. That's what you look for in training partners. Also, I could see they were like me, trying to build on the success they had as college athletes, aiming for the next road race. No more scholarships to win. No chance of prize money. When I think of our focus, I think of the Greek virtue of excellence that was behind the Olympic games. This was just love of the sport.

There was a great feeling of brotherhood, and excitement, in all of us aiming to fulfill the same dream. None of us were getting paid and yet we thrived on the physical challenge. We were like a struggling rock band. A couple of the runners lived together in a house. Whenever we traveled to a race, there'd be five or six of us piled into a hotel room, sleeping on the floors, the sofas, wherever. We were not doing too much better financially than the Kenyan runners living together in training camps, sleeping in primitive huts without electricity and running water.

Although we faced the same dire money woes, we were all constantly joking around, sharing funny stories, trying to one-up one another. We all gave one another interesting nicknames. Some of the guys used to call me "Feather Shoes" because of my light, effortless stride, but my most popular nickname was "Will-ha." "Will" was the name that showed up in the press, thanks to a local reporter who mistakenly stated my name after my Falmouth Road Race victory in 1974. The "ha" was added to make it sound Finnish. We so greatly admired the "Flying Finns" for their legendary running prowess—and their *sisu*, the Finnish word for "pure will" or "guts"—we called ourselves by Finnish nick-names. Most of these Finnish names ended with a "ha" or "ho" as in Paavo Kotila, the three-time Finnish champion and winner of the 1960 Boston Marathon, or Vomma Iso-Hollo, two-time gold medalist in the 1930s. So I was "Will-ha," Scott Graham was "Scott-ha," and Vin Flem-ing was "Vin-ho."

Four months before the Boston Marathon, in the middle of winter, eight of us from the GBTC piled into a couple of beat-up cars and drove to Philadelphia to compete in the city's marathon. After two of our run-ners secured a hotel room with two double beds, the rest of us snuck up the back stairs. We tossed the mattresses on the floor so that all eight of us had a place to sleep—a pair on each mattress and a pair on each box spring. We woke up the next day and ran the marathon in the wind and cold and rain. I crossed the finish line to win the race in a time of 2:21:57, then we packed into the cars, and headed back to Boston. By then, we couldn't scrape up enough money between the eight of us to pay for the tolls on the Mass Turnpike; we had no choice but to stick to the back roads.

These group excursions were a common part of our lifestyle. Run-ning meant everything to us. It sustained us like oxygen. It mattered because we believed it mattered.

I would have a great time going out on a long training run with my friends. And we would run together all year round. It didn't matter if there was a blizzard. Of course, not everybody was happy to share the roads with us. Some people saw us as threats—we might cause them to crash or something. We definitely felt picked upon by the drunk, macho part of society, members of which would on occasion roll down a window and toss a beer bottle and yell some big obscenity at us. I had friends who wanted to fight back, but these guys outweighed and out-muscled us two to one, so I didn't like those chances.

You have to imagine a completely different climate from today—running was not part of the mainstream. The attitude was, "You skinny guys go running like crazy for hours, running in your underwear, and then you puke from exhaustion—and then what happens? You finish third in the marathon. What's the point of finishing third? What do you mean, the prize is a bowl of beef stew?" Despite the wide chasm between any normal part of society and us, we knew what we were doing was good. We had a self-righteous feeling, which I suppose was bad in a way. But we had chosen a certain path and we knew it was the right path.

I would never suggest that running made me better than somebody who didn't run, but maybe I was making a statement with my running. A statement for personal freedom and against collective inertia. I did not think it was right that people were told that running for long distances might kill them. Careful, or you might end up like poor Phidippides, your heart exploding due to the exertion. I couldn't stand that phony Greek myth and the way it was used to scare people and keep them from exploring their full physical and mental potential. What's the worst thing that could come from that? Luckily for the defenders of the status quo, the ranks of us shaggy outcast runners were too small to pose a real challenge. But that was about to change, starting in the summer of 1972, with Frank Shorter's gold medal victory at the Munich games.

Shorter's stunning triumph was a bolt of lightning, a call to action, a game changer. His win triggered a mass soul awakening. But this awakening was different than the counter-culture awakening that came before it. First of all, it wasn't political. It was personal. It didn't manifest itself in a physical place—a college campus, a farm in Woodstock, the Washington Monument. It occurred quietly, imperceptibly in the hearts of certain people. How many? Fifty? Five hundred? A thousand? Who knows the exact number?

I can tell you that they were a lot like me. Born into a middle-class family. Went to college. Competed on the track team. Graduated. Probably drifted a bit on the fringes of the mainstream. Put off getting a professional job. At the same time, they knew they couldn't make a living from their passion of running. They were jocks, but not an aggressive, knock-some-guy-on-the-turf kind of jock. Just a guy who enjoyed working out and lived for competition—whose idea of fun was chilling by the campfire with friends, strumming on an acoustic guitar, as opposed to pounding beer, chasing blonde former sorority girls, and shooting rifles at deer.

With our "us against the world" mentality, we were bound to develop a tighter unity than most clubs. I remember, that winter, running through Natick with Bobby Hodge, Vin Fleming, and Kirk Pfrangle. There was a rule: no stopping to go to the bathroom. If you did jump into the woods to get some privacy, the rest of the guys would take off at a sub-six-minute pace. I'd have to kick up some serious dirt to catch back up to them.

Sometimes while we were running as a pack up a particularly tough hill, we would pysch ourselves up by naming it for someone in the club. For example, we had a "Dickie Mahoney Hill," which he trained on near his house. We got the idea from the Kenyan runner John Ngeno, who was famous for his epic battles against Steve Prefontaine while a student at Washington State University. Ngeno would train daily on this brutal hill near the Pullman campus, which became known and feared as Ngeno's Hill. We admired Kenyan runners like Ngeno and Kip Keino, Olympic gold medalist in 1968 and 1972, for having the will to push their bodies to the extreme, doing painful hill repeats, and so to have a hill named after you was a great honor in our club.

I remember one time we were out on a run near Boston College. Leading the pack that day was a guy named Ken Mueller. He was an old warhorse from the BAA who had conducted field endurance training while serving in the army in the 1950s. He's gone now, but back then he logged as many as two hundred miles a week and ran the

Boston Marathon nineteen times. He was a trail runner like Amby and Johnny Kelley and he knew all the trails around that area. Anyway, we got caught in one of these classic Boston snowstorms, where you can hardly see your hand in front of your face.

We were running along both sides of the road and there was this guy driving behind us, honking away, and yelling viciously at us out his car window. We got pissed at him. It was, like, Share the road buddy. We surrounded his car. We weren't going to let him go. Things got a little heated. We started throwing snowballs at his car. We finally let him go, still slinging a few choice words at him as he drove off. It was the classic Boston feistiness that we all had. Later that night, we would laugh about our snowball assault over drinks at the Eliot Lounge.

Besides that incident and perhaps a few others, I didn't aggressively defend my lifestyle. That's just not who I am. I would rather quietly go my way and let them go theirs and hope they don't run me over next time around the block.

It did seem like crazy things always happened on our training runs. One time, there was a group of about ten of us doing a twenty-miler. As we were passing through Natick, we came up on this big mansion set back from the road. I spotted a big Great Dane in the yard, about sixty feet away. Next thing we know, the Great Dane was galloping toward our group with his teeth showing and foam dripping from his jowls. The pack of us started running for our lives. For some reason, he singled out Alberto Salazar, nicknamed "the Rookie" because he was seven years younger than the rest of us. As Alberto recalls in his book: "Snarling, snapping, slobbering, the beast comes close in on me. I'm frozen. I can't move. But just as the dog is about to spring—it's just like the movies—he yelps in pain and slinks away. I look over, and there's Bill. Among his eccentricities was the fact that he always ran carrying this heavy key ring—I never realized why until that moment (although, being Bill, he might not have realized why he carried it either). He had chucked the key ring at the dog and scared him away. We continued our run. Bill Rodgers had saved my life."

We soon became more than an athletic club, a tight-knit group of runners and their wives that would hang out socially. Practically every weekend, we would all pile in a couple of cars and drive down together to a local road race. While we were serious when it came to the competition, there was plenty of partying going on before and after the race. We had our big annual events like the Falmouth Road Race, which Tommy Leonard made sure every year morphed into a colossal summer blowout party.

I remember one New Year's Eve Tommy had been celebrating pretty hard and he told everybody to meet up the next day at the Eliot Lounge. We all showed up and ran twenty-five miles to Sharpless Jones's house on the South Shore. None of us planned to kick off the year on a little fun run, almost the distance of a marathon; it was a quirky, lighthearted "let's do it" kind of thing, like most other club happenings. A huge celebration commenced at the home of Sharpless Jones with big vats of chili and kegs of beer. He owned a running shoe outlet in Hanover, Massachusetts. I don't think Coach Squires ever found out about our New Year's Day workout.

On a summer day, a group of us would be in the middle of a long run, dripping with sweat, when we would jump into the Eliot and say hello to Tommy. He would greet us with a big grin and quickly serve us cool drinks on the house. A few minutes hanging around Tommy is all it took to feel happy and refreshed and ready to go back out there and conquer the world.

There was a great feeling that took hold during the first years of the running boom. Maybe it was the newness of it all, and the sense that something was happening here, that the sport was growing and our community of good friends was growing with it. Whenever you passed a runner on the street in those days, you would wave and they would wave back. Today, people often run with earphones and tune out the world around them, including other runners. If you wave to a woman you don't know in the park, she might not take this as a sign of solidarity. She may even take offense. Yes, I know time marches on, and you can still see amazing connections being made between runners, especially on the fund-raising side. But I'll never forget the unique bond shared among all runners back in the seventies, and how this great camaraderie became a powerful force for change.

Although I ran faithfully with the GBTC on Tuesday and Friday nights, officially I was still a member of the BAA. As much as I loved Jock Semple, I felt that my loyalty should go to the guys I was training with. Sev was elected to go down with me to tell Jock that I would run for the GBTC. We went down to his little training clinic in the back of the Boston Garden. We were scared out of our minds. Sev didn't know Jock that well but I had seen him in action—tearing some guy's head off on the phone or grabbing some clown by the scruff of his neck and running him off *his* marathon course.

I knew it was Jock's dream to see a member of the historic club win the race, something that had only occurred one time in history, when Young Johnny Kelley captured the laurel wreath in 1957. Jock, being one of these classy guys said, "Billy, those are ya training partners. You should run with them." He didn't give me any grief at all.

Amby Burfoot once told me he wished that a club like the GBTC had been around after he'd graduated from college. Instead, he went back to little old Mystic, Connecticut. His mentor, Johnny Kelley, was there, but on the downside of his running career, and so Amby had to continue to train on his own. Meanwhile, I now had five or six Ambys to push me on workouts. Being able to count on a group of guys to go on long training runs with me during the week, or put in speed work on the track with me at night, was a huge factor in my physical conditioning for the marathon. My teammates spurred me to train even harder; they motivated me to give it my all during workouts.

With months of speed work under my belt, I prepared for my next big test: the World Cross-Country Championship trials in Gainesville, Florida, which would determine who would make up the U.S. squad at the championships in Morocco.

FOURTEEN

Duel in Morocco

APRIL 21, 1975
BOSTON, MASSACHUSETTS

By the time I passed Coolidge Corner, I was over a minute ahead of Ron the Hill's course record, not that I had a clue I was running that fast. Nor was I aware that Jerome Drayton had dropped out on Heartbreak, close to where I had stopped to tie my Prefontaine shoes. I was now running within the city limits of Boston. Less than two miles to go.

While I remember going up a slight upgrade near Fenway Park, I didn't see the famous giant Citgo sign. It's almost impossible to miss, but that's how single-minded I was at the task at hand. I was getting closer to the finish with every step. I took off my gardening gloves and ran with them in my hands. I was just going for it.

With less than two miles to the finish line, I finally began to think I might win if my legs didn't cramp on me. I knew I'd get across that line. I told myself that if my legs went on me with one hundred yards to go, I would crawl across the finish.

Turning onto Hereford Street, I skimmed around the corner like a leaf driven by the wind. You could see the focus in my eyes as I sprinted through the narrow gap between thousands of screaming, rowdy spectators, urging me on to victory. The fans were frenetic. They felt the intensity of the race. They pushed me on, no question about it.

The onlookers were swept up in the drama, and brought alive with excitement at the first sight of the runners approaching, especially the leader. Boston loves a winner. They love the feeling of witnessing a great performance, and will become mesmerized watching as an athlete performs the unimaginable with equal measures guts and grace. They know the rich history of the event, and they will pass on the stories of triumph and tragedy to their children. They appreciate the nature and cost of the battle being waged by the men passing mere inches in front of them. And if you emerge the victor, they will put you on a mantel, as they did with Johnny "the Elder" Kelley, who competed at Boston a record sixty-one times, and for whom a bronze statue is erected at the foot of Heartbreak Hill. "One time I met a woman at a dinner," recalled Kelley. "She said, 'I've always wanted to meet you.' I said, 'Why?' She said, 'I live in Natick and I got married on Patriots' Day. My husband wouldn't come inside the church to marry me until you went by in the marathon.'"

The same cheering crowds that had lifted up hometown boys like Johnny "the Elder" Kelley and Young Johnny Kelley decades earlier were now doing the same for me as I ran past them with BOSTON written across my chest.

With about a mile to go, I remember thinking to myself, I ran my first five-minute mile in high school. Can I do one now? Of course, this one would be after running twenty-five miles.

I went straight up Hereford and tearing for the finish area at the Prudential Mall. With a burst of speed, I entered Kenmore Square. The thick crowds spilled onto the streets and sidewalks, leaving me the narrowest path to slice my way through. I glanced over and saw the Prometheus Unbound statue. I thought back to that night, five years earlier, when Jason and I raced across the imaginary finish line in the middle of the night, drunk and laughing and smelling of cigarettes.

Here I was, running that same stretch of road, a sea of people flanking me, shouting "Boston, Boston!" in unison with every step I took toward the finish line. The spectators a little farther along the course heard the noise and picked up the chant. "Boston! Boston!" I'd like to think that the woman who'd shouted, "Go, Jerome!" was somewhere in the midst of the crowd, her voice being drowned out by the beautiful roar from all directions.

"Boston! Boston!"

ONE MONTH EARLIER
BOSTON, MASSACHUSETTS

Three years ago, I'd stopped running completely. I'd been working as a lowly hospital orderly, pushing bodies to the morgue, hanging out at bars with Jason, drinking and smoking and trying to meet a girl. Suddenly, I was now the best road racer in New England. Some guys might have been content with that sort of rapid rise. Not me. I was on a mission to win the Boston Marathon.

Step one was to quit smoking. I did that by tossing my last pack of Winstons in the garbage. Next was to build up my base. I did that by running thousands of laps around Jamaica Pond. The next step was to test myself on the local road-racing circuit. By 1974, I was dominating the competition. That told me something. Then came San Blas. My first international competition. I had hung with Lasse Virén. That told me something. Then I took on the great Marty Liquori at Falmouth and blew him out of the water. While that win gave me a big lift, I felt that I should beat him, a miler, over a longer distance. What I needed now, before I knew I was ready to achieve the ultimate prize, was a true test of my mettle. I couldn't have asked for a tougher challenge than the third annual World Cross-Country Championships held in Rabat, Morocco.

It's hard to appreciate the magnitude of the World Cross-Country Championships today, but forty years ago it was the ultimate showdown for long-distance runners—on par with the Olympics. What made it the greatest—and toughest—single running event on the planet was that it assembled the world's best track and field athletes in the same place at the same time to compete at one distance—twelve kilometers. Everybody from the world's best miler to the world's best marathoner showed up to compete.

Our team of seven American runners, led by 1972 Olympic champion Frank Shorter, would be taking on teams of champions from around the globe. The awesome collection of talent included future 1976 Olympic fifteen hundred-meter gold medalist and world record holder John Walker from New Zealand, future two-time Olympic champion Waldemar Cierpinski of East Germany, 1972 Olympic ten-thousand-meter fourth-place finisher Mariano Haro from Spain, 1972 Olympic bronze medalist Ian Stewart of Great Britain, and 1974 Boston Marathon champion Neil Cusack from Ireland, who had beaten me a few weeks earlier in the 20K.

My claim to fame was that I had won a bunch of road races around New England; suddenly I was about to go head to head with the greatest collection of champions from around the world. Up for grabs was no less than this title: greatest distance runner in the world. I should have been petrified, but I wasn't. I was excited to see what I could do.

The U.S. trials were held in Gainesville, Florida. I had gone down with Scott Graham and a bunch of other friends from the Greater Boston Track Club. Someone in our group had a friend who lived in Gainesville and agreed to put us up. We ended up sleeping on the floor in sleeping bags; it was one of those deals.

When I arrived in Florida, I was still battling a nasty cold. My first day there I went for a forty-minute run at a slow pace. I felt dizzy and weak. I took some cold medicine but nothing helped. The day before the race I ran five miles over the 15K course and practiced some hurdles, which I had never done before in my life. That night, I felt gloomy about my chances, noting in my journal: "Felt spacey and I'm still sick. Depressed about the race tomorrow but praise the Lord I luck out." I was nervous.

The trials at Gainesville would decide who earned a berth at the World Cross-Country Championships, but the event was huge for another reason—for the first time ever, I would be facing off against Frank Shorter. I couldn't imagine this reality back in August of 1972 when I was sitting on a couch in my dingy apartment, eating junk food, watching Shorter obliterate the field in the Olympic marathon to become a running legend.

I remember Shorter arriving at the trials in a nice sports car. He was definitely the big gun. I would also be going against my former college teammate Jeff Galloway, who smoked me on the track when he was a senior and I was a freshman. I was always thankful to Jeff for finding time to help me with my homework and, along with Amby, showing me that long-distance running could be a blast. I would also be competing against my mentor, Amby.

The race itself was in a huge cow pasture—totally insane. It was a beautiful day. They had these big steeplechase hurdles. I didn't know how to hurdle at all. I was totally finessing it. I ran solid, despite feeling under the weather. Somehow I managed to tie Gary Tuttle for third place. Of course, Frank Shorter was victorious. He beat me by thirty seconds. The important thing was that I had punched my ticket to the big race in Morocco. As for Amby, he had the worst race of his life and finished far behind me.

I remember how excited I was to receive my U.S. team uniform in the mail. I relished the chance to proudly represent my country after being labeled unpatriotic for my opposition to the Vietnam War. Of course, I felt that I was doing my patriotic duty by refusing to fight in a war that did not represent either American values or national interests. At the same time, I understood that many people didn't see it that way. I was excited to be an ambassador and to shine brightly for the red, white, and blue.

By the time I left on a plane for Morocco with my U.S. teammates, I had fully recovered from my cold. I was sitting on the plane with Shorter and Galloway when I mentioned that I was in dire need of a new pair of shoes for the Boston Marathon. Shorter said he knew someone at Nike. Who could have imagined that "someone at Nike" would mean running superstar Steve Prefontaine? Not me.

We arrived in Morocco a couple days before the race and checked into a hotel. At some point, I left the hotel and went down to this little old market and bought a rug—a memento from the trip. When I got back to the hotel, I made a surprising discovery: I didn't have any racing shoes. I'd forgotten to bring them. I went to Gary Tuttle, who I had hung out with a little at the trials, and asked him if he had any extra shoes. He loaned me a pair of beautiful Asics spikes that, as luck would have it, fit me great.

Race day was perfect for running—sunny, dry, 70 degrees. I was so wired—wired out of my mind. I had been pushing myself for months, building my speed under Squires, building my strength on long runs with my teammates. I was putting in eight-mile runs at a 5:10 pace, two hundred-mile training weeks. I was ready to go for it.

Early on, Frank and I ran shoulder to shoulder but just as he started falling back I made a break for the front. I kept passing runners until I was in the lead. I was moving! The hurdles? I felt like I could jump over anything. I could not be stopped. Man, that feeling. I did hit it good: what they call a sweet spot; I hit the ball just right. It was an audacious thing for a total unknown like me to break from the pack. I just felt on.

I have a picture of me going over this hurdle in the lead with two other runners—Ian Stewart of Scotland and Mariano Haro of Spain. I held off the two challengers until the final one hundred meters when they both outkicked me.

It was a breakthrough feeling when I crossed the finish line in third to claim the bronze medal. I'd just run the race of my life. I'd never run a race like that, ever before. Nobody had given me a chance against the world's best—I didn't even think I had a shot at a medal—but an unstoppable feeling came over me during the race and I flew. I had no idea what the hell was going on, but I suddenly went from being fourth in the trials to third in the world and the second American man to ever medal at the World XCs.

Everything changed, really, starting that day. Frank Shorter took twentieth that day; Olympic gold medalists were behind me. He didn't run poorly. He ran steady, but I don't know if he ran as well as he did at the trials. Frank was a four-time national cross-country champion in the United States, but you're talking about the whole world of distance running at the time. So, I knew I could run with anyone then; that was the feeling I had. I can run with anyone.

I was so sky-high after that race that I went out for a seven-mile run on my own; I just kept going, I was so psyched.

When I came back from my run, an official approached and told me, "Give us a urine sample." Yes, they actually did drug testing in 1975. I don't know what they were looking for, maybe steroids. I was just shocked. I couldn't pee; I was dehydrated from the race and then running an extra seven miles in the heat. So, when I came back for the awards ceremony, I gave them a urine sample. They probably couldn't believe that somebody like me could take the bronze medal.

I remember the next day seeing coverage of the race in the newspaper. It was in French so I couldn't read it, but I could see the photos and that was exciting. To this day, I treasure my third-place prizes: a bronze medal and a strange-looking gold candlestick, which still sits on my fireplace.

This breakthrough set me up for Boston. My mind, after that race, changed; my attitude changed. I was always a competitive runner, training to be a competitive runner, and it had been a long haul. I had this strange, circuitous route that took me on all these detours. But after that race, that mentally gave me the strength of mind where I thought, Whoever's there at Boston, I'm going to go with them. It was dangerous to think like this as a distance runner. Get too cocky and that's when you get brought down in this sport. The marathon loves nothing more than teaching the fittest among us lessons in humility.

During this whole time, nobody in the press noticed I'd become only the second American ever to medal at the World Cross-Country Championships. (To this day, I'm only one of four American men to have medaled.) It wasn't a big deal to them, or to anybody else, for that matter—with one exception. Amby Burfoot.

By then, the once heir apparent to the New England running legacy had missed the 1972 Olympics, then gotten asthma working on a house, and settled down in Groton with his wife and kids. He was now a writer for *Runner's World* magazine. Amby asked if he could come to Boston and stay with Ellen and me, and interview me for the magazine. As Amby recalled: "For a New England road racer coming off the slush-covered winter training roads to place third in this Olympic-caliber event was virtually unthinkable. Maybe nobody at the *Boston Globe* took notice, but I did. Something was up. I wanted to find out."

Three weeks before the Boston Marathon, Amby and I sat at the kitchen table of our tiny basement apartment in Jamaica Plain, drinking wine and eating spaghetti. In those days, runners ate tons of pasta, almost every single night. The place was kind of frumpy—after all, Ellen and I were living a kind of low-key, low-expense life. I remember Amby and I having one of those fun Italian dinners. We chatted a while about our lives and running.

For a couple of years after his victory in 1968, Amby entertained optimistic thoughts about repeating his success in the Boston Marathon. But for Amby, our college years—when he was so focused on running and all he did was go to classes and do his homework and work in the cafeteria and run—had been conducive to training to be the best.

Once he entered the real world, and found himself working in an elementary school classroom for seven hours a day, it wasn't as easy to find the time to train and to keep the dream afloat. Amby had a few years when he went back to Boston and thought he was in 2:14 shape and thought he was going to run well and finish in the top five, but those races never developed. He also had other years when he was in miserable shape, because the teaching load just sort of ground him down, and he wasn't ready to run well. He kept trying, more or less, for eight years; he sort of gave up the ghost in '76.

The New England running scene was like one big family, so I would still see Amby before and after a race. We would shoot the breeze. Sometimes, we would jog around together during my warm-up. But also, in the years I was running at the top, he was always very careful about not wanting to bother me before a big race. But seeing my good friend would never be a bother to me.

Amby looked over at me and asked about Morocco. "How the heck do you think you ran so fast?"

"I'm not sure," I said, taking a sip of wine. "I went into the lead at about three miles and really felt good—not fatigued at all. It didn't feel fast at that point and I kept expecting people to go past me."

Amby gave me the same bewildered look sitting there in the kitchen as he did during our long training runs through the trails around campus, when he would be running with a look of intense seriousness and turn to see me wafting easily at his shoulder. He couldn't comprehend how I could feel that relaxed and easy while racing stride for stride in a grueling battle of wills. Or how I could have a superrelaxed approach toward so much in life and running, but I could snap into another gear, and another intensity and aggressiveness, when I got to the twentieth mile of the marathon. To be honest, I don't either. All I know is that I had this ability to be relaxed ninety-eight percent of the time, which is what you want over long distances. But I also had the ability to turn it on that crucial two percent of the time.

Listening to me describe my Morocco race, Amby sensed that something big was in the wings for me. But what? He couldn't tell me. He didn't know. He just sensed it. Maybe, he thought quietly to himself, if Bill had a good day at Boston, he could finish in the top ten, perhaps even crack the top five.

Sometimes a runner's career is one of gradual improvement, but my performance in Morocco amounted to an abrupt leap forward, even if Amby was the only person in the world other than myself who could see this clearly. Now the question was, could I do it over the full marathon distance? There was no way to find out but to line up at Hopkinton and fire the gun.

FIFTEEN

I Can't Run That Fast

I don't recall every moment of my 26.2-mile journey to victory, but I'll never forget turning the corner on to Boylston Street for the home stretch and seeing thousands of people erupt like a rumbling geyser that can't hold back any longer, shooting out a powerful spray of emotion. Many runners have gone on record saying that the final downhill parade along Boylston Street to the finish line at the Prudential Center is the best stretch of road in marathoning. I couldn't agree more.

"Dreamlike" is the only way to describe how it felt as I ran through the tiny path cutting through the unruly mass of Boston fans, spilling over onto the streets and sidewalks. I let myself succumb to the thunderous madness all around me. I let myself get swallowed up in the wall of ecstatic noise. I let the crowd's energy carry me home. It was fun and exhilarating. The greatest thrill of my life.

Unbeknownst to me, as I turned for the finish line, Jack McDonald, the former college miler who had founded our little track club one night with six other runners in a Boston College locker room over a six-pack of beer, scampered up a tree to see me break the tape. "As he came by, down Boylston Street, I'm up in the tree, holding on to the tree and trying to clap my hands at the same time, screaming," McDonald said. "It's like, 'I know that guy. He's my friend. I drank beer with him two days ago.' It was a lifetime memory."

I coasted to the finish line with the next closest racer two minutes behind. In those final steps of my twenty-six-mile journey, I thought about Amby, who had first inspired me to start running marathons. I was glad my former roommate had dragged me out of bed that one Sunday morning to run the full twenty miles with him through the outskirts of campus. He knew the power and beauty of distance running and, in the acts of his daily life, he communicated this to me. At the same time, he taught me that to succeed at the marathon took the passion of his mentor, Johnny Kelley, the courage of our barefooted hero, Abebe Bikila, the Lion of Ethiopia, and the commitment that he himself showed to the highest degree.

As I closed in on the finish line, I also thought about my brother, Charlie, who had been in my corner ever since I was a kid. He had been there for me since the day began, getting me to Hopkinton for the race start, finding gloves for my cold hands in the nick of time, and then giving me water along the course. Charlie would later tell me that after he told me to slow down on Heartbreak Hill, he flew down to the finish line with his friend. He didn't know if I could hold on and so he craned his neck around the corner, waiting anxiously for me to come into view. When he finally saw me coming down Boylston Street, he leaped up in the air, and for the first time he thought to himself, Oh my God, he's gonna win this thing.

I thought about Ellen, who had been there with love and understanding and rent checks: I thought about Coach O'Rourke, who had given me that initial confidence and Coach Squires, who had been there with his crazy, ingenious workouts: I thought of Tommy Leonard, who had been there with sea breezes and blue whales, offering shelter and warmth to maligned runners fighting for respect on the streets; Jock Semple, who drove me to races in his car, shouted encouragements to me along the course, and gave me sage advice at his Boston Garden training clinic; and my teammates, who had been there every day, pushing me on runs and aiding my recovery after workouts with food, drink, and laughter. Lastly. I thought of my pal Jason, who had been there on his bike to inspire me as I was coming down the home stretch.

I felt like I was floating on air the last fifty yards of the race, my elbows practically grazing the spectators who pressed thirty deep along the narrow pathway. As they screamed, clapped, and urged me on to triumph, I glanced down at the racing shoes, taking me those last steps to victory. In a way, Steve Prefontaine had been there for me, too. His gift had carried me to victory just as surely as the crowds had. What did Edison say? "Success is one percent inspiration and ninety-nine percent perspiration"? It might be the other way around in the marathon. Inspiration is everything.

It was a nuclear explosion of cheers as I broke the finish line tape. As the tape drifted to my feet, I saw Ellen jumping for joy and that's when I knew for sure I'd won it. I still had no way of knowing if I'd hit my target—2:15. I was too swallowed up in the surrounding excitement to care.

"After he crossed the finish line," Charlie recalled, "my friend and I put our arms around each other and started jumping up and down and yelling. I'm sure the people around us thought we were insane. Next, I fought my way up through the crowds—which were out of control back then—to the victory stand."

Meanwhile, Amby Burfoot was now running with all his remaining strength to get to the plaza in time to see me receive the laurel wreath. Soon after reaching the Prudential Center, he found a lonely-looking Ellen and took her by the hand and led a blustery charge through the police and press to get her to my side.

At that moment, my mother, who was a nurse's aid at a children's hospital, was driving home from work with my sister. The radio was on and they announced that William Rodgers had just won the Boston Marathon. She nearly drove off the road.

As for my dad, he was handing out exams that day at Hartford State

Technical College, where he was a professor of mechanical engineering. He told his students, in a tone of mild exasperation, "My son is running in that crazy Boston Marathon today." He thought it was a goofy and perhaps dangerous thing to do. The next day he came in and all the students were waving newspaper accounts of my Boston victory. Pretty funny.

On the victory stand, the winner's wreath was placed on my head as I become the first Boston resident to win the marathon since John "the Elder" Kelley in 1945. The torch had been passed. As the wreath was put on my head, I saw Charlie leaping up out of the crowd, calling out my name. There's a picture of him reaching his hand up to me and me grabbing it and we're laughing with joy.

Charlie said, "You broke the American record! You ran 2:09:55!"

"That can't be true," I responded. "I can't run that fast. I just can't."

I had just taken ten minutes off my personal best marathon time. It didn't seem possible to me. I was shocked.

Now, everybody was there—Ellen, Amby, Charlie, Jock Semple, Tommy Leonard, Coach Squires, all my GBTC teammates. It felt like a homecoming, and we were all wired. We were like the same team— New England road racers. Great fun. I was as high as a kite.

In that moment, to have that laurel wreath, which you know has been on six-time champion Clarence DeMar, Tarzan Brown, John "the Elder" Kelley, Young Johnny Kelley, and all of a sudden—I'm this no-body Boston grad student and it's being placed on my head. Winning had been on my mind in my training for months and months. But at that moment, standing on the podium, I was like, "What the heck just happened?" because I had gotten my marathon time down to 2:09:55, which was, at the time, the fourth-fastest marathon in the world. I had suddenly run the marathon race I'd always wanted to run and to win was a great honor. That's how I felt about it.

I posed together with the female winner—a West German named

Liann Winter, who dwarfed me in height and size. As photographers snapped pictures of us, I felt I should congratulate her on her victory. I gave her a big smile and said, "You had a great time. You must be very happy." She turned to her interpreter and started speaking German. The interpreter looked at me: "She said, 'I am. But could you get me a beer? I'd really like a beer."

Her wanting a beer right then flipped me out. But that's the way runners were—very down to earth. It was like, "Hey, we both won the Boston Marathon. Let's have a beer and celebrate."

I was quickly ushered down to the makeshift media room deep in the basement of the Prudential Center. There I was besieged by hundreds of flashbulbs and a horde of reporters. They shouted out questions at me as I sat there with a look of awestruck wonder on my face and a green laurel wreath on my head.

"How does it feel to have run a 2:09:55, breaking Frank Shorter's American record?"

"Are you sure it's a new record? 2:09.55? Honest? This is absurd. I can't run that fast. This is ridiculous. I must be dreaming this whole thing."

Everyone laughed, but I was serious. The moment felt so surreal.

I have a photo of myself lying down on my back, laughing my head off, because there was a tradition at Boston where a podiatrist would take off your shoe and your sock and take a picture of your foot. This was a big deal because they wanted to show bad blisters and stuff. A totally corny photo. They would never do that today in a million years, but I didn't care. I was floating.

The podiatrist removed my Prefontaine Boston '73 shoe. I didn't have a single blister on my foot. It was a great ad for Nike.

Questions continued coming fast and furious from the reporters. "What were you thinking, stopping four times for water?"

"I can't run and drink at the same time."

More laughter.

"You also stopped to tie your shoelace?"

"Yeah. On Heartbreak Hill, a good place to stop, don't you think?"

The crowd erupted again.

"What are you going to do now?" somebody shouted.

I said, "I'm going to the Eliot Lounge to have a blue whale."

Again, everybody laughed. But I was just speaking the truth. I wasn't going to Disney World. I was off to the Eliot Lounge to celebrate with Tommy and all my friends.

If I had thought of it, I would have invited Liann Miller to the Eliot Lounge for a Hefeweizen.

The scene at the Eliot Lounge that evening was uproarious. I remember being there with Ellen in this sort of floating state. Surrounded by friends and family, my face radiated with joy. To celebrate my victory here in this small club, a runner's club, with pictures of runners hanging on the walls, felt perfect. A part of me wanted to run around town and thank each and every spectator who had lifted my spirits as I ran for the win. A nice thought, but I don't think my tired legs would have allowed such a thing.

While the place was packed, it was still very much a local runners' party. It was fun and we were just laughing our heads off. Young Johnny Kelley was there and I got to know him better. Having Johnny show up really made it a New England thing. The New England road runners— cranking it out for the past hundred years.

If the Greater Boston club reached its peak in '79, then this was the kickoff. Coach Squires was there, pumped out of his mind, as were all my Greater Boston mates. Everybody was trying to grasp what my victory meant, including me. To hold my own against Olympians in Morocco was a major deal—real runners like Amby and I understood that. But I was far from an established marathoner, so to run the way I had that day in Boston was beyond comprehension. Nobody could conceive that I could run that fast. I ran out of my body and my mind.

"For me as a sports fan," says Jack McDonald, "Billy's win in '75 is right up there with Carleton Fisk's home run that won game six in the World Series. It's up there with the top things I've seen in sports, seeing your buddy run and set the record."

People think the marathon is a loner sport, but that's not so. It's a powerfully emotional sport, and that's why you see so many things today, like the Run for the Cure. These organizations have realized the emotional power of the sport and what it means to try so hard to do something and for someone other than yourself. I don't know if I was doing it for someone else, but I did feel part of a close fraternity of runners. My teammate Scott Graham, who would later make a scrapbook of newspaper clippings of that race from around the world, came over and gave me a big hug in the middle of the crowded bar.

My faithful training partner Sev was also there, but the tough Vietnam vet opted for a hearty slap on my 125-pound Kermit the frog frame. "Bill doesn't even know this," says Sev, "but the day he ran 2:09:55 I was with Dickie Mahoney. Dickie and I were sitting in a car outside the fire station near mile seventeen where the runners turn onto Commonwealth Avenue and start their climb through the Newton Hills. Dickie and I are trying to fly to the finish—he's driving because I have a cast over my foot—and the freaking radio announcers aren't saying crap because they didn't know who Billy was. One minute they're talking about how he stopped for water going up Heartbreak Hill. After that they said nothing. We had lost him. Then suddenly they announce that he'd won. I remember Dickie and I stopped the car and started crying—matter of fact, I'm probably going to cry now—because we knew him so well and had watched him grow."

I did, in fact, order a blue whale, a concoction of blue curaçao, vodka, gin, and rum. The Tommy Leonard specialty looked like a large Guinness pint of Windex. Only Tommy Leonard, the usual ringmaster of our festivities, was bizarrely nowhere to be found. It turned out that

Tommy had rented a room at the Eliot Hotel, where he fueled up for the party with a dip in the hot tub that included a few pints of friend rice and more than a few beers. "The next thing I knew," recalled Tommy, "I woke up freezing with a ring of fried rice around the tub and a flotilla of beer bottles. I wouldn't want to say I drank too much." Only Tommy, the man who could turn a regular Tuesday at the Eliot Lounge into a triumphantly good time, could end up missing the biggest celebration in his bar's history.

I could see from the glowing blue drink in Charlie's hand that he had just been introduced to the blue whale. He put his free hand on my shoulder and said, "I can't believe you really won. You were flying along so smoothly out there, it looked like a lark."

"I felt great," I said. "I was having fun."

"You know how I told you to slow down out there on the course?"

"Yeah."

"Well, I'm making a vow to never question you again."

I laughed and then so did he.

That night I wrote in my running log: "Won 79th BAA Marathon in 2:09:55. New personal record for that distance. Total miles run today 26.2."

The next day I was back in my tiny basement apartment, finishing up my interview with Amby while we shared a pizza. I was sore, but it was a pleasant soreness. I tried my best to recount the events of the previous days, which boggled both our minds. I asked Amby to tell me about his race. "Well, as I was running, I kept asking people how you were doing," Amby told me between bites of pizza. "They kept telling me that you were with the leaders and I got more and more excited. Around eighteen miles, I saw Coach Squires and he said you were a quarter of a mile ahead and then he screamed out, 'and a minute under the course record pace!' At that point, I started begging people to drive me to the Prudential so I could see you finish but everybody kept telling me there was no way to get through the traffic. So I just ran as fast as I could to the finish line." In fact, Amby ran so hard he crossed the finish line in 2:21:20—almost a full minute faster than his winning time in 1968.

I took great pride in being only the fifth American to win Boston since John "the Elder" Kelley had won it twice, in 1935 and 1945. I marveled at the thread connecting my achievement with my New England road-running predecessors. The Younger Johnny Kelley, who won it in 1957, studied the Elder Kelley and called him "a great confidant and mentor." After Young Johnny Kelley revolutionized the sport in America in the 1950s—daring to push beyond the old grind-it-out plodding style, embarking on a whole new level of training that allowed him to sustain his innate speed over 26.2 miles—he then passed down this sacred knowledge to his protégé, Amby Burfoot, one of his runners at Fitch High School in Groton, Connecticut.

Propelled by his dream to follow in Kelley's footsteps, Amby became the next American to win the Boston Marathon, in 1968. And, of course, it was Amby, my roommate at Wesleyan, who persuaded me to try running long-distance races (I still recall running that thirteen-miler in a blizzard!) and gave me an appreciation for the Boston Marathon and all that it represented. He introduced me to the sheer joy of going on long runs through nature. He showed me the dedication, hard work, and sacrifice required to race in a marathon. "At one point in the mid-1960s, Frank Shorter, Bill Rodgers, Jeff Galloway, and I all lived in Connecticut within fifty miles of Kelley's home in Mystic," adds Amby. "Our proximity to Kelley, and our resulting marathon careers and assorted contributions to road running, is no coincidence. Kelley was first, the path breaker. The rest of us followed in his footsteps. The entire American running boom thus traces a straight line to him, and the road he explored." Now that I had been crowned with the laurel wreath of victory, it sunk in how blessed I was to be part of such a great heritage of New England marathon runners.

It was a powerful feeling to have won the Boston Marathon and suddenly be called Beantown's newest hometown hero. I was high as a kite for a long time. I remember driving up a week or two later to Connecticut to visit my family. My sister and my father had made a big sign on Styrofoam board and hung it on the front porch. It read, GOOD RUN, BILL!

To this day, when people ask me what's my favorite marathon, I tell them Boston 1975. I would run other great marathons over the next five years, but this was where I broke through. I was now a world-class marathoner, and someone who I believed could contend against anybody in the world, even the mighty king of the sport, Frank Shorter.

I knew I would get my chance to knock the reigning marathon champ off his five-year throne the following summer on the sport's biggest stage—the Olympic games in Montréal. Such an audacious thought would have never crossed my mind before, certainly not in 1972 when I couldn't make it more than a couple of laps around the local YMCA. Or when I was smoking Winston cigarettes and living off potato chips and soda. Or when I was lying on the couch, watching in awe as Shorter pulled away from the field at the Munich games. If Shorter was worried about the challenge I posed to him now, he sure didn't show it. "I wasn't concerned that Bill broke my American record," he said. "He ran a very good race at Boston. I was concerned with my own training."

The day after my victory, I went running alone around Jamaica Pond. I ran three or four miles, a traditional distance the day after Boston. Nobody recognized me. Nobody stopped to ask me for my autograph. It was just another ordinary day of training; I was just another anonymous face in the park.

Thirty-seven years later, on the afternoon of the Boston Marathon, I would find myself on a leisurely run through a nearby park in the city. I hadn't gone two hundred yards when I heard somebody behind me shouting, "Bill!" I turned around and saw a Kenyan runner in his warm-ups approaching. He jogged right next to me.

I said, "How're you doing?" I had no idea who he was.

"Good," he replied.

"So, how did you run?" I asked, our feet hitting the ground in unison.

He said, "I won."

It was Wesley Korir. I had met him a few days earlier at a press conference, but he looked different. He had shaved his beard. He was doing a recovery run like I had done around Jamaica Pond in 1975. We were running past all these people in the park and nobody recognized us. I thought, Here goes the Boston Marathon champion. How does nobody know who he is? Thirty-eight years later nothing had changed— for some reason this was more beautiful than sad.

The day after I set the Boston course record, Jock Semple called to tell me that the Mexican team had left me a special award. I went over to Jock's clinic at the Boston Garden and he presented me with a block of wood about six-by-six inches with a ceramic dog's head on it. Mario Cuevas had written a congratulatory note on the underside of the figure. I ran into Mario at the Fukuoka Marathon later that year. I spoke a little Spanish and thanked him for the gift. For many years, I treasured that ceramic dog until one day it disappeared. I've always wondered if the canine was a special cultural symbol in Mexico. Most of all, I understood the gift to be a message of international friendship and respect, conveyed from one athlete to another.

A month later, I remember coming back to the apartment and Ellen telling me a famous American runner had died in a car crash. I thought it was Shorter. I was wrong. It was Steve Prefontaine. Gone at the age of twenty-four.

The tragedy of Pre's death hit me hard, maybe because of how much we shared in common, despite training on opposite ends of the country. The press had labeled us both rogue runners, probably because of our long blond hair and tendency to go against the establishment. We both ran with fearless, aggressive heart, guaranteeing that we'd know disasters as spectacular as our triumphs. Neither of us was interested in second place. Neither of us shied away from a fight. Some might say we sought them out, knowing that a head-to-head duel was sure to ignite our inner fire and drive us to run even harder. Pre left it all out there on the track, and I left it all out there on the road.

I flashed back to the day I received the waffle-soled running shoes in the mail, along with the handwritten note from him wishing me success in the marathon. Those "Boston '73" racing shoes had to be one of the last gifts Prefontaine ever presented to another person. And what a gift they turned out to be. Despite running in the brand-new, oversize shoes for 26.2 miles, I didn't suffer a single blister. Judging from the way my feet looked after the race, you'd think I'd jogged down to the grocery store around the corner for milk. It defied logic.

I'd like to think those shoes had been sprinkled with a little of Prefontaine's magic, propelling me to great heights that I didn't even think possible. I think he would have liked how I took on Drayton, dueling with him mile after mile, then taking off. Going for broke. After all, he once said, "A lot of people run a race to see who's the fastest. I run to see who has the most guts." Prefontaine had more guts than a thousand runners combined.

In the end, Prefontaine and I were both on the same solitary quest to discover our potential as runners; to answer what Roger Bannister called the challenge of the human spirit. Doing so required us both to embrace a whole new level of training. For Prefontaine, this meant lung-burning workouts on the track. For me, it meant running up to two hundred miles a week on the roads. The relentless intensity of our workout regimens was born out of the same desire to explore our physical and mental limits. Although I never got the chance to talk to Prefontaine before his shocking death, I think he knew what I did—going beyond those limits was the real challenge of the human spirit. Maybe, in the end, he sent me those shoes so I could do just that. At least I'd like to think so.

For the next thirty-five years, the shoes, along with the handwritten letter from Prefontaine, would hang in the Bill Rodgers Running Center in Faneuil Hall, the shoe store I opened with my brother Charlie in 1977.

SIXTEEN

Lunch Break Runs

By winning the Boston Marathon, and breaking Frank Shorter's American record, I had achieved the Holy Grail of long-distance running. I was sky-high. My life changed almost immediately. Suddenly, I got invitations to compete in major road races around the world. One of them was a marathon in Enschede, Holland, run every other year in late August. I was thrilled to receive the invite, knowing the race officials picked only one or two Americans to come and compete against the top Europeans. They offered to pay for Ellen and me to fly over there and put us up in a hotel, but they couldn't pay me a fee under the table. Around that time, Frank Shorter told me, "Ask for a thousand dollars. That's what I get." I started to become more curious; maybe I could make a living at this.

One problem: If I was caught asking for a racing fee, the AAU would strip me of my amateur status and I'd be barred from competing in the Olympics. I felt this system of tight control over athletes was backward and un-American; it equated not getting paid with integrity but expected runners like Steve Prefontaine and myself, who were striving for the highest level of excellence, to do so with almost no resources. Geoff Hollister explains, "In the world of amateurism, an athlete was on his own to qualify for the very competition the AAU controlled. The AAU pocketed all of the ticket money, advertising money, and television money without giving any back to the athletes who brought all that money in."

The very rules that were supposedly in place to ensure integrity forced top athletes like myself to make shady backroom deals. I needed somebody to act as a go-between; somebody I trusted wholeheartedly. I trusted Ellen. I was apprehensive about involving her in this messy business, but she was eager to help; as she pointed out, the backward rules of amateurism were impacting her life, too.

Ellen wasn't asking for big money. She would tell a race official over the phone, "Well, could you cover Bill's airfare and maybe an appearance fee, a per diem fee?" If I went to Japan to race in the Fukuoka Marathon, I would get thirty-five dollars a day to buy my own food. This was the seventies. Today, if you're a top marathoner and get invited to a major race like that, you might get fifty or one hundred thousand dollars, so it's all changed. The first time Ellen negotiated on my behalf—the marathon in Holland—she asked for a thousand dollars and they agreed. We were a little in shock. We were a couple of small-town kids entering a brave new world.

While race invitations came my way, job offers did not. I received my graduate degree in special education at Boston College. I remember going down to the Boston School Department with Bobby Hall, a twenty-four-year-old from Belmont, Massachusetts, who had just become the first athlete to race the Boston Marathon in a wheelchair. Race director Will Cloney told Bobby, who had contracted polio as a child, that he would recognize his time but only if he finished under 3:30. Hall crossed the finish line in a time of two hours and fifty-eight minutes. The stunning landmark achievement, along with the official finisher certificate, was all his. As a result of his daring feat that day, he helped wheelchair racers earn the respect and legitimacy they'd always been denied and soon formal wheelchair divisions were established at most marathons, including the Boston Marathon, which in 1977 was declared the National Wheelchair Championship.

Bobby and I showed up at the Boston School Department. What we realized very quickly was that our highly publicized breakthroughs didn't mean as much as we thought. In fact, my title of Boston Marathon champion made very little impression on them at all. They offered us no help in securing a job and we left.

What followed my win at Boston was a whirlwind of activity. I landed a job as a special education teacher of emotionally disturbed children at the Edward Everett Hale School in the city of Everett, a few miles outside Boston.

To be closer to my new job, Ellen and I moved into the second-floor walk-up of a dark green three-story frame house in Melrose. For some unexplained reason, the floors sloped down to the middle of the room, causing plates and cups to slide off tables as if we were out on the roaring seas. On the walls, above the TV that didn't work and the radio that needed repair, hung flags and medals and, of course, my prized childhood collection of butterflies.

We also got married in Jamaica Plain that summer. Our wedding was anything but typical. It was conducted so fast and casual-like that I don't even remember our exact wedding date, which is terrible. It felt very spur of the moment: "Oh, what happened? We got married." There was pressure on us to tie the knot, which we should have ignored. Her mom was a devout Catholic and didn't want us living in sin. Of course, we were already living together, but this was a big secret, which required me to leave the house (and hide all evidence of our cohabitation) when her parents came to visit. Ellen was an only child and I don't think she wanted to offend or hurt her mom. Neither did I. She was a nice person. The conversation probably went something like, "Oh, honey, it's not a big deal. Let's just do this!" It's just a wedding, after all. Just a vow of love that bound our souls in eternal sacrament. What's the big deal here?

We didn't have a big reception with lots of guests and a wedding cake. Neither of us had money. It wasn't like that. This was a very low-key event. My parents weren't even there. It was me and Ellen; her parents; maybe one or two other people; the priest. I can see now that it was weird that my parents weren't at my wedding. They liked Ellen. There were no problems like that. I was very much a member of the counterculture. As with most things in my life, I was winging it. It was just another day. When I got home, I went for a long run. No honeymoon. Her parents did give us a brand-new Dodge Van as gift. That was cool.

In retrospect, I don't think her mom was the sole reason we got married. I had just won the Boston Marathon. I was getting invited to big-time races around the globe, reporters were calling me up at the house, I started to get offered some money under the table. It was a heady time—I needed Ellen by my side. We needed each other. I didn't want to try and ride this massive wave on my own. I wanted to share all the new experiences I was going through with Ellen and she was excited to see I was finally going somewhere with this running thing.

We didn't think the way young people do today: Most of them plan their lives out together in advance, but we weren't like that. All we knew was that we were friends, we cared for each other, and we were both happy about the changes taking place in our lives. I knew Ellen wanted to protect me and take good care of me. She was also very low-key and friendly and easygoing, all the words most people would apply to me. We were a good match in our ability to tolerate each other's casual attitudes. Ultimately, I sensed that not everything was right in our relationship. And I think she did, too. But we were certainly in love.

The four months leading up to my trip to Holland should have been devoted solely to preparing for the marathon, but that wasn't the case. While I continued to run every day, my training fell off a little. My life was busy beyond belief and I lost some focus. I suddenly had to cope with the prospect of a new job, a new wife, a new home, a new city. I wasn't getting my normal amount of sleep.

I did feel pressure to follow up my breakthrough at Boston Marathon with another victory. I started hearing some chatter around town, in the newspapers, other runners saying that my record time at Boston was a fluke. I had been unfairly aided by a twenty-mile-per-hour tailwind and the fact that it was a downhill course. I remember after setting the American record, Ron Hill saying to me, "You may run that fast again. But then again, you may not." At the time, I thought, Well, that's kind of like sour grapes. Who was he to tell me that I might not run any faster? I would show him and the others I wasn't some one-hit wonder. I could always run faster.

I saw no reason why I shouldn't win in Holland. I had just run the fourth-fastest marathon in history. I felt unbeatable. What gave me that incredible confidence? The mileage. I was putting in 150 miles a week and sometimes thirty miles a day. I knew that few runners could match my training intensity. Lasse Virén, Jerome Drayton, Frank Shorter—not many others. Also, Shorter wasn't going to be in Holland. Even had he been racing there, I still believed that I could and should break the tape first. After all, I had just beat him at the World Cross-Country Championships in Morocco and broken his American record. Our showdown would have to wait for now.

My trip to Holland didn't start off well. Ellen couldn't make the trip because of work so I flew to London alone. Once there, I suffered jet leg from hell. My body was lethargic and my head a bowl of thick New England clam chowder. I changed planes and boarded a smaller plane to Amsterdam, where I waited in the airport for two hours for another runner to arrive, and then we took a two-hour train ride, followed by a fifteen-minute drive to Enschede and my hotel.

All I wanted to do after my fatiguing journey was get to sleep. Instead, I tossed and turned in my unfamiliar bed. My brain and body craved rest, but something just wouldn't let me drift off. I was awake for forty straight hours. Finally, the night before the race, I managed to get some shut-eye.

I showed up to the start of the race feeling sluggish and fuzzy-headed. The hot sun scorched my long hair as I waited with the other runners for the starting gun to explode. Another hot-weather race—just what I didn't need.

Despite my skull feeling like it was filled with warm mud, I clung to the belief that as the American record holder, I had a decided advantage over my competition. I never entertained the idea of holding back a little. Never once considered running cautiously to assure a top-ten finish. My focus was on winning. So when a few of the runners broke from the pack, I went with them.

I battled it out with the leaders until around the twenty-kilometer mark, when a painful side ache struck me out of nowhere. I gritted my teeth and pushed on. A little farther up along the course, I came across Neil Cusack of Ireland, the 1974 Boston winner. He was throwing up in the middle of the road. We were both hurting, but neither of us wanted to throw in the towel. We decided to run slowly together.

As we trudged on through the countryside, the unrelenting heat worked to strip us of our remaining strength. At this stage, there was a spirit-crushing awareness that any chance of victory had vanished. But sometimes two people can carry each other along through a hard trial without exchanging a single encouraging word. Sometimes just being at each other's side is sufficient.

Around thirty kilometers, my legs felt liked cooked spaghetti. The sun was beating down on me and I was dizzy with dehydration. About six miles from the finish line the cramps became too severe to take another step. I thought I was going to hit the deck. The next thing you know, I'm lying on a stretcher on my back, being pumped with loads of fluids.

Once I started to regain my strength, I was taken to the finish area, where I learned that Ron Hill, whom I had beaten soundly at Boston, had won in a course record of 2:15. He wasn't Ron Over the Hill that day.

The thirty-six-year-old Brit in the Union Jack shorts had beat the two previous Boston Marathon winners—both much younger than him. Why didn't he end up getting dehydrated and cramps like us? I don't know. He was running smarter somehow.

I thought back to Hill's comment after my win in Boston. "You may run that fast again. But then again, you may not." I suddenly realized. Hill was just speaking from experience. He had already learned the lesson that Holland taught me—it doesn't matter who you are, or how good you think you are, the marathon will humble you.

When you run a great marathon, like I did in Boston, and then you don't even finish your next one, that messes with your head. Majorly. I had run one great marathon, my record race in Boston. But I had a perfect day and I was in peak shape. I expected to improve from there. I didn't. I went backward. It was disappointing, frustrating.

I knew my flameout was due in part to the heat. I hadn't consumed enough sports drink. (Although there might not have been that much available along the race.) But I also knew that I had acted foolishly by rushing into a major marathon without making sure I was prepared. The marathon is serious business. The difference between excelling and bombing out is razor thin. If you're not performing at your highest potential, if you've let yourself get distracted by other issues in your life, when the time comes to race, the course will think nothing of eating you up alive. After my disaster in Holland, I swore to give every marathon my complete attention; I couldn't afford not to.

Progress in the marathon is not a steady upward curve. It's an uneven, jagged trajectory, where one minute you're on top of the world and the next you're a heartbroken wreck on the side of the road. Perhaps this is even more true for someone like me—a more aggressive runner, a more emotional runner. Sometimes you get great days in the marathon and everything comes together. Other times, things go very badly in a race, and you don't know what happened to you. I think partly it's that, in those days, I raced a little too much—three or four times a year—in the marathon, whereas today's marathoners run once or twice a year, with more of a focus and more concentrated training for fast times and for a higher-level effort. Runners like me and Tom Fleming went all over the place, hardly ever turning down an invitation to race.

Shorter didn't race too much. He was careful and that got him his gold and silver medals. But I just loved to race.

Soon after returning home, I started my job as a teacher of special education at the Hale School in Everett. Special ed had just become law in Massachusetts; this was the early days of special education in America. I thought I would be working with people who were mentally challenged, the old word used was "retarded," but I soon discovered that I would be teaching emotionally challenged kids, as well.

Working at the Hale School was a unique experience, both fun and frustrating. I had a class of five boys and one girl between the ages of ten and twelve. A couple of the kids had no interest in doing anything except lashing out. I found it hard to discipline them, maybe because I didn't have kids of my own, or because it's just not my nature to crack the whip. Mostly, I felt sorry for these kids. I tried to give them focus and incentive. I would take them outside so they could be active, and then we'd come inside and practice writing, or do some math work or reading. I remember taking a couple of them on a fishing trip once; it was kind of crazy, but it was also fun.

Later, I was lucky because I got a teacher's aide, Ms. Conley. She was a mom and had kids herself. She helped so much. She knew how to discipline the kids to a certain degree. Once in a while a kid would become aggressive with one of the other kids and even with me—physically. You had to try to deal with these kids rationally when they were being irrational. Emotionally, they were struggling.

The kids I taught were isolated from the rest of the student body. We weren't given a regular-size classroom. We were in a small book storage room or something converted to a special ed classroom. The other teachers were afraid of the emotionally disturbed kids. No one knew what special ed was really about then. This was the first time we, as a society, started to take a look at kids with more serious issues and try to still teach them subjects. Arithmetic, reading. Simple life skills. I liked being part of this new educational movement—especially after Ms. Conley arrived on the scene to lend a hand.

The first year I was there an elderly principal ran the school. She told me to think of the school as her home. She was the matriarch. If we had a meeting after school, she'd say, "Please listen up. Ladies. Mr. Rodgers." I was the only guy in the whole school. At times I felt like an interloper.

Making matters worse, the principal, who was in her mid-seventies, couldn't wrap her mind around the concept of special education. I think she was trying to come to grips with the new realities. She ran the school strictly, putting as much emphasis on teaching appropriate behavior as she did on teaching the times tables.

I recall coming downstairs once and finding the principal talking to my students. There was a heavy religious component to her message to them—as if their behavior problems were due to a lack of religious teaching at home, rather than some type of emotional or cognitive issue. I don't know that I would have been able to explain to the principal why my kids needed special support and guidance. In the end, I was left alone to do my own thing. They figured I knew what I was doing, which I did a little.

I remember taking the kids outdoors for half an hour. We had to stay on school grounds—a small parking lot on the back side. We played basketball and four-square—that's about all we could do in the space. And still it was the happiest time of their day. They were angry at the world. Being outside, they could run around and play and blow off some steam. I would concoct games for them to play and give them incentives to win my trophies. They really got into the contests. They liked it a lot. We would come back inside for class and they were more engaged and less misbehaved. One time, I had the kids playing outside and the principal came out and yelled at me in front of them: "Mr. Rodgers, I wish you would have these kids concentrate on their school work!"

Runners have a long history of employment as teachers. It was one of the few jobs that allowed runners the time for marathon training. In theory. After college, Amby tried to balance a full-time teaching job with a career as an international-level marathoner. "I found that every September I'd be in forty-nine-minute, ten-mile shape, and every June after the school year was over, I'd be in fifty-six-minute, ten-mile shape."

I got invited to run the Fukuoka Marathon in Japan, which serious runners like myself considered the Super Bowl of marathoning. I used to call it the Japanese Boston. Of course, this meant I'd have to miss three days of school. When I explained this to the principal, she was none too pleased. I suppose I could have told her Fukuoka was the Super Bowl of marathoning but she probably would have replied, "What's the Super Bowl?"

I'd learned about Fukuoka from Amby. Back when we were roommates at Wesleyan, he spoke of the race with reverential awe. The race, traditionally held on the first Sunday in December, was established in 1947. It begins and concludes at Heiwadai Stadium, winds through the city, and proceeds on a crescent course along Hakata Bay. Over the years, the race has taken on an almost mythical status, due largely to the superior field, the remote and idyllic rural setting, and the deep respect that the Japanese people have for the marathon and those who succeed at it. They are as knowledgeable about the sport as Boston fans are about baseball, and worship their marathon champions as if they were gods.

Since 1966, when for the first time Japanese amateur athletic officials invited a select group of top foreign marathoners to compete with as many as eighty Japanese runners, it has been considered the unofficial world championship. By then, the Japanese had established the marathon as an event that they did very well in. Not to put it in a negative way, but they were quite fanatical about those things at which they, as a culture, excelled. It's not surprising that in light of the pride that they took in producing so many top-flight marathoners, the Japanese put the most time and money into organizing their marathon and established it as the best in the world. In many years, the caliber of competition at the Olympics was less impressive than that found at Fukuoka.

After he won the Boston Marathon in 1968, Amby was invited to race at Fukuoka. To him, this was a dream come true. A chance to claim the highest status in the sport against the world's very best. Now it was my turn.

Before leaving for Japan, New Balance offered me five hundred dollars for the year to wear and endorse their shoes. I was on my way to Japan when I stopped off at the Nike offices in Oregon. They were a tiny shoe company at the time and didn't have much money. They offered me five hundred dollars. I told them I would think about it.

When I got to Japan, Asics, which was the number one athletic shoe company in that country, offered me three thousand dollars for a one-year contract—six times what New Balance and Nike had offered. For a special education teacher with very little income, that sounded like a lot of money. Of course, by making the deal I left myself open for stiff sanctions by the authoritative AAU. Therefore I had to keep the contract a secret. That bothered me a little. Still, three thousand dollars—I was rich! Things were looking up.

The moment we arrived at the airport, the press was waiting to take our picture. They put us up in the Nishitetsu Grand Hotel, a beautiful hotel in downtown Tokyo. Everywhere you went you were showered with gifts and kisses. I remember one schoolgirl presenting me a doughnut after the race. Others would gather in the hotel lobby for autographs. Back home, we were invisible. In Japan, we were rock stars.

Because the marathon was such an honored tradition in Japan, we were treated first class. We were wined and dined. We were given a tour of a factory where traditional Hakata dolls were made, shown around ancient temples, and taken shopping. I remember picking up a Nikon camera for Charlie because I knew he was into photography.

At the city hall the Saturday before the race, a beautiful opening ceremony took place with traditional folk dancers in kimonos. We were introduced on the stage, given bouquets of flowers by Fukuoka school-children, and presented with gifts. Boston was the oldest marathon in the world, but all you got was a bowl of beef stew at the finish line.

Also, unlike Boston, the race was carried on live national television. The race itself was run like clockwork. I was stunned at how well every-thing was organized. Japanese officials, dressed in clearly identifiable uniforms, ensured an orderly race from start to finish. No kamikaze starts down steep hills. No shortage of water stations. In fact, they have officials who call out your splits at every water station. I thought, Why can't marathons in America be run like this? Why can't all people ap-preciate the marathon the way the Japanese people do?

I did not win. I came in third place. Jerome Drayton took the vic-tory while setting a Canadian marathon record that, amazingly, still stands today. While I was a little disappointed to not win, I was thrilled to be soaking in the reverential pomp and pageantry.

The finishing ceremony inside Heiwadai Stadium was very formal, yet moving. Government officials and members of the royal family looked on as the top finishers were presented their awards. The whole feeling of running for my country was powerful. I could feel the lure of the Olympics.

That evening, I attended a party back at the hotel. There, I met with politicians, Princess Nichitibi, reporters, and all the athletes and coaches from around the world. We were served a lavish buffet. I re-member meeting the Soviet runner Leonid Moseyev, a staunch Com-munist. He was one of the best in the world. In 1980, he finished fourth in the marathon at the boycotted Olympics in Moscow. I started talking with him about Russian literature and American life. Leonid wanted American jeans, so I gave him a pair and he gave me a bottle of vodka.

Leonid and I were representing our countries; we were acutely aware of that during the cold war. But we respected each other; we respected the effort the other runner put forth on behalf of his country and himself. He's not my enemy, I thought to myself. Maybe he's somebody else's enemy, but that's for them to resolve.

In the early 1990s, I went with a group of around fifteen American runners to the first Moscow Marathon. I ran into Moseyev there, totally by chance, out of fifteen thousand runners. He was there with his son and his wife. Again, I felt like, This guy's real. He's just another person with a family. Later, we brought him to the Boston Marathon, he stayed with my brother, Charlie, and ran for our store. Kind of wild.

That was another part of being a marathoner: I saw how the sport could break down national barriers. I've always said I think we should get all the world leaders together to go out on a run together. I know it's a Pollyanna vision. But I don't think it's totally Pollyanna. On the road, people get real. They get to know one another. All the barriers fall.

SEVENTEEN

The Trials

In the fall of 1976, I began my new job teaching emotionally disturbed children at the Edward Everett Hale School. Dealing with the pressures of a full-time job while at the same time getting ready for the Olympic trials proved tricky from the start. Nowadays many people wake up early to get in a run before work. You can do that—but can you make the U.S. Olympic team doing that? Meanwhile, some of my competitors, namely Frank Shorter, were training full-time. Frank was a lawyer, but not actually practicing law. He was in Colorado, training at a five thousand-foot altitude. He was preparing for the marathon under perfect conditions. My situation was less ideal.

At first, I would wake up at six in the morning and go running in the freezing cold of winter. It was a nightmare. The snow had accumulated on the sidewalks, forcing me to run in the road with the cars. Since it was still dark out, drivers often had trouble spotting me as I ran alone down the street. The roads were narrowed by the snow drifts, piled so high it was difficult for vehicles or runners see around corners or maneuver out of the way. I think I lost a year of my life every time I went for a morning run—it was that dangerous and stressful.

I can recall one day going out for a run, getting a few blocks in the near darkness, and freaking out. I rushed back home and started to jog in place in the living room. I felt every bit of positive feeling draining from my body and mind. I pictured Frank Shorter running mile after mile in the high-altitude splendor of Colorado while here I was, preparing for the Olympic marathon trials by jogging in place in my tiny apartment in the city.

I decided that I was going to ask the school committee for permission to run during my lunch break and if they turned down my request, I would quit. I would feel bad about giving up a job that I liked, but I was driven to strive for the next level, to go forward, to achieve the very best in me as a runner, no matter the personal cost or private sacrifices along the way.

Thankfully, there was a new superintendent at our school, Frederick Foresteire, who's now the superintendent of all the schools in Everett. He gave me the chance. He said, "Yeah, you can go out on your lunch hour, just be back here at a certain time." So as soon as the lunch bell rang, I would fly downstairs to a small room in the basement, change into my running gear, wave to the kids, vanish out the door, and start cranking five-minute miles on the road. On most days, I'd run between six to seven miles, but if I was lucky I might get in as many as nine. I'd then slip back inside, jump into the shower in the basement, wash in record time, and rush upstairs to teach the next period.

Once I got home from school, I changed back into my running gear and went on a ten- to twelve-mile run. By the time my day was done I was wiped out. At the same time, I never lacked the motivation to wake up and start anew. I believed in what I was aiming for and did what I did—teaching, running—not out of an obligation to others, but because of a passion from within.

All the kids would be scampering down the stairs and grabbing their lunch and milk, and here comes Mr. Rodgers, exhausted and sweating from his run. I don't know what they thought of my whole Superman in a telephone booth routine. While the female teachers were friendly to me, I doubt any of them were runners. These were the days when there were only thirty thousand runners in the country. Now there's over half a million. So they probably didn't understand the marathon or the goal I was trying to fulfill. They probably thought of the marathon in the usual mythological terms, not worth taking seriously.

It was probably hard for the teachers to relate to me. Most of them couldn't appreciate the fact that I was trying to push myself to reach levels in the sport that were previously thought unattainable. In those days, the concept of training to be a marathon runner was not understood. I would come back from running eight miles at a five-minute-mile pace during my lunch break and a handful of female teachers would be standing around the entrance, smoking cigarettes in their buttoned-up blouses and drab skirts. They probably thought I was crazy. Now, you see people across the country incorporating physical activity into their schedule like biking to work, or hitting the gym at lunch, or taking breaks for a walk. You see this everywhere. But in 1975, the idea of daily fitness bordered on the ludicrous.

My principal was not happy that the school committee agreed to let me run on my lunch break. She watched me like a hawk, trying to catch me coming in late from my run so she could convince the school committee to revoke my privilege. She would even direct kids—her own personal Stasi police agents—to wait by my classroom door to make sure I returned on time for my next class. As fast as I ran the Boston Marathon in 1975, it paled in comparison to the record speed in which I climbed the stairs from the basement, where I changed back into my work clothes after a run, to my classroom. There were many times when I made it back just under the wire.

I wanted to make the Olympic team more than anything in this world and so I was willing to put up with the harassment at work, but it didn't make it right. The truth was, many amateur U.S. athletes had to contend with uncooperative employers. Tom Fleming had to go up against his school committee in Bloomfield, New Jersey, who were unsympathetic to his need to prepare for the Olympic trials. He, too, kept trying to get up at five in the morning in the winter, when it was dark and slippery outside. He came in fifth at the trial and didn't make the team. He was an alternate. But he did great under those circumstances.

Circumstances he should have never had to face as a serious contender to make the American squad.

While athletes from countries like Sweden and the USSR received tremendous support from their country, this wasn't the case for American amateurs. Simply put, you were on your own. When I traveled to a race to run for the United States, I had to pay my own way to get there. As a member of the United States team you were lucky if you received an American team uniform in which to compete for your country. If that sounds ridiculous, that's because it was.

I was so fearful of asking for time off work to race that I arrived late to the Olympic trials in Eugene, Oregon. I missed more than a few major races because I knew that my emotionally challenged kids would bring the substitute teacher to their knees. That happened a few times; I came back to discover some incident had occurred in the classroom. While the principal didn't need more justification for her persecution, I could see from the look on her face that she was pleased to present more evidence of why I should quit running to focus entirely on teaching. Believe me, if I was going to quit anything, it would be the job.

I remember the whole weekend was very intense, almost more intense than the Olympics itself. I came there as the American record holder, but I still didn't put myself in the same class as the man who I had watched become a legend in Munich four years earlier while sitting on a couch, broke and unemployed. As far as I was concerned, there was Frank Shorter and then there were the rest of us.

Once I arrived in Eugene, Oregon, late on Thursday, I had a hard time falling asleep and generally felt light-headed and queasy. At the time, I blamed it on jet lag from my long flight, but in hindsight I think it was nerves. I bought junk food from the vending machine and dumped the trans-fat bounty on my bed. After devouring all the snacks, I felt better.

An hour before the race start, I jogged the mile from the hotel to the starting line. Once I got there, I realized I was the only runner warming up without a racing number attached to his singlet. I immediately raced back to my hotel, searched for my bib amid the ruins of junk food, found it, clumsily affixed it to my shirt, dashed out of the hotel, and ran a mile back to the starting line. Thanks to my principal I was accustomed to nail-biting, high-pressure dashes to get to my destination on time. Of course, in this case it wasn't my next period I was trying to get to in time, but the start of the Olympic trials.

With no time to spare—and my heart pounding like a racehorse—I made it to the starting line. Before I could catch my breath, I was off.

At the eight-mile mark, Frank tried to run away with it like he did in the Olympics. A runner by the name of Barry Brown and I went with him. I was going along with Frank and Barry when I was suddenly hit with a painful side ache. This is like a nightmare, I said to myself. It's like a bad dream. Why is it happening to me?

I fell back a few strides behind Frank and Barry. I could feel my Olympic dreams slowly slipping away. But I knew that if I panicked then I would be sunk. I knew if I tried to stay up with them I would be ruined. I needed to run at my own pace and wait calmly for the pain to pass. And if it didn't? I guess that's the meaning of faith; doing what you know needs to be done and trusting it will work out in the end. I think earlier in my career I would have tried to stay up with Frank, I would have lost control of my emotions, I would have let my emotions control me. By not losing my head, I was able to save myself from a perilous situation. By doing less, not more, the issue was resolved, the trouble was overcome, the side ache passed.

I began to breathe and relax, more or less. I took a quick physical inventory. I was okay. As a matter of fact, I was better than okay. I felt amazing. Twelve miles into the race I picked up the pace. Confidence surged through me as I closed the gap on Frank and Barry. Running down the road with newfound resolve, I finally chased down the two leaders and, from there, matched them stride for stride. I felt so fearless that when Barry started to slip behind I considered for a moment saying to Frank, "Why don't we wait for him?"

Frank and I were cranking through the middle section of the course, knocking off ten miles in forty-nine minutes. The early part of the race had been nerve-racking, especially with my rushed start, but once we got out there—well, it was still nerve-racking because we were running at a sub-five-minute pace, but it was also exhilarating. They didn't run much faster at this year's Olympic trials—and we had tough weather. Much tougher weather. To command your destiny under the power of your own legs was a tremendous feeling. Something you can't really describe.

For well over an hour, I ran elbow to elbow with Frank and we even talked a bit. I think in a way I kind of helped him because I forced the pace and we were able to put the rest of the field away early. Around mile 13, I said to Frank, "We've got this." It was my way of telling him, let's just run smart and steady now. It was clear we were the two top Americans. There was no reason to turn this into a showdown between us. There'd be plenty of opportunities in the future for us to take each other on.

It was a sunny day, mid-to-high sixties—by no means overbearing, but warm enough to elicit a healthy sweat early in the race. Unlike me, Frank ran well in the heat. Also, he had made sure to have his own special water bottles, probably filled with Gatorade, waiting for him at each water station. I didn't.

Frank would run along and pick up his own plastic bottles, which had a long, curved straw, allowing him to take a sip without disrupting his perfect running posture. I, on the other hand, was trying to swipe cups off the tables as we flew down the road—most of the time, missing my mark. On the occasion that I managed to secure a cup, most of the water splashed out before it ever reached my lips. I was tilting my head back, breaking my stride, and trying to throw the contents into my mouth, coughing out the water I had taken in too fast.

The weather in Eugene had been cool in the days prior to the race so I made no arrangements to station plastic bottles, with or without perfectly cupped straws, along the course. Looking back, I should have been filling up bottles with hydrating sports drink instead of emptying the hotel vending machines of Ring Dings. As a result of my serious (water) drinking problem—I barely consumed any fluids after the first few miles—my calves and legs stiffened up about five miles from the finish line.

We came into the stadium with two miles to go. Frank started pulling away. I could have tried to stay with him, but what was the point? A second-place finish would earn me a spot on the team; I knew we had a two-minute lead over everybody else and I was concerned about my calves. I eased up and watched Frank widen the gap between us.

I remember seeing the finish line up ahead and feeling a rush of euphoria. I started to count down the steps to the finish line. Ten, nine, eight, seven, six, five, four, three, two, one . . . . I had never felt such elation and relief as I did crossing that line. I had fulfilled more than a goal; I had realized a dream. I had refused to let anything, not snow-clogged streets or brain-clogged principals, take away my dream of representing my country at the Olympics.

I thought back on the long road I had traveled to get here. After not running for three years, after being in such poor shape I could only run a mile around the dinky YMCA track, after losing my job, losing my bike, going on food stamps, after all the days and nights spent running alone around Jamaica Pond, after sneaking out on my lunch break to get in an eight-mile run, coming home and running ten more miles, after all the pavement I had covered on foot, all the training, all the early marathon failures and heat-related collapses, I was on my way to Montréal. Unbelievable.

In the end, Frank beat me by seven seconds with a time of 2:11:51. At the stadium, we shook hands. Frank and I were both running for

Asics at the time and I remember the Asics shoe rep coming up to me and giving me a big athletic bag, which I thought was cool. That night, back in my hotel room, I was already thinking about what I needed to do to win gold. "In the next few weeks," I wrote down in my running log, "1. Need two or three 25–30 mile runs at good pace; 2. Need to take ERG or Coke during race; 3. Need little more speed; 4. Need lots of rest."

That last thing—get rest—was the toughest to follow. The next day I was running five miles at the San Francisco Airport during a layover. I got two hours of sleep that night. I was so wired, thinking how I was going to be running in the Olympics. The word "Olympian" has always struck a deep chord within me. I felt that I was running for more than personal glory; I was running for my wife Ellen, for my coach, my teammates, my family, my friends, for my brother Charlie and my best friend Jason. Most of all, I was running for my country. If all this comes off sounding romantic, that's because for me it was.

As soon as I got home, I leaped right back into my training. Two days later on Monday I ran sixteen miles. The day after that nineteen miles. Today top runners wouldn't do that. They would rest more. But I was one of those people who had no time to rest, only time to train.

I think my mentality was typical of runners during this, the running boom. After Frank Shorter's gold medal victory, there was a no-limits attitude in our sport, a feeling that you've got to aim high. Because the Finns and the Russians and the Spanish were training harder than ever before and reaching new levels. It was an intense time when you had runners who were hungrier, who were willing to sacrifice more, who were willing to drive themselves to the limit, maybe over the limit.

The old approach was to do a moderate level of training because there were more important things to do. The prevailing attitude was, "Your job was all-important and don't take this running thing too seriously. After all, it's not a realistic pursuit." But this was a different approach. The approach of professionalism was that this was a very worthy and high-level goal in itself, and that's why the training mileage started increasing and the records started falling.

It was this no-limit attitude that convinced me to return to Eugene in June for the ten-thousand-meter trials; also, I felt that training for the ten thousand meter—which would require lots of speed work on the BC track—would actually help me bring down my time in the marathon, and so did Coach Squires.

At the Penn Relays in April, I shocked myself by scoring the fastest American qualifying time in the ten thousand meter; how could I not try to make the Olympic team now? In Eugene, I made it to the ten-thousand-meter finals. Before the race, Squires and I talked it over and decided not to try and make the team. Our reasoning was that the two ten-thousand-meter races I would have to run in Montréal would take a lot out of me and it would be better to conserve all my energy for the marathon, an event I had a real shot at winning. Meanwhile, I was a serious long shot to medal in the ten thousand meter.

Just because I had decided I wasn't going for the Olympic team didn't mean I didn't want to set a personal record. On a cool day, I hung with the leaders—Frank Shorter, Garry Bjorklund, and Craig Virgin—until half a mile from the finish line. That's when I fell off the pace. I was still in third place, good enough to earn a spot on the Olympic team. Bjorklund, who had lost a shoe earlier in the race, saw me slip back and began sprinting to catch me. He passed me with ten yards to go to make the Olympic squad. I was happy for him and for the fact that I had set a new PR—28:04:04. But my cheerfulness would be short-lived.

One day, shortly after returning home from the trials, I went over to Boston College and tried to run the track. I felt a stinging pain on the ball of my foot. Not good. Not when you run on the balls of your feet, like I did. Turns out I had aggravated an injury in my right foot while running in the Olympic ten-thousand-meter finals. The foot had given me trouble over the previous winter; my guess is that the culprit was overuse. The shoes I was wearing were too narrow for my foot, the metatarsal bone in the bottom of my foot became inflamed, and scar tissue formed, which led to a pinched nerve between the toes. Simply put, the ball of my foot hurt like you wouldn't believe.

I knew that the speed work Squires had insisted I do on the track had played an important role in achieving my American record time in the 1975 Boston Marathon, but I felt I had no choice but to forgo that part of my training regimen; my foot couldn't withstand the heavy pounding. I feared that if I made my injury any worse I might not even be able compete in Montréal and there was no way I was going to let that happen.

Because I relegated my training to long, easy runs, I saw less and less of my GBTC teammates. Most of the time I would run alone through the streets of Melrose, waging my own personal war with the blistering summer sun. While I was training at a slower pace of 6:30 a mile, I told myself that I wouldn't need to run as fast as I did at Boston to take home the gold. Even without my normal speed work on the track, I knew I'd be among the top conditioned athletes at the starting line. The Olympic marathon would be run in August, likely on a hot day, when nobody would be thinking about breaking any records.

I figured that if I ran around a 2:13, I would have a great chance of winning.

EIGHTEEN

Feet, Don't Fail Me Now

The only real difference between the first Olympic marathon and the one I was preparing to race in 1976 was the distance. At the 1908 Olympic games in London, the original twenty-four-mile distance was extended another two miles to cover the ground from Windsor Castle to White City Stadium, with 385 yards added on so the race could finish in front of King Edward VII's viewing box. The American Johnny Hayes won it in a time of 2:55:18. Other than that, they're both simple footraces. And yet running a great marathon is dictated by any number of variables, some of which, like weather or illness, are beyond our control.

Oftentimes, putting together that perfect race can feel like catching lightning in a bottle. I've always said if the marathon is a part-time interest, you'll only get part-time results. Total devotion, however, doesn't guarantee success. So much has to go your way, not just during the race, but in the months leading up. Running a great race means all your training comes together at the right time so that you peak on the day of the race. It also means your body has survived the day-in, day-out rigors of a relentless training schedule. You've got to make it to the starting line in one piece. Easier said than done.

On July Fourth, I ran in the seventh annual Peachtree Marathon, a ten-kilometer road race held in Atlanta. The first race in 1970 featured 110 runners and was sponsored by a local brewery. By 1976, the number of participants skyrocketed to 2,200. Everybody was shocked and excited by the rapid growth in popularity. Of course, today more than sixty thousand people run the 6.2-mile route from Lenox Square to Piedmont Park, making it the largest 10K running event in the world.

Although my foot was still bothering me, I decided to race the Peachtree to test my fitness, break the monotony of training, and lift myself up—assuming I ran well. You're always playing these little psychological games with yourself during the training phase for a big race, designed to get you to the start line feeling confident. Otherwise, doubt will infect your thoughts during the race and erode your concentration. You'll lose your ability to hear what your body is telling you and to monitor your effort level as you go. It'll be tough to read the subtle movement of your competitors. In a blink of the eye, all those months of careful training can be washed down the drain. So great is the power of the mind in relation to the body that *believing* you are ready to handle whatever the course throws at you is often the very thing that makes it so. In the end, belief is all you can attain because it's never until you're out on the course, when Mother Nature finally reveals her mood, that you discover just how prepared for battle you are.

A 26.2-mile journey on foot is fraught with unknown perils, especially while running at a sub-five-minute-mile pace. How many sporting contests go two hours straight without a single break? The boxer can go back to his corner to get his eye examined. The tennis player can sit down and regroup after losing the first set. The baseball pitcher waits in the dugout when his team is up to bat. The football player gets halftime. There are no timeouts or reset buttons in the marathon. The punishment for performing at less than peak efficiency during a marathon is not just defeat, it's total destruction.

On the day of the Peachtree, I ended up losing by two seconds to Don Kardong, a collegiate track champion at Stanford. I knew I'd have the chance to face him again—and our fellow American Frank Shorter—at the upcoming Olympics. So I licked my wounds and got back up.

Over the next three months, I stuck to a moderate running schedule. I threw in some speed work on the track, but not as much as I wanted. I felt pain every time my foot pounded the ground. I knew I had to keep up the high mileage, in spite of my foot issues and the brutal heat of summer. I felt that I couldn't let anything stop me. I might run at different times in the day or slow up my pace. But if you need to go twenty miles, you're going to go twenty miles. Guys like me and Jerome Drayton and Tom Fleming and Alberto Salazar were from the era where we were trying to achieve times which had never been done before in the marathon. Long periods of rest weren't an option. Our mentality was always keeping pushing. Run more, run harder.

On July 9, I drove up to the Olympic Training Center in Plattsburgh, New York. The next day, President Ford showed up in Plattsburgh and met personally with all of us who would be representing America in the Montréal games. Afterward, he delivered a speech at a ceremony outside the SUNY Plattsburgh Field House. "All the wonderful people of Plattsburgh and your fellow Americans know that you will bring the Olympics the same dignity, the same dedication, the same magic blend of hope and talent, humility, and pride which has characterized American Olympians and made them so successful and so respected over the years. Good luck, God bless you, and as the Olympic motto suggests, may all of you be swifter, higher, and stronger."

As I stood there listening to the president speak, I couldn't help but experience a deep patriotic feeling. It's always an honor for anyone to run for their country, but for me, it was a unique situation because I had been a conscientious objector during the Vietnam War. I was thrilled to represent my country at the Olympics, and to show all the people who ever doubted my love for America that it was as deep and as strong as anybody's.

From Plattsburgh, we were bused up to Montréal and assigned dorm rooms. Along with Frank Shorter, I arrived in Montréal as America's hot favorite to win a gold. Only I didn't feel so hot. To be more specific, my foot hurt. They'd stuck me in a dorm room with a group of sprinters who all knew one another. I was definitely the outsider. I asked to be reassigned and was put in with a couple of distance runners, which was better.

After the tragedy in Munich, they made sure no one could just walk into the Olympic dorms by erecting a security fence. But a huge number of people waited outside the gates, hoping to trade pins or get a few autographs, and that was tremendously exciting.

From the dorms, it was a long walk to the cafeteria. The task of traversing the distance with my aching foot made it feel even longer. As a marathoner, I had learned to run races with a certain amount of soreness and pain, but I didn't want to add to it. I wanted to reduce it. Today, I think the trainers would have done more to try to speed my recovery. They didn't give me a cortisone shot or something to make the pain subside. The truth is, I felt like I barely existed there. Probably because I was a marathoner and, back then, our sport was considered on the edge of the track and field world.

I attempted to run on the golf course next to the Olympic Village, but the rolling terrain was far from the remedy my ailing foot begged for. Neither were the five flights of stairs I had to walk up to reach my dorm room. Neither was the long walk to the dining room. And, God forbid, if I had to meet Ellen or some friends at the entrance gates of the Olympic Village, which was some distance from the dormitory, the trek left me limping in pain.

However, no physiologist ever inquired about my training regimen. No podiatrist asked to examine my injury. I never thought to ask. I'd hardly heard of a podiatrist in 1976. No coach offered up any words of wisdom. Here I was, the athlete with the fastest qualifying time for my event, the American record holder, hobbling around the Olympic Village, and it was like I was invisible. Was I the only American runner who felt neglected by the staff in Montréal? Was I the only Olympic athlete who felt like he was all on his own?

I finally got fed up with it. Three days before the race, I fled the Olympic Village to go stay with Ellen in a rented house outside the city of Montréal. Nobody noticed that I had left. Not my coaching staff, not my teammates. Nobody cared.

Unbeknownst to me, Ellen called Coach Squires and told him about my foot and how none of the trainers were offering much assistance. At the last moment, Coach Squires tried to come to my rescue. Despite the military-style security, he managed to get into the Olympic Village and locate the head American trainer. He convinced him to find me and to give me ultrasound treatment on my foot and ice it down. After receiving the treatment, I actually felt some improvement in my foot. It was as if Ellen and Coach Squires were the only ones who cared as much as I did about how I performed in the most important race in the world.

Squires drove over the course with me and he helped me work out a game plan. Like with the Boston Marathon, he had me run sections of the course so there would be no surprises. We sat down and talked late into the evening about strategy. By the next day, we had our plan in place. I was going to let the front-runners go early and bide my time in the middle of the pack. At thirty kilometers was when I'd make my move.

I was a little nervous because this was the opposite of how I had always raced before. I was known for pushing the pace early, but I knew that I couldn't force a fast time in the early stage, not the way my foot felt. All the same, I would run hard, but no harder than I needed as I patiently chewed up the miles, and then I'd turn on the jets at the end.

Even though I knew I was not going into the race at my top fitness level, I never doubted that I would find what I needed to make a hard charge for the win. As I've said before: My thoughts and fears were always pushed aside by hope. An athlete is always hopeful, and always should be.

I gather that Frank Shorter, Jerome Drayton, and the other race favorites didn't spend the days leading up to the marathon lying prostrate in an unfamiliar bed, watching hours upon hours of Olympic coverage on the TV. I did. I managed to go out on a few easy training runs, but for the most part my time was spent resting the foot and trying to recover from my injury. I knew I was missing important fitness training, but putting as little weight on the ball of my foot was necessary if I hoped to have any chance of being ready for race day.

It was 77 degrees at race time. Warm conditions, just as I had predicted. Yes, a hard race at a tempered pace! All of a sudden the most unexpected thing happened: It started to rain. The air immediately cooled off several degrees, indicating a fast race. Heck, maybe a record-setting race. And here I had stopped doing speed work on the track weeks ago, fearful of aggravating my injury. Any other marathon day I would have thanked my lucky stars for the cool breeze I felt brushing against my cheek. On this day, it was comically cruel.

Standing on the stadium track next to the other runners aroused an unmistakable foreboding. At the start line, I talked to some of the runners, shook a few hands, including Frank Shorter's. A thin rain drizzled down on us as the gun went off. We did a lap on the track and then out the tunnel—the classic Olympic marathon.

Out of the stadium, Shorter quickly shot up to the front and set a very fast pace to follow. I was part of a tight pack shadowing him, determined to keep him in our sights. We moved as one—Waldemar Cierpinski of East Germany, Jerome Drayton, Lasse Virén, and me—focused on the back of Shorter's head.

The streets of Montréal were lined with people, many of them holding umbrellas, urging us onward. And with that, the carefully thought-out strategy that Squires and I had decided upon went up in smoke. Maybe it was the adrenaline, but I went out hard with the leaders. My competitive fire had gotten a hold on me again. And maybe I was compensating for the fact that I was worried about my foot.

I was pushing away, leading almost. I was forcing the pace. Not a good thing. After all, you're not going to break a field of Olympic marathon runners early. They are the best-conditioned athletes in the world. They deteriorate gradually. They don't fall apart.

After only six miles into the race, I felt none of the good feelings I experienced at Boston in 1975, none of the fluidity of each stride, none of the confidence of knowing I could run with anybody over any distance. Yet, I kept pressing hard. Hunger has a knack for shutting out any rational messages being sent from the brain. At least, that's the way it's always been for me. I wasn't going to lay back because, well, I didn't know how to lay back. It was second nature to go all out in a race; it was unnatural to take my foot off the accelerator.

I was forcing the pace because that's how I had won before. I'd rushed out to the front to inflict a fast pace on my rivals. It was my way of saying to them, "Think you have what it takes to stay with me over 26.2 miles? Let's find out." Only this time I was in no condition to pose such a cocky challenge, especially to the greatest assembly of running talent on earth. But the emotions kicked in, desire rose in me like a fever. To be honest, I didn't even feel any pain in my foot.

I glanced over and saw Finnish runner Lasse Virén matching me stride for stride. A switch went on inside me. I liked and respected Virén. We had competed hard against each other in San Blas, Puerto Rico, and afterward partied together at the local bar. But it irritated me that Virén, who had never run a marathon before in his life, had the gall to think he could waltz in and take the gold from those of us who had dedicated our lives to conquering the longest distance.

I understood why Virén had entered the marathon. He had a chance to repeat the famous triple crown of long-distance running achieved by Emil Zátopek in Helsinki in 1952—an Olympic sweep of the five thousand, ten thousand meter, and marathon. I believed that it was up to one of us true marathoners to make sure this track guy earned it the hard way.

I figured Virén was pretty beaten up after he'd just raced against the world's best in two long-distance races, and that he'd likely collected a few sores and blisters for his efforts. I knew if I set a torrid early pace, he'd feel those blisters practically popping under his feet. You see, I was not out there to make friends; I was not out there chasing butterflies with Charlie and Jason; I was out there to win the war. The eternal wide-eyed kid—everybody's harmless little brother—was now a tiger with the soul of a warrior.

Fifteen kilometers into the race, I was still maintaining my position up with the lead pack, but my body was working harder than it should have been. It was the foot thing, as well as a lack of hydration. While I had made sure to have bottles of Gatorade stationed along the course, I missed some of those bottles in the heat of the competition.

Meanwhile, Lasse Virén was heeding the advice of his coach: "Stay on Shorter's shoulder. When he surges, you surge. If he holds back, you hold back." Good strategy—if you could do it. Keep in mind, the best runners in the world couldn't do it at Munich. Sure enough, through the next five miles, Shorter would throw in the occasional surge to test the rest of us and see the level of our fitness. Shorter was gradually able to shake four of the runners, and the lead group shrank to eight.

I felt I was already running beyond my capacity when, around twenty-five kilometers and one hour and sixteen minutes into the race, Frank broke into another fast mile of about 4:40. I could feel whatever energy reserves I had remaining drain down to nothing. Just the same, I willed myself to respond to Shorter's relentless string of uppercuts. Hold on, I told myself.

I passed the halfway point and continued to match the killer pace of the leaders, doing my best to ignore the rain needling my skin or the pain gnawing at my hamstrings. I'd suffered dehydration before and the distressing leg cramps that accompanied it, my first two Boston Marathons come to mind. But those cramps came on Heartbreak Hill—a mere five miles from the finish line. Here they made their rude entrance with only half the 26.2-mile journey completed. I knew I was in trouble, but what could I do—call a timeout?

With the rain continuing to fall hard, Frank held his firm grasp on the lead with five remaining runners strung out behind him—Waldemar Cierpinski of East Germany, Shivnath Singh of India, Drayton, Virén, and myself. Frank inserted one more surge to see how many of us, already at maximum exertion, could stay with him. This time the answer was one—the East German Cierpinski. As for me, that was the back breaker.

Cramping up like I was, my muscle energy wasn't being distributed in a normal way. My right leg was doing much more work than it was used to. The strain was too much for me to bear. I faded and my dreams of Olympic victory faded along with me.

One second I was in contention for an Olympic medal, and the next I felt I'd be lucky to survive to the finish line. I'm not kidding when I say that, either. If this were any other race, I'd probably have taken the DNF and just as quickly started pumping large amounts of fluid into my body. But there was no way I was going to drop out of the Olympic marathon—not while wearing the USA colors. I couldn't live with myself if I didn't at least cross the finish with my head held high.

Runners were going by me and I recognized Mario Cuevas from Mexico and Jack Foster, a runner from New Zealand. These were runners I'd finished ahead of in the Boston Marathon, Fukuoka, and the World Cross-Country Championships in Morocco. It was a very devastating feeling, a flashback to my first marathon failure. But as beat up as I was, and my legs were really shot, I shrugged off the voice in my head telling me to surrender.

About thirty kilometers into the race, my teammate Don Kardong came up alongside me. There was nothing I could do to prevent him from passing me. At that point, I couldn't have prevented a kid on his tricycle from passing. Kardong had run the race that I should have run. He had hung back early and conserved his energy and stuck to a smart game plan. Now he was blowing past runners like me who had pushed themselves beyond the limits and red-lined with miles left to go in the race. Don told me not to give up and I thanked him for the encouraging words. I've always liked that part of the sport. When another athlete is out of it, there was nothing but shows of support and pats on the back.

My face showed immense strain as I ran those last eight miles, hobbled with each step by brutal hamstring cramps, too tired to avoid the puddles in my way. I had been so caught up in the emotion of the fight during the early stages I ignored all the warning signs blaring, "Slow down! Danger ahead!" Now it was too late. My muscles raged all-out war against me. All attempts to weaken the painful, iron grip of my cramping hamstrings proved laughable. While I gritted my teeth and pushed on, those were the toughest eight miles I've ever had to run in my life.

Though I was still in the top ten with only three miles left, at that point, I had only one thought in my head: finish. I was reduced to doing the marathon shuffle—an inelegant walk-run motion—and grabbing my boiling legs. Those final miles back to the stadium were a slow, un-abiding destruction of body and soul. As running guru Hal Higdon once said, "The difference between the mile and the marathon is the differ-ence between burning your fingers with a match and being slowly roasted over hot coals." Yet I knew I was going to finish. How? Because not fin-ishing wasn't an option.

Finally, I found myself back at the entrance of the stadium. As I emerged from the tunnel onto the vast track, I was a broken-down, sputtering piece of machinery, walk-limping underneath the darkening sky. The scattering of people that remained in the cavernous stadium urged me on with shouts of support. Then I heard somebody shout, "Why don't you quit, Yankee?" I yelled back, "I haven't quit yet," and started running a little.

As I struggled through my final lap around the track, I had no clue which runner had taken the gold medal, but I assumed it would be

Frank Shorter. I glanced up at the giant scoreboard and to my surprise I saw that the East German Waldemar Cierpinski had chased down Shorter, besting the reigning Olympic marathon champion by fifty-one seconds. He won in 2:09:55, cutting over two minutes from Abebe Bikila's Olympic record. So much for the slow, difficult race in the summer heat I had expertly forecasted.

Twenty years later, a German doctor named Werner Franke uncovered hidden documents that revealed the country's systematic doping program and showed that Cierpinski had been taking androgenic steroids when he competed in Montréal. I felt for Shorter. He was cheated out of a second gold medal despite running 2:10:46—his fastest-ever time in the marathon. I also felt for Don Kardong, who made a brave late charge for third place, only to miss out on a bronze medal by three seconds. Of course, if Cierpinski's win was voided—which it never was—Kardong would move up from fourth place to the bronze medal. As for me, I finished in fortieth place in 2:25:14.

I was in a mental fog as I made my way back to the rented house after the race. The hardest part for me was the finality of it all. My legs were cooked and I was not in a good mood. Making the Olympic team was a terrific high. Now I fell down to a terrific low. To have a terrible race on that day was worse than frustrating, worse than dispiriting, worse than any feeling I can come up with.

During the awesome pageantry of the closing ceremonies, I remember looking up at the giant screen and seeing hundred of Russian girls dancing and a banner that read, "See you in Moscow in 1980!" It hit me like a ton of bricks: Whoa, that's four long years from now. I was struck by a desolate feeling in my heart. For the next couple of days I did nothing. My foot was in too much pain to go running; besides, I was too deep in the doldrums.

Ellen and I made the long drive back to Melrose. Later, I tried to make lemonade out of the lemons. I ran in the Olympic marathon. I did my best. I recorded a time. I represented my country. I experienced the pageantry of the opening and closing ceremonies, and soaked up the beauty of the city, its streets bustling with people from lands far and wide dressed up in flags and singing their anthems. I got to meet other athletes, trade pins and jerseys with them, and learn a little about their culture. All in all, I wouldn't trade my Olympic experience for anything.

Two weeks after Montréal, I entered a 7.7-mile road race in Chelmsford, Massachusetts. I think the other runners were shocked to see me racing again so soon after getting the stuffing kicked out of me at the Olympics. Though my legs were still achy from the marathon, I breezed to victory.

A couple of reporters came up to me after the race. I assumed it was to talk about my victory, but instead I was bombarded with questions about whether I was going to quit running after my poor showing in Montréal. Quit running? To them, I was washed up. My fortieth-place finish in the Olympic marathon was a career death sentence. My breakthrough win at Boston the previous April—nothing more than a fluke.

The last time anybody had asked me if I was going to quit running, it was my parents and I was graduating from college. Back then, I assumed that I would need to find something else to pursue in my life; but running was no longer some hobby, but an all-encompassing lifestyle and a essential part of who I was. I was not alone.

For me, for Frank Shorter, for my GBTC teammates, running was not an escape from the real world. It was a necessary, life-sustaining passion, the way painting was to Vincent van Gogh or writing was to Ernest Hemingway. As runners, we embodied a new attitude; and it would be this new attitude that led to the running boom, and the last golden era in American long-distance running.

NINETEEN

Showdown in New York

I n my log a week later, I wrote how my legs were still tight. Having the terrible race in Montréal was really depressing. It wasn't like I couldn't get out of bed, but the disappointment was hard to shake. In terms of failures, it was like going back in time to my first Boston marathon. But these are the kinds of missteps you can get in distance running. Like I said, the marathon can humble you, no matter who you are. It will do it. Everyone falls. So, how do you get yourself back up? You get yourself back up by looking to the next race. You get yourself up by setting a new goal.

I was eager to get back into competition after my debacle in Montréal—something to remove the bad taste in my mouth. There's no way to describe how bad I wanted a chance to race again after being stripped of my status as up-and-coming star and given the new label of "one-hit wonder" in whiplash speed. I knew the 1976 New York City Marathon was my chance to rectify things. A chance for salvation.

The next Sunday I returned to the Falmouth Road Race, along with my Greater Boston teammates Scott Graham, Bob Hodge, and Vin Fleming. A year earlier, in 1975, as a favor to my good friend Tommy Leonard, I wrote a letter to Shorter, asking him to run at Falmouth. After all, I knew that Tommy's dream of holding his own world-class road race in Cape Cod was born the night he watched Shorter's gold medal run on the TV above the bar he tended.

Shorter, who was on his way to Europe for a ten-thousand-meter race, agreed to show up for the race, but only if he was given six hundred dollars and a plane ticket. Tommy convinced Billy Crowley, the owner of the Captain Kidd, the Woods Hole bar where the race kicked off, to pony up the money and the ticket. Shorter accepted the invitation. I thought I had a great shot against the gold medal champ, especially after my record-setting triumph at Boston four months earlier, and the fact that I had won Falmouth the previous year in 1974.

Shorter and I gapped the field of 850 runners by two minutes over the seven-mile route along the shore, from Woods Hole to Falmouth Heights. But in the end, Shorter won the shootout, pulling away around mile 5 and coasting to a fifteen-second victory in a record time of 33:24.

The real winner, however, was Tommy Leonard. With the national media playing up the showdown between the top two American runners, Falmouth quickly became one of the most popular and celebrated road races in the country, and eventually the world. Tommy's dream from that night in 1972 had come true.

By 1976, the field at Falmouth had exploded to 2,090 runners but all anybody could talk about was my rematch with Shorter. Could I finally step out of Shorter's shadow? I think we made each other nervous. I knew I could beat everyone else here—but what about Shorter? He was a great strategist in terms of how he ran his races, how he exerted pressure, how he paced himself. He knew when to go for the kill.

The night before the 1976 race, I met up with Shorter at a nightclub on Main Street in Falmouth called The Oar and Anchor. I asked him, "What have you done since Montréal?" He answered: "All I've done is lie around a pool, go waterskiing, eat and drink too much, and live the life of laziness. I feel terrible."

"That's great," I replied. "That's the way I feel."

I might have been too easily taken in by the wily Ivy Leaguer because the race proved to be a repeat of 1975, with Shorter beating me by eleven seconds. He broke his own course record with a time of 33:13.

New York City Marathon race director Fred Lebow, a charismatic and street-smart promoter, approached Shorter and me after the race. He told us that, for the first time ever, the New York City Marathon would be staged through the streets of all five boroughs of the city. He planned to sell the extravaganza to the public as an epic battle between the two American heavyweights of marathon racing. Our head-to-head duel would add lustre to the event and set the media abuzz. But I wasn't interested in attention. I was after redemption.

The strongest wind couldn't blow me off course as I prepared for my showdown with Shorter in New York. (Feel free to start humming the *Rocky* theme right about now.) I woke up early to train before school and ducked out for an eight- or nine-mile run on my lunch hour. I took advantage of the weekends to rack up more miles. I coasted through the streets alone, monotonously chewing up distance with each stride, my running shoes gliding with rhythm over the pavement. My shirt was drenched in sweat. My mind didn't wander. I concentrated on my breath. I thought about my form. I went over race strategies in my head. Everything I did was geared toward making sure I was in the best shape of my life when I stepped up to the start line in New York.

I trained more miles per week leading up to the New York Marathon than I had during any other time in my life. Over the next eight weeks, I ran between 130 and 150 miles per week. One week I racked up 180 miles. In September, I set a new personal record for miles in a month—673.

I ate like a horse, consuming four thousand calories a day. I stepped up my ritual of raiding the refrigerator in the middle of the night, drinking bottles of honey, devouring boxes of Oreo cookies, scooping out gobs of peanut butter or mayonnaise from the jar and, for the grand finale, submerging them in a bottle of bacon bits. On this diet, I was a whopping 128 pounds with seven percent body fat. The normal standing heart rate for most people is between sixty to ninety beats per minute. Mine was thirty-eight.

Feeling like I was making a comeback gave me strength. It invigorated my spirit. My desire burned at full flame. I ran with friends. I ran alone. I ran in the heat. I ran in the rain, one long, steady run after the next.

Despite my all-out commitment to training, I was careful to give my body the rest it needed. I knew how hard I could push myself without overtaxing my body. Injury is the biggest risk a long-distance runner faces: Perhaps no athlete in any other sport can less afford to be knocked off his training program than the marathoner. Miss a couple of days to injury or sickness and you can be sure to lose some fitness. For every day you take off, it takes twice that long to build your mileage back. Every run matters.

I would psyche myself up on training runs with my friends, even once telling Sev that I was going to "take Frank out." He had the legacy to protect. I could only acquire mine. Still, I knew that no one expected me to answer the bell in New York, not after Shorter got the best of me in Montréal and Falmouth. But when race day finally arrived, I was in the best shape of my life. If I was going down, I wasn't going down easy.

I was so broke that I drove all the way to New York City on back roads in order to avoid paying tolls on the turnpike. I figured if Shorter could get six hundred dollars under the table for running in Falmouth, maybe Lebow would pay me something to run in New York. Of course, it was illegal for me to directly ask for money, so I let Ellen handle the negotiations, while I stayed in the dark. She called up Lebow and asked for two thousand dollars. He agreed.

On the morning of October 24, 1976, I parked my car in Manhattan and shared a cab with *New York* magazine publisher George Hirsch to the race start. Fortunately, it was a different taxi than world-class marathoner Jack Foster of New Zealand had stepped into after arriving at Kennedy Airport. Two men who were already inside the cab robbed him on the way to the hotel.

I arrived at the race start on the Staten Island side of the Verrazano Narrows Bridge to find overcast skies and 40-degree temperatures. I couldn't have asked for more ideal conditions to race in. A beautiful day for a tour of New York City.

The top runners and I toed the starting line. I was wearing my lucky white gloves, my Greater Boston Track Club T-shirt, and a pair of borrowed red soccer shorts. Around two thousand runners crouched directly behind us, waiting to go off like a time bomb. Half the field consisted of first-time marathoners, a clear sign that the country was on the crest of a running boom.

Among the world-class assemblage of competitors at the starting line with me were Ian Thompson, a linguist from England who ran a 2:09:12 in 1974, then the second-fastest marathon time in the world; Great Britain's Ron Hill and Chris Stewart; Akio Usami of Japan; the always tough Tom Fleming, and, of course, the man everybody was trying to beat, Frank Shorter.

When Shorter and I finally lined up on the Verrazano Bridge for the start of the marathon, the whole nation was tuned in. Lebow had set up New York as a personal grudge match between Shorter and me, but in my own mind, it had less to do with taking down Shorter and more about setting things straight about where I stood in the marathon world. I felt in my heart that I was one of the best. I came to the conclusion that the only way to prove this, and erase the dark blemish of that failed Olympic marathon, was by fighting and beating the best in a head-to-head competition.

I had a little nerves at the starting line. I was about to leap into the unknown. What awaited me could be pain, misery, and heartache. If you're not feeling a little anxiety before taking off on a 26.2 mile race at unrelenting, break-neck speed, you might want to make sure you're still breathing.

Former Manhattan Borough President Percy Sutton fired the starting gun and we were off. A twenty-seven-year-old Finnish Olympian named Pekka Päivärinta broke from the Staten Island toll plaza at the start of the race as if blood-thirsty mobsters were chasing him down with tommy guns. Frank and I hung back, rather than try and match

Päivärinta's fast pace across the world's largest suspension bridge, sloping into Brooklyn. Both of us knew Päivärinta was more of a miler than a marathoner and doubted he could maintain the blistering 4:45-mile pace he'd run for the first five miles.

Surprisingly, Päivärinta maintained his grip on the lead as we passed through Williamsburg and a number of bewildered-looking Hasidic Jews in black coats and fur hats. At around eight miles, I threw a light shrug to some people in the press bus that was ahead of us but trailing Päivärinta. Go figure.

Now that the race had started, the nervous energy quickly dissipated, replaced by the excitement of being in the middle of the hunt and hearing people cheer for me as the New York City streets flowed under my shoes. Through Brooklyn, I continued to trail four blocks behind Päivärinta, content to run in a pack with Frank and nine other runners.

For a time, Shorter and I ran shoulder to shoulder along the course. *Sports Illustrated* would describe after the race: "Shorter's stride was the more fluid. His feet falling more softly, yet Rodgers' was the more beautiful. There can be something hard in Shorter, a scornful quality, especially when he is out front and applying pressure. But Rodgers, blond and open-faced, simply ran faster, ghosting away with a look of amazement."

Around the twelve-mile mark, somewhere in Queens, I caught up to Päivärinta and passed him. Chris Stewart, a thirty-year-old stamp seller from Great Britain, went with me. Shorter did not.

As we neared the Queensboro Bridge, Stewart pulled even with me.

"What's your name?" I asked.

"Chris Stewart," he replied.

I didn't know a lot about the British runner except that he had run a fast marathon time before and that he was a serious threat. I watched as Stewart surged past me into the lead. It was a clear challenge to my dominance. Maybe he thought I would start to fade now as I did in the Olympics.

At about the 14.5 mile point, we came off a long, flat stretch onto a steep half-mile climb up the Queensboro Bridge. I said to myself, Okay, time to challenge, and picked up the pace.

We were running stride for stride up the incline. I could feel his breathing growing heavier and his form breaking down a bit, and the more I sensed he was laboring, the more I put on the afterburners. While I floated over the metal grating that covered the road surface on the Queensboro Bridge with my light running style, Stewart ended up with bloody feet and missing toenails from pounding on the surface. (For later races, they installed a 3,975-foot strip of nylon carpeting, or what was hailed as the "world's longest runner," over the steel expanse.)

Once I broke away from Chris Stewart at the bridge, I felt like nobody in the world was going to catch me. It was the first and probably last time during a race that I just knew I was going to win. It didn't matter that I still had ten miles to go. I felt that full of confidence.

Once in front, I started to relax. I was feeling strong and feeding off the buzzing energy of the crowds that lined the streets. A couple months earlier, traversing the same distance, I almost had to crawl to the finish. Now I ate up the miles, stride after effortless stride. I glanced over my shoulder; there was nobody behind me. Shorter was nowhere in sight.

While I no longer feared any of the other runners, I had to stay alert about following the course. It wound itself in every strange manner through the unfamiliar urban jungle. A painted blue line was supposed to guide me along the race route, but the early morning rain had washed it away. Suddenly, the screaming crowds provided more than inspirational support, they made sure I didn't get lost and end up in Yonkers.

As I came into Manhattan, I expected to be greeted by the roar of fans along the shops of First Avenue but I was unexpectedly rerouted to the East River—and the start of a harrowing adventure.

I can't say I enjoyed sucking in car fumes from the cars zipping by me on the FDR Drive. I did, however, derive amusement from the strange looks I got from the bums, prostitutes, and drunk guys fishing as I whizzed by them in my racing singlet. The trickiest part was navigating flights of stairs on the drive's sidewalks. Sure, flights of stairs seventeen miles into a marathon. Why not?

I ran up through the mean streets with a "bring it on" attitude. If I had to leap over garbage cans, dodge fashion models, somersault over livery cabs, and outrun the two robbers that had held up Jack Foster at Kennedy Airport, so be it. Nothing was going to stop me from reaching Central Park and crossing the finish line for victory.

At eighteen miles, I passed Dick Traum, a thirty-five-year-old competitor who had set out to finish the marathon in under eight hours. Not the most difficult task unless, of course, you accounted for the fact that he was running on a prosthetic leg. Traum had begun his attempt to become the first amputee to run a marathon at 6:49 that morning. Traum was now four hours into his journey when I came up on him. I guess Traum was feeling a little discouraged, the faster runners making him feel like he was "going backward."

"Attaboy, Dick," I shouted to him as I roared past him.

My little pat on the back gave him the lift he needed. Traum said after the race: "I was blown away that he knew who I was. It had to be one of the most exciting moments of my life." Traum went on to complete his first marathon in seven hours, fifty-one minutes, beating his goal by nine minutes. Maybe it's true, as Alberto Salazar said, that we all start out the marathon as cowards. But Dick Traum is all the proof you need that all of us who finish the marathon finish as heroes.

I crossed over the Willis Avenue Bridge, which carried traffic over the Harlem River into the Bronx. Coming off the swing bridge, I had reached the twenty-mile point, a spot that would later be dubbed by runners as "the wall." But if this was a wall, I'd smashed through it without a scratch. I was sailing.

I expected to see crowds of spectators cheering for me as I descended off the bridge leading into the Bronx, but the area was oddly vacant. I took no more than a few steps into the fifth borough when I suddenly came upon a light pole where the faint blue line on the road seemed to come to an abrupt end. Do I make a sharp U-turn and head back into Manhattan? Or do I keep running into what the *New York Times* called "the nation's most infamous symbol of urban blight, a bombed-out relic and a synonym for hopelessness and decay"? I made the call. I swung around the pole and started back over the bridge.

Going back over the Willis Avenue Bridge, the olive-colored river merging with the misty sky, I spotted a runner approaching me from the other direction. It was Shorter. He gave me a nod and a little smile. "Way to go, Billy," he said. The moment didn't last more than a second but, looking back, it was a symbolic moment in American marathon running, the passing of the torch from one champion to the next. Shorter had reigned for the first five years of the decade; I would reign over the final five years.

A lot of people started slowing down after twenty-one miles, but I was floating along like a feather as I made my final assault through Harlem down Fifth Avenue. The crowds in Harlem kept me running hard with their boisterous cheers of support. I entered Central Park feeling on top of the world.

The exhilaration I felt running that final stretch though the park, sandwiched between screaming throngs of New Yorkers from every walk of life, young and old, urging me on to victory, was indescribable. I braced for the daunting hills at the north end that were part of the old New York course. A guy riding his bike kept telling me the hills were just up ahead. But they never materialized (for all I know, the bicyclist had just escaped from Bellevue) and I just kept coasting along, free and easy.

The crowd was screaming like crazy as I squeezed between them. I felt like I was running a cross-country race in high school, except instead of dodging bushes and rocks I was navigating around people, potholes, cars, bicyclists, you name it.

The scene was utter chaos as I approached the finish line. It made for great dramatic theater. Of course, at that stage, all that I was thinking about was getting to the finish line, wherever the heck it might be.

Crowds pressed in all around me. Cops were trying to hold back the frenetic crowd and keep stray vehicles from running me over. I was veering in and out of the insanity when suddenly the lead vehicle stopped short.

At the last second, I weaved around it and shot through the narrowest of openings between the car and the wall of yelling spectators. I broke through the tape. A roar of cheers ripped through the crowd.

In spite of all the wild obstacles I had to navigate along the 26.2 miles of urban frontier, I had crossed the finish line in 2:10:10, beating runner-up Shorter by more than three minutes. I was sweaty, exhausted, and my ears were ringing. I was in heaven.

In the winner's circle, Mayor Beame handed me a Tiffany sterling silver tray and then crowned me with a handmade laurel wreath. As he pushed the wreath down on my head, the wire tips used to hold it together pierced my skull. "Ouch," I exclaimed.

That 1975 Boston Marathon will always be my favorite because it was the breakthrough I had worked so hard to achieve, but New York might have been the best marathon I've ever run. I broke the course record. I set the fastest marathon time in the world for that year. I ran the eighth fastest marathon in history. I was only fourteen seconds from breaking my own American marathon record, which I had set in Boston in 1975.

After three attempts, I had finally beaten the great Frank Shorter in a marathon. (Shorter hadn't run Boston during his marathon peak because the BAA, in their infinite wisdom, refused to pay the champ's airfare and travel expenses. He wouldn't run Boston until 1978, when he was getting past his prime.) Even after my failure in Montréal, I believed I was good enough to beat the Olympic champion. Few others did. But everything came together that day in New York. I had shown people that Boston hadn't been a fluke. It's hard to put the emotions into words. I felt redeemed.

After the awards ceremony, I returned to the spot where I'd parked my 1973 Volkswagen Beetle and discovered it was no longer there. Apparently, I had parked illegally, and it had been towed away. Fred Lebow didn't want my great day to end on a sour note, so he took up a collection of $100 so I could retrieve my car from the impound lot. I was grateful to Lebow for his help. It wasn't until many years later that I found out he had given the money to me out of his own pocket.

After beating Frank Shorter in a head-to-head competition, I was no longer able to masquerade as the underdog or the marathon runner on his way up. I was now the man to beat.

I asked myself, How am I going to live up to the expectations that my triumphs in Boston and New York have created while holding down a full-time teaching job? I'd seen how my job had impacted my training for the Olympics. Running on top of snowbanks at the crack of dawn was not the best way to train.

One morning, the elderly principal called me into her office.

"Mr. Rodgers, I'm afraid we can no longer allow you to run on your lunch hour."

"But I have permission."

"And that permission is now revoked," she said sharply.

I let out a frustrated sigh.

"It's time you decide what's more important to you, Mr. Rodgers," she said in a lecturing tone. "Your avocation or your vocation."

I looked straight ahead at the crotchety old lady demanding that I choose between my job and running—the thing that brought me the most pleasure in life, the thing that I lived and breathed.

I liked teaching. I really did. But I didn't want to be a part-time amateur anymore—I wanted to be a full-time professional. I was done messing around as a marathoner. I made up my mind. I said, "I'm going to go for this."

The question was, how?

TWENTY

More Than a Shoe Store

After my victory in New York, I felt the doors swing wide open. I knew I had a shot to compete at the highest level. I also knew my window of opportunity to become one of the top marathoners in the world was small. I had to strike while the iron was hot, make my mark while I was at my physical peak. I'd worked years to build up to the kind of shape I was in. I was determined to win as many marathons and road races around the world as I could. But I knew there was only one way I could do this: find a job that allowed me a more flexible schedule to train than teaching had. I needed a plan.

Tommy Leonard and others suggested I open up an athletic store around Boston College, which by then had become a big running area for the many students living in the vicinity. I called up Charlie, who was still living in Connecticut, working as a drug counselor, and said, "I'm opening a running store at Cleveland Circle, right along the Boston Marathon course. Want to be manager?"

Charlie's initial response was skepticism. Were there really enough runners to support that kind of business? I explained to him that runners in Boston were no longer a tiny group rustling on the edges of society, getting pelted with empty beer cans by passing motorists. From the banks of the Charles River to the brick sidewalks of Harvard Square, people were running through the streets in their Nike and New Balance shoes with their iron-waffled soles. They were humming the theme to *Rocky*. I told Charlie, "I think we can make it work."

The phone went silent. Then I heard my brother's voice. "Oh, what the hell. Let's do it."

Ellen and I pooled the money from our teaching jobs and the under-the-table income I'd made from appearance fees. Together, we invested forty thousand dollars to get the store off the ground. Running friends like Bob Sevene helped build the store in the basement of a former laundromat with saws and hammers and two-by-fours.

In November of 1977, the Bill Rodgers Running Center was open for business. I remember we did one hundred and twenty-seven dollars our first day. We thought that was great. My easygoing, bushy-bearded brother presided over a tiny staff of enthusiastic runners, who roamed the aisles proselytizing about the joys of running.

Charlie and I brought Jason in to be our assistant manager. I remember after I moved out of our place in Waltham, Jason ended up dropping further out of society and delving deeper into psychedelic drugs. He was still drifting while I had found my purpose with the marathon. The store gave him a way to return to the fold. He rediscovered his passion for running, which Coach O'Rourke instilled in us in middle school. He got up to the point where he was running seventy miles a week. He started running after work every day, which he continued to do for the next thirty-five years. He was like Charlie and me in that he knew he was lucky to have gotten into running, and he wanted to help others to discover the sport. The Three Musketeers were back!

Between long training runs back and forth from the store, I'd go into the store and help customers find shoes and give them advice. I made sure we sold only top-of-the-line running gear—Asics, Nike, New Balance. No junk shoes allowed.

With that said, I was convinced that it could be more than just a shoe store. That's why I called it a running center. I wanted it to be a source of information for runners. We provided beginners with an extensive collection of resources. I also ran coaching clinics for kids and adult joggers. I would talk about how to avoid injury, pick the right shoe, and the proper way to train for a marathon. We even brought in a nutritionist and podiatrist to give lectures.

Charlie, Jason, Ellen, and myself were a team—a funny kind of team. We weren't your typical store. We were an off-the-wall store. We didn't know what we were doing at first. None of us had a lick of retail experience. What it came down to in the end was that we all loved running. We all felt that the sport should have a much wider audience. It should be better understood. More people should join us on the roads, not just hardball types, but everyone. Dentists, firemen, daughters, and grandmothers. We had an eager welcome, open-door policy.

Every day, more and more people gravitated to our store. It soon became this vibrant hub of activity for Boston runners, and a central place where they could hang out or meet up for long runs. Word of our fantastic local running community spread and, one by one, great runners from around the world started moving to Boston to train with us.

Greg Meyer was one such person. I had gotten to know Greg at the World Cross-Country Championships in 1978—we were teammates and we passed the time together playing poker. He was just a young Turk out of the University of Michigan, unsure about where to go next in his life. "Why don't you move to Boston and join the GBTC?" I told him. "I'll give you a job at our store."

Greg took me up on my offer and he was suddenly part of our tight crew. He became good friends with all of us. If I couldn't go to a race, I'd tell them to invite Greg. I wanted to support the young guys on their quest, just as Amby had done for me.

In our heyday, we were the golden bloom of running stores in the country. We had twenty guys working in the store. One day, I saw this sixteen-year-old kid sitting quietly in the corner, reading running magazines all day long. So Charlie and I finally walked up to him and asked, "What are you doing? You've been here all day." With his Texas drawl, he told us his name was Dave Dial and that he was a runner. That's why he'd come to Boston. His mother and father had put him on an airplane and he'd flown here by himself. Charlie and I basically adopted the kid for a while. He ended up working for us at our store for years. Over time, the staff became so close to one another that the store felt like a family.

Another great part of opening the store was that I could sneak out twice a day—fourteen miles in the morning and another ten miles in the afternoon. I rarely ran through the streets of Boston alone. I could always count on a group of my Greater Boston brothers—Bobby Hodge, Dickie, Sev, Scott-ha, Vin-ho, the Rookie—to follow me through the hills around Boston College or the bike paths along the Charles River.

We used to churn through the streets in packs sometimes as large as thirty people. Greg Meyer recalls the sudden outpouring of support that Bostonians showed us, their local boys in running shorts, as we raced by: "Heads would literally pop out of manhole covers and yell, 'Kick their asses, Billy!'"

As was customary, we'd stop partway through our long run at the Eliot Lounge, where "startled businessmen looked up from their martinis" to see a motley bunch of sweat-drenched young men clamor onto barstools. Tommy Leonard would instantly respond to the uproar, quickly pouring us sea breezes and uncorking raunchy one-liners. After a quick drink and some boisterous conversation, I would lead the jumble of bodies out the door and we would continue on our long run.

Following a hard workout, there might be another reconvening at the Eliot Lounge, a place that some claim inspired the show *Cheers*. Just switch running for baseball and Tommy Leonard for Sam Malone.

As always, Tommy would make sure to keep the beer flowing for the club—and for himself. I stuck with a gin and tonic or a blue whale. I never indulged too heavily, unlike some of the working-class heroes who frequented the bar. I always made sure to try and get ten hours of sleep.

I was conscious of the fact that other guys in the club pushed themselves further on training runs because I was there. They would tell themselves, If he can run a 2:09 marathon, and I'm hanging with him in our daily workouts, that means I'm not far behind. Everybody felt they had an open shot—Hodge, Graham, Mahoney, Fleming. Of course, it worked both ways. I had a pack of hungry runners pushing me on long runs. I couldn't give somebody the self-satisfaction of having whipped my butt in practice. If one of them did, I'd have to hear about it for the next couple of days.

On a regular basis we'd jog a mile to the Boston College track to work out with Coach Squires. Workouts would get competitive from time to time. Somebody would want to go hard the last four hundred meters. The runners with good, fast twitch muscle fibers would sprint across first. Guys like Alberto and I were in the back getting stomped.

People would beat me on the track and, therefore, assume that they could beat me in the marathon. Once they made that effort at New York or Boston, and got to a point at fifteen or eighteen miles, they discovered I was a different kind of animal on the roads than they'd encountered during practice. My philosophy was always, You can win the workout. All I care about is winning the race.

In the end, we were just a bunch of neighborhood guys, but we were going out and winning races. A lot of runners, not just folks in the Boston area but all across the country, had the sense that "if a guy like Billy can win, a regular guy just like me, then I can too." And they were right—a lot of Americans were succeeding on the roads and on the track, like no time before or after. Randy Thomas won the Ohme-Hochi 30K in Japan. Bobby Hodge won the Mount Washington Road Race four straight years. Alberto Salazar won the New York City Marathon back to back. We were all having our own successes, athletically and financially. But at the same time, we still remained friends and saluted one another and the club and Billy Squires. The feeling was, "We worked for this together."

On April 16, 1978, I held off a hard-charging Jeff Wells by two seconds to win my second Boston Marathon. But what made that day even sweeter was watching with joy as two more of my Greater Boston teammates, Jack Fultz and Randy Thomas, finished in the top five. The next year, I broke my own course record in a time of 2:09:27. But what really shocked everybody was that four of us from the GBTC finished in the top ten. Bobby Hodge took third, Randy Thomas came in eighth, and Dickie Mahoney, a full-time mailman, placed tenth. As Scott Douglas wrote in *Running Times*: "If you scored the race as a team event, Greater Boston, a seat-of-the-pants club with a minimal budget, would have beaten all other countries, including the rest of the Americans."

I look back at our achievement and feel pride, but also gratitude that I got to be part of a group of running brothers who felt the same spark of electricity, and limitless possibility, shoot through their veins that shot through mine. The marathon may be run alone, but nobody makes it in the long run without close friends to lean on.

The team model of the GBTC—which led to astounding results for U.S. distance runners in the late 1970s and early '80s—was all but given up by the 1990s. At the 2000 U.S. Olympic marathon trials, we only had one woman and one man qualify to compete in the Sydney games, which is pitiful. The same year, only twenty American men had run a sub-2:20 marathon, compared to 267 in 1983. After hitting this low point, the people over at U.S. Track and Field finally did what they were supposed to do—they created a high-altitude track and field training facility in Mammoth, California. That's where our current crop of high-level marathoners train.

While American athletes train more in groups now, the sense of unity and shared conviction is nothing like in the days of the Greater Boston Track Club. If you want to see the tight club mentality of the seventies running boom, you need to travel to Kenya and Ethiopia. It's no surprise they now dominate the distance events. Meanwhile, this common spirit of enthusiasm and devotion to the cause, and to one another, is missing among our best distance runners. We need to change this if we are to recapture an era of American marathon success, when athletes like Frank Shorter, Alberto Salazar, Greg Meyer, and myself came out of our running clubs to triumph at Boston and around the world.

Charlie and Jason were part of a second level of runners who would meet up at the store for long runs. Maybe they couldn't keep up with my Greater Boston teammates and me, but they were training hard, too. They might be running seventy miles a week, not 110. Charlie and Jason and their crew would gradually pick up the pace and begin surging and thrashing against one another. They called them "hate" runs. We had our Greater Boston Track Club—they dubbed their crew the Sick Puppy Running Club. In the end, it didn't matter that we were all at different levels. We shared the exhilaration of pushing ourselves beyond our normal limits.

The local running scene was made up of a crazy, fun-loving group of families and friends. I remember it being 100 degrees and we'd all go running to Hal Gabriel's birthday party on July 10. Then we'd have birthday cake and ice cream outside. There was a very strong neighborhood feeling. Patti Catalano would be there, the American female record holder for almost every distance from five miles to the marathon. No one talked like Patti, with her thick Boston accent. Dickie Mahoney, the fastest, hardest-running mailman in the world, talked the same way. Like many local runners, the store gave Patti a place to go where she felt she belonged.

In December, a month after we opened the store, Charlie and I decided we should have a group run to celebrate the season. We called it the Jingle Bell Run. As far as I know, it was the first of its kind in the country. Today, you'll find them in practically every major city. A group of the employees and some friends we knew decided on a whim we would run down to Boston Common. I wanted it to be purely for fun. Not a race. Not at holiday time.

When I first came to the city, I was awestruck by the sight of all the spectacular Christmas lights in Boston Common. I'd never seen anything like that. It must have always been in the back of my mind how beautiful it would be to run through there at night. When we got down there, it was even more striking than I had remembered. Running together with my friends around the Common was not that different from running around the woods with Charlie and Jason as kids. It's the eternal childhood.

After that, we ran back to the store for food and refreshments. It ended up being four miles there and another four miles back. I'm not sure we realized it was going to be that far. But in those days we were young and running a lot and nobody seemed to mind.

The story of our Jingle Bell Run spread through word of mouth. The first year seventeen people participated. The next year we had over two hundred people take part in the run. It became a big annual event and then we started raising money. We raised money for Massachusetts Special Olympics for years. I had been a special education teacher, so this seemed right up my alley.

I later got more involved with the Special Olympics in Massachusetts. Once Tom Grilk, who was head of the BAA at the time, and I handed out medals to the athletes at the Mass Special Olympic state championships. Working at the Fernald School, I understood the power of just recognizing somebody, letting them know you saw them and they mattered, especially people who had been rejected by their families and society. Very small things could make somebody happy—a Tootsie Roll, a smile, a walk outdoors.

One of the reasons that I still love traveling around to different road races is that it's a chance to see all my old running friends from those days: Coach Squires, Amby Burfoot, Bobby Hodge, Alberto Salazar, Greg Meyer, Joan Benoit Samuelson. Sadly, some of my friends are not here anymore. This year, we lost Jason—one of our Three Musketeers.

Charlie, Jason, and I were the best of friends for sixty-four years. We were like brothers. He left a gaping hole, not only at the store where he worked since it opened in 1977, but in my heart. In thirty-five years, he almost never called in sick. He was incredibly committed to the store, just as he was to his running—to the last days of his life. Our lives were intermeshed. We were both conscientious objectors. We both lived together in Boston. We rode that same wave during the running boom. I would give him the shirt off my back because I know he would do the same for me.

I still remember the time he gave me the money to buy my first motorcycle and how excited we were to go cruising around town. Jason was the guy who drunk-jogged down the finish line of the Boston Marathon with me—and was there by my side, riding alongside me on his bike, as I ran toward the finish line and an American record. I'll miss him.

As for Charlie, he's still my ace in the hole. He's been a good big brother. He's had to carry the weight of looking out for Jason and me all these years. He was the one who really kept the running center going steady for all these years. As far as I'm concerned, it became his store. He earned that. I think our shared love of running brought us close as kids and that connection between us endured through the peaks and valleys of our individual lives.

My mom and dad were quietly focused people. Charlie became that way running our business and I became that way with running marathons. Most of what we learned from our parents came through osmosis. Never sit back on your laurels. If you persist and keep plugging away, you're going to do all right in life. And that's a marathoner's message, too. There's no way to excel as a distance runner without putting in the nitty-gritty, day-in, day-out effort.

I used to always say, if the marathon is a part-time interest, you will only get part-time results. That's true of anything in life.

TWENTY-ONE

The Forty-Foot Wave

In college, nobody would have ever imagined that the top two American marathoners would be Frank Shorter and me. Anyone who trained with us back then would never in a million years have predicted that he would become an Olympic gold and silver medal winner and I would become a four-time New York and Boston Marathon winner. So how did it happen? I got my chance after losing my job and motorcycle. I suddenly had the time and motivation to aim for the marathon. As for Shorter, it wasn't until he was in law school that he found the time and hunger to start excelling. We each had our own internal timetables, I guess.

Our stories are proof that passion and purpose in life can lay dormant for years. But then, one day, you find your desire, your dream, your strength. It was in you the whole time. And once you find it, nothing will ever be the same. From that day forward, you will put everything on the line, make every day count, test the limits of your heart, and embrace the challenge of your spirit.

You don't know when it might come—this spark—which is why you should never lose all hope. The spark came for me after years of getting knocked down by life. But it did come. It did come. And I always knew it was a matter of time before others would discover the power of running to elevate, to inspire, to reshape their destiny, as it had mine.

When I ran my first Boston Marathon in 1973, running was a fringe activity. The tiny band of us bounding through the streets, in our running shorts and training flats, were viewed as drifty freaks of nature. After Jim Fixx came out with his book *The Complete Book of Running* in 1977, running became a bona-fide craze in America. Suddenly, hundreds of thousands of people were lacing up their sneakers and taking to the streets. Nike shoes were flying off the shelves. Road races sprang up all over the country. The Boston and New York City Marathons became major social happenings with the newly converted showing up to the start line in mass droves. Other major cities, besides Boston and New York, decided to hold their own marathons. The running boom was on.

Fixx had all these chapters where he detailed the physical and psychological benefits of running, but the most compelling thing about his book was his own personal transformation from overweight smoker to dedicated runner. He also included a whole chapter about visiting Ellen and me in our little second-floor apartment in Melrose. That day, we'd gone out for a seven-mile run around Spot Pond. He wrote about how I ran easily and how it was harder for him. Ellen had cooked him dinner. I remember we had macaroni and cheese—a high-carb feast. He asked me about my training. He got a glimpse into my simple life as a top distance runner (he wrote about how our kitchen table wasn't level, the kind of food I ate, all the running shoes in the hallway). I hated that runners had always been viewed as weaker athletes in America. Fixx showed that it actually took a lot of strength to live this lifestyle—and also that it was fun.

At the time of his visit, I thought Fixx was working on a little running book, but then it came out and topped the *New York Times* bestseller list for sixty weeks in a row. I was stunned. His story inspired hundreds of thousands of average Americans to lace up their running shoes and take to the streets. It also got a lot of people interested in trying the marathon for the first time. Suddenly, every lawyer, doctor, professor, and housewife in town was a reborn runner, espousing the virtues of "runner's high."

When I saw everything that resulted from Fixx's book, my reaction was: Well, yes, this is the way it should be. Our sport has always had a lot of power to it—now people are finally waking up to the benefits of running, and you didn't need to be Bill Rodgers or Frank Shorter to get them. Everybody gets something out of this sport, everybody gets results, both physically and psychologically.

I was doing what I'd done my whole life, since I was a kid in Newington—run. Only now the whole world was running with me. It was thrilling, addicting, and more than a little mind-boggling. I suppose people liked the fact that I was this homegrown kid from Boston— friendly, warm, and easy to talk to. I also didn't resemble the typical athlete of the day: I was this five-foot, nine-inch, 128-pound Peter Pan who liked to run marathons in Snoopy hats and oversize white gloves and eat pizza with mayonnaise. Up until then, the image we all had of professional sports athletes was somebody like Joe DiMaggio. People you could watch on TV and cheer for up in the stands—but you could never see them, touch them, feel like you shared a whole lot with them. In the world of running, we all felt like we were on equal footing, because everybody ran 26.2 miles, it's just that some people ran it in two hours and some ran it in three hours.

After a road race, I would hang out with the guys, go to the pizza joint, have a beer and a few laughs. Somebody would say, "Hey, you want to run tomorrow at seven?" And I would say, "Yeah, come and get me and I'll run with you guys." And people would say, "Really? You'll run with us?" And I'd say, "Yeah, sure. Why not? That's what I do: I run with people." That's how I ended up going out on more runs with local running clubs than probably anybody in history.

I remember once running with the guys from a running club in York, Pennsylvania; another time a group from Binghamton, New York. I didn't go out and run them into the ground in the morning; I went out and ran a nice, easy, relaxed eight or ten miles with them. Probably most of the guys in the club were three-hour marathoners and probably most of them could stay with me every step of the way, much to their amazement and delight. There were groups of people who, when they ran together, turned all their runs into races, but that was not the tradition I came from. It's not the tradition Johnny Kelley passed on to Amby and it's not the tradition Amby passed on to me. Running was just the fun, relaxing, social thing that we did in New England.

I was the biggest star in the sport, a household name among both runners and nonrunners. It was like being a surfer and being on top of a forty-foot wave. I knew the wave would eventually crash, but I was excited to ride it as long as I could.

I wasn't the type of guy who saw a good reason to change my lifestyle even after the store was starting to make money and I landed on the cover of magazines. Ellen and I continued to live in our sloping one-bedroom apartment in Melrose. I continued to putter around in my beat-up VW Beetle. I would sometimes sneak off by myself with a pocketful of quarters to play Asteroids and Space Invaders at the local video arcade. I turned down the assorted invitations to movie premieres and celebrity parties, preferring instead to hang out with my small group of friends.

People from as far away as Russia and as close as two blocks away would show up at the store, looking to meet me. I'd say, "Come on. I'm about to go on a run. Let's go." At first, I'd get a shocked reaction—You're the Boston Marathon champ. You can't be serious? I didn't care if the person was a top marathoner from Kenya or a recreational distance runner from Tennessee. You've got two feet that work—let's hit the roads. For me, this was the best part of our sport—making long-lasting friendships with people from different cultures and backgrounds.

Ellen and I made a great team. I needed a smart, no-nonsense person in my life like her. She acted as a buffer between me and aggressive race directors who wanted me to come to their races, reporters who wanted to interview me, and people who wanted me to show up to charity events or lead running clinics. When we attended some corporate event, she always brushed me up and put on some clothes for me. I just didn't do the suit-and-tie thing.

Ellen always made sure I stuck to my busy schedule, which wasn't easy. In 1975, I ran the Amsterdam marathon too soon after Boston. I wasn't going to make the same mistake again. I wrote the organizers a letter, telling them I wasn't going to be able to make it. The race officials kept calling the house and pleading with me to come. I finally said yes. My agent/wife wasn't happy.

Sometimes she would try to break my pledge to race, but mostly she would just shake her head with exasperation. It wasn't in my nature to say no to race directors, hang up the phone on reporters, brush off a low-level racer who wanted to bend my ear, or deny somebody an autograph. I always wanted to please my fans and show them my appreciation. As a result, I'd end up staying around for hours after a race, embracing people with a warm smile. Ellen often had to step in and say, "Well, Bill can only be here for an hour."

When Ellen met me, I was down and out. Drifting aimlessly through life. She had literally watched me pull myself up by my bootstraps. I give her thanks and credit for being my sole support through those lean years when I was trying to rediscover my talent. After I won Boston and things started to really improve, we had a great time riding the wave together. We found adjoining passions in this world of running. At the peak of my success, she traveled with me to races around the globe, joined me on business trips to the Big Apple, and was my date to dinner at the White House. We went everywhere together, and it was a blast.

I wasn't getting rich, nothing like that, but there was quite a bit of media and excitement surrounding me. Everything was changing rapidly for both Ellen and me; it was pretty heavy for two small-town kids to be caught up in this whirlwind. I think if you're with someone you care about and they care about you, life is easier.

At the time, the AAU, our national federation, ruled over track and marathoning with an iron fist. They pocketed two-thirds of any purse won by an amateur athlete. The rest went to a charity of our choice.

They insisted that I only own fifty-one percent of any store that used my name, making it virtually impossible to franchise or spread my business. We were being hit and nickel and dimed and treated poorly, and it fueled my anger toward the international governing bodies.

I was capturing national media attention with my repeated wins in Boston and New York City. The press began asking for my opinion on everything under the sun. I suddenly had a venue to express my disgruntlement. Reporters would ask me why the AAU rules were so strict and I'd tell them, "Because we're living in the Dark Ages. Amateurism in this country is treated like mother and the flag and apple pie. And it's all hypocrisy. All over the world, there's always been under-the-table money in track and, now, in road running. But people want us to be the last bastion of amateurism."

So, what are you going to do about it?

"Well, I talk to a lot of American runners and tell them to fight for compensation, and to not let themselves be exploited. But there are some types of personalities that just want to be hammered. Masochists, I guess. I'm not a masochist—I want to be compensated. I'm being exploited, which is another word for slavery."

If it sounds like I was trying to make some waves, that's because I was. I knew that I wasn't the only one bothered by our treatment—Tom Fleming, Frank Shorter, all of us chafed at the system. And we weren't the first ones. Previous generations had chafed, too. In many ways, I felt I was carrying on Steve Prefontaine's legacy. Our motivation for railing against the status quo came from the same place—the desire to be treated just like any other "professional athlete" in America. We wanted to lift our sport up and bring it a whole new level of visibility, appreciation, and excitement.

The running boom was the catalyst that gave our calls for change momentum. Due to the sheer number of new converts to running, and the marathon heating up into a hot media event, the financial opportunities for runners like me and Shorter skyrocketed. Meanwhile, our spirited rivalry transformed us into the "stardust twins" of American distance running; people were suddenly very interested in what we had to say.

As I kept up my fight in the press, the pressure was mounting on the AAU to make reforms. They eventually agreed to make some modest amateur rule changes. One way an amateur runner could now get around the money ban was by opening a clothing line.

With a PhD in textile chemistry, Ron Hill of Britain was the first runner to press the limits of amateurism when, in 1970, he started a clothing line and opened a running store. Shorter paved the way in America. With the blessing of the AAU, he formed Frank Shorter Running Gear and hired his Yale classmate and former miler Rob Yahn to operate the business. They figured they would make a profit of $250,000 in the first year; they ended up booking $3.5 million in orders in their first month. I realized I could also take advantage of this change in the amateur rules and start my own clothing line. After all, Shorter owned the entire marketplace. There had to be room for one more.

My battles with the AAU and the Olympic Federation came to a head in 1980. That year, I did two national TV commercials. One was for Visa and one was for Life Savers. I was supposed to be paid $25,000 for each one, but the head of the AAU told me I couldn't receive the money. They demanded that I give the money to them, and it would be used for our Olympic athletes.

Later, I spoke to Frank Shorter. I asked him, "What's your situation?" He'd done a national TV ad for Hilton Hotels and I wondered if he'd had to send the money to the AAU, too. And he said, "No, yeah. I kept the money." The fact that Frank was a lawyer probably made the difference. I guess he went in there and told them, according to the law, he was entitled to keep it all. But the AAU felt that they could pull the wool over my eyes. Of course, America ended up boycotting the Olympics, anyway, and the ads never were used. To this day, who knows whose pockets the money ended up in. Not the athletes'.

At the same time I was jetting around the globe, establishing myself as the world's top distance runner, our clothing line was growing by leaps and bounds. In 1981, we did $3 million in sales, earning a reputation as the hottest company in the running clothes industry. By 1984, we were number 29 on the INC. 500, the highest-ranked apparel business on the list.

Although Ellen and I owned sixty percent of the company's stock, I wasn't very hands-on. I was focused on running and winning races. My head-to-head battles with Shorter generated huge amounts of national press coverage. While the media often overstated the personal nature of our rivalry, I was thrilled that our sport was finally getting the attention it deserved. With everybody from newscasters to race directors billing us as the Ali/Frazier of running, a record number of people were brought into the sport, and many themselves started competing in road races, and local running clubs sprung up overnight.

Amby said of Shorter: "He was the Olympic champion, a little more distant and imperial than Bill, but Bill was the champion of races that the people themselves ran in—Boston and New York and Falmouth. He literally reached out and touched people, like God on Michelangelo's Sistine Chapel, and that was a big part of the spark that created the running boom." In 1976, an estimated 25,000 people finished a marathon in the United States. In 1980, that number ballooned to 143,000. By 2009, that number had jumped to 467,000, an increase of 1,768 percent.

After I beat Shorter at the New York City Marathon in 1976, the scales started to tip in my favor. At that point, he had done three more years of hard racing than I had. That's because he kept running after college, whereas I retired to fully enjoy the Boston nightlife with Jason. I think some of the wear and tear from those extra years started to take their toll. He suffered some injuries that slowed him down. He still remained a force, but I don't know if he ever beat me again. I don't think he did.

We didn't really know each other as people, and I think that kind of enhanced the rivalry. Later we both had stores and clothing lines and that bolstered our competition. I think the nature of our sport also stoked the flames. The marathon is a "tremendous glory or complete destruction" event. In the Olympic 10K, you never see people collapsing five times in the final lap and getting dragged across the finish line by officials, which is what happened to Italy's Dorando Pietri in the 1908 London games. Also, there was a certain amount of bombast and ego floating around with the marathoners. This is like heavyweight boxing a little bit, boxing without touching each other. Mental exertion without fisticuffs.

We might have been bitter rivals in the eyes of the world, but in the end, we joined together to fight for better treatment for American runners—that meant prize money, so that a runner could train full-time and compete with the rest of the world. The governing bodies of the time fought us tooth and nail but in 1981, at the Cascade Run Off, America's best distance runners came together to openly revolt against the Olympic Federation, racing for prize money. History had been made. We had finally come out of the Dark Ages and into the light.

In 1976, I had trained hard for the Olympic trials and came close to knocking off the Olympic champion there—seven seconds back. How could I *not* get a medal at the Olympics? Finishing in fortieth place was a wake-up call: I couldn't count on anything in this sport. Nobody could. I had to strike while the iron was hot, make my mark while I was in my physical prime.

New York was the beginning of a five-year stretch of big victories, during which time I finally dethroned Shorter at the top. I traveled to Japan to race at Fukuoka, the race I had always dreamed of winning. Frank Shorter had won the race an incredible four times while this was only my second time I'd gotten an invitation. I knew the challenge wouldn't be coming from Shorter that day, but rather from the USSR's Leonid Moseyev and Massimo Magnani of Italy. Both men had beaten me soundly in the Olympics. Japan's best hope was a pair of twin brothers—Shigeru and Takeshi So. The Japanese put a lot of pressure on them to win Fukuoka and their pictures were in all the newspapers. The other top American was my pal Tom Fleming.

Fleming and I broke away to an early lead. Around six miles in, I turned to Fleming and said, "I'm going to pick it up a little. Do you want to come with me?" He shot back, "Are you crazy, Rodgers?" I made the surge, but failed to shake the lead pack.

Mile after mile, the competition was breathing down my neck. I was running a scorching 2:08:40 pace as I hit the halfway point. The pressure of being in the lead was wearing me down. I peered over my shoulder and saw Moseyev and Takeshi So stalking me. It irritated me.

When Takeshi fell back, the Japanese spectators standing along the route went dead silent. But as they watched me give it everything I got, the chorus of cheers for me gradually grew louder and louder. Then an incredible thing happened. The crowds that lined the streets erupted into cheers of "Rodgers-san! Go hard, Rodgers-san!" I practically had tears in my eyes as I roared along the ancient coastline.

I saw Moseyev wearing his little hat. It was the same hat he had worn on that day in Montréal when he'd beaten me. Flashing back in my mind to Montréal spurred a feeling of extreme feistiness. Here we are again. But this time, the results would be different. The cries of "Rodgers-san" continued to ring out from the crowd as I flew past.

When I reached Heiwadai Stadium, I stopped for water. The crowd of Japanese spectators looked stunned. But I felt the same way I did at Boston in 1975 when I stopped three times for water on my way to victory. It was my way of celebrating and saying, "I worked hard to get to this point. I had to use a lot of energy to break this far away from the pack. It's time to take a drink."

As I stood there calmly drinking the cup of water, I could hear firecrackers going off inside the stadium. I entered the stadium, did a lap around the track, and crossed the finish line in a time of 2:10:56.

Sometimes you get great days in the marathon and everything comes together. This was one of them.

To win Fukuoka was a great honor. I valued it as much as winning either Boston or New York, and winning it made me the first and only runner to win all three. Fukuoka is a prestige race. It is a Mecca for serious runners. In those days, it was the race that top marathoners dreamed most of winning, other than the Olympic marathon. Frank Shorter's ability to win Fukuoka four consecutive times perhaps speaks more of his greatness than even his gold medal at Munich. The best used to always compete in Fukuoka, but not anymore. This saddens me.

To celebrate my victory, Ellen and I attended a party at the Nishitetsu Grand Hotel that evening. We'd all thrown a party to raise money to send Tommy Leonard, the spiritual leader of our running club, to Fukuoka along with me. Tommy, who had probably had a few beers by then, bounded toward the stage and started singing "You Are My Sunshine." One by one, we all started joining in. After that, it became a tradition for runners to sing songs from their homeland. I remember watching Leonid Moseyev and his coach singing a depressing Russian folk song and seeing Lasse Virén howling with laughter. Leave it to Tommy to start a new tradition halfway across the world.

We spent a night in Tokyo, flew to Honolulu, and spent a week relaxing in the warm sunshine. I even tried surfing at Waikiki. I needed to learn how to ride those big waves.

That April I won my second Boston, finishing eighteen seconds off my American record, and the second-fastest Boston time. In six months time, I had won the three major marathons—Boston, New York, and Fukuoka. Nobody had ever achieved this Triple Crown.

Amby pointed out that to make it an official sweep I had to do it all in the same calendar year. The media made a big deal over the quest to win Boston, New York, and Fukuoka all in the same year. While that never happened, over the next year or so I won forty-five of the fifty serious road races I entered, stringing together a streak of twenty-two consecutive victories on the roads in 1978. On the track in Boston that August, I also set the American records for fifteen kilometers (43:39.8), twenty kilometers (58:15), and for the one-hour run, a world record (1:14:12).

I slaked my thirst—my Olympic thirst—at Boston and New York. Between 1977 and 1980, I won four straight times in New York, three more times at Boston, and three times was ranked the world's top marathoner. In all, I won eighteen of the twenty-nine marathons I entered, and ran nine sub-2:12 marathons.

I felt like a pioneer, trying to take marathoning to a place where it hadn't been before, particularly in terms of the large number of high-quality international races that I ran. I probably overraced, to the chagrin of my de facto manager, Ellen. I didn't rest my body much in those days, and didn't start getting massages two times a week until the eighties. But I felt the true measure of a marathoner was continued success racing on a global scale. Perhaps what I admired most about Frank Shorter was that he proved his greatness, not that one time in Munich, but sustained a level of excellence over years. I won significant marathons on five continents; Frank on at least four. I had less respect for somebody, perhaps from the track side of the sport, who entered the marathon to see if he could win it once. For me, consistency was the ultimate mark of a marathon champion.

Does winning marathons on five different continents mean as much for today's marathon runners? I don't think so. The dynamics have changed. The money is bigger. The big five—New York, Boston, London, Chicago, and Berlin—will always draw runners back because of the big purses. But I think it would be worth it for some of our top American runners, like Ryan Hall, Deena Kastor, or Shalane Flanagan, to go to places like Fukuoka, Japan. Alberto went. I take my hat off to Alberto for doing that. Alberto knew what the sixty-seven-year-old race stood for—long before marathons began popping up in every big city around the world, there was Boston and Fukuoka. To this day, Shorter and I are the only Americans who've won it, but I'd love to see others race Fukuoka because it's a great, historical race that reflects Japan's long love affair with the marathon. I don't care what anyone says, Fukuoka is the equal of any marathon in the world.

I think about all the failures in my life. Each one set me up for an even greater success. I was destroyed after dropping out of my first Boston Marathon in 1973; I returned two years later and broke the American record. I was torn apart by my fortieth-place finish at Montréal; I rebounded and beat Frank Shorter at the New York City Marathon in 1976. I suffered another painful dropout in Boston in 1977; I erased that bad memory by climbing the winner's podium the next three years in a row, breaking my own American record in 1979. My career as a marathoner taught me much—but perhaps nothing more important than to never surrender. Never quit. Always keep moving forward. But if resilience was the one trait that ensured my success as a marathoner, it was also the one quality I would need most in the months ahead.

After my Boston Marathon victory in 1979, I was off and running toward my next big goal: the 1980 Moscow Olympics. I knew it would be my last chance to set things right after bombing out so badly in Montréal—my last opportunity for redemption. I was thirty-one years old and determined to make the most out of the physical strength I possessed, and resolved to make the most of my remaining days at the top.

When I didn't have a race to travel to, I woke up early each morning, had a cup of coffee, drove down to the store, and from there went out on a ten-mile run. Most days a couple of the guys from the store would go with me. Even Ellen joined me for three or four miles. I'd still run around my old stomping grounds, Jamaica Pond. Other times I'd run along the Charles River or the crowded sidewalks of Beacon Hill. As I glided through the city streets, my shoes striking the ground, my hair bouncing with each stride, people would shout out to me, "Win gold in Moscow, Billy!" Their calls of support pushed me to run harder and faster.

I kept a journal with information on my main Olympic contenders—Drayton, Shorter, Cierpinski, Moseyev, and Bjorklund. Over the past two years, I had raced and beat them all. This gave me great confidence. Of course, I knew Seko would be my main challenger. He had won Fukuoka; I had won Boston. The stage was set for an Olympic showdown. I couldn't wait.

Then I heard the news: President Carter announced we would be boycotting the Summer Games as a protest of the Soviet invasion of Afghanistan. I thought back to my trip to the White House; I had hit it off with President Carter. I left that night with a positive impression of him; I admired his sincerity, his straightforwardness and honesty. But I didn't see what he was hoping to gain with his decision.

On April 12, 1980, the U.S Olympic Committee voted by secret ballot to endorse President Carter's boycott, effectively killing my dream of winning an Olympic medal. All I ever wanted was a chance to come home with a medal. It was the only thing I felt was missing. I thought, If I get that medal, I'll retire. Happily. I was devastated. My heart was broken. Only this time I couldn't blame a hill in Newton.

Through my life, I've been branded a radical, but I only ever did what I thought was right. I spoke out against the Vietnam War because I felt it was immoral, unjust, and not good for the country. I tried to organize a union among the hospital orderlies because of the cruel labor practices I witnessed. I protested on behalf of the mentally disabled patients of the Fernald school, and later, the Hale School in Everett, because I felt they deserved to be treated with understanding; I brought them outdoors because I thought they should taste the joy of freedom. I fought against the AAU because, like Prefontaine, I felt runners should be treated equal to athletes in all other sports. And now I spoke out against the boycott because I felt the Olympics should transcend politics and unite in friendship all the people of the world, in spite of their cultural, religious, or political differences. I didn't think it was right for athletes to be used as pawns in a political chess match between nations. Maybe I was radical.

I loved to run and compete. I was driven to be the best distance runner on the planet. That, and the allure of bigger appearance fees, pushed me to run more and more races. My busy schedule was taking me to marathons in Europe and Asia. By now, I was squeezing in training runs during layovers, whisking back and forth on airport access roads for two hours. One time I ran around the six hundred-meter loop of a Vietnamese zoo. I had no choice. I had to keep to my usual twenty-mile-per-day training schedule, which had become increasingly hard, between the escalating demands of TV and magazine interviews, running clinics, speaking engagements, and charitable visits to local hospitals. The clothing line kept growing more popular, and dealers who carried my running gear wanted me to make appearances at their stores.

Back when I broke through in 1975, race directors were offering me a ticket, a hotel room, and a small per diem fee. By 1979, I was getting as much as $20,000 for a marathon, and $3,000 to $10,000 to show up for a road race. I had done what I had set out to do—become the first professional road racer. I hoped my efforts would benefit the next wave of runners to come after me—that promising American talents like Alberto Salazar would finally have the necessary resources to compete with the top foreign runners from around the world, and to fulfill their true potential.

Perhaps when Steve Prefontaine handed off to me those racing shoes a week before the Boston Marathon, and a month before his fatal car accident at the age of twenty-four, he was really handing off to me his fight for amateur athletes everywhere to be treated fairly. I hope he would be happy looking down from heaven, knowing that his spirit of rebellion against the tyrants of our sport lived on with me, and that today American runners have the freedom to earn a living through the kind of tireless, passionate effort on the track that made Prefontaine the most electrifying runner of his age.

I used the success of my clothing line to sponsor other athletes. After getting a grant from the AAU, I split it up into smaller pieces, paying emerging U.S. track stars like Benji Durden to wear our athletic gear. Throughout my life, I was lucky to encounter a host of teachers— Frank O'Rourke, Amby Burfoot, Jock Semple, Coach Billy Squires— who trained and inspired me in the craft of distance running. Now that I was an older, more experienced runner, I felt it was my duty to help the up-and-comers as much as possible, whether it was on or off the track. I would take young runners out on the Boston course and run with them, pointing out critical areas, answering questions, and offering strategic advice.

In the early eighties, I was committing myself to run thirty to thirty-five road races a year, which was too much, especially with the draining demands on my time in the public eye. Perhaps it was inevitable that I would start to lose my edge. A group of hungry young lions, including Alberto Salazar, Craig Virgin, Herb Lindsay, and even my own employee Greg Meyer, stormed the gates.

I did my best to hold off the youngsters. Eventually, it was impossible to keep them at bay. They were training harder. They were in better shape. They had that intense devotion and willpower that the marathon demanded. Five years earlier, Shorter had opened a crack in the door for me to take over the top spot. Now it was my turn to do the same.

It was frustrating to feel like my career was on the downside. But, at the same time, my life was changing. My first child, Elise, was born in 1985. She was more important to me than racing.

As Shorter and I aged, we both started to mellow. Winning marathons was no longer the be-all, end-all. We both had kids. Our kids became the be-all and end-all. We both got married and divorced. We both went through tough times with our businesses. We both dealt with the health issues that come with aging. So, we both thought, Okay, I can understand where he's coming from. We realized that we were alike in a lot of ways. These days, we get along very well; we have for years. I'm a big supporter of Frank's. I saw him at the Olympic trials; it was great to see him be recognized for his golden performance in 1972, which set me on the road to my destiny.

Shorter and I have more hard-racing miles on our bodies than anyone in American history. I'm pretty sure of that. So, we both can relate to each other on that level, too. I estimate that I have around 165,000 miles of wear and tear on my body. I'm sure that Shorter has a similar number of miles on him. For people to expect us to race hard now is absurd to us. But some people do. People who do not understand—new runners—will come up to us and say, "Frank, you won a gold and silver." Or "Billy, you won Boston and New York four times each. Why aren't you winning races in your age group now?" They have no idea.

Only he and I know the physical and mental toll of running that many hard races over several years. At some point, I'd run sixty competitive marathons. Frank has run fewer, but he's still done a lot of hard races. He started his marathon career when he was around twenty-two years old; I started at twenty-five. We both competed into our forties. We both have marathon wins on four continents. That's a lot of hard racing, just the marathon alone. That doesn't count the road racing—twenty-five races a year—or the track races, or the cross-country races. We had been going a long time.

Shorter and I know we are lucky to have come of age as marathoners during the running boom of the 1970s. While I know running is going to be a huge sport for a long time to come, there's never going to be a period quite like the one we lived through. We were at the birth of something extraordinary, when the first flowers came up through the spring soil.

For five or six years, a small group of us shared a crazy excitement for the sport. Watching the rest of the world suddenly catch on to the wonder of distance running was an overwhelming experience. The best part is that the Boston Marathon goes on and on. The New York City Marathon goes on and on. And all the people who were part of the circle of my life during that golden time, they are a part of the circle of my life now.

Back in college, when I followed Amby along the trails around campus, I never imagined in my wildest dreams I would race marathons on five continents or that there would be a Bill Rodgers Running Center or that I would get invited to the White House. But that's life. That's the marathon. At first, it's this unimaginable thing. Like climbing Everest. The journey is hard, and riddled with setbacks, but it can be conquered. The unimaginable becomes the imaginable. The impossible dream becomes just the dream. The important thing to remember is that the quest to win a marathon, or even to finish a marathon, starts where all great quests are born—within the heart. That's where it started for me.

The heart is always the true starting line.

Still Chasing Butterflies

Patriots' Day. April 21, 1980. As I broke the tape to cross the finish line, I held up four fingers, signifying the fact that I had matched Gérard Coté's four laurel wreaths, leaving only the great Clarence DeMar with his seven victories. I also joined DeMar as the only other man to win Boston three straight times—he did it from 1922 to '24 and I did it from 1978 to '80. Kenyans Cosmas Ndeti and Robert Kipkoech Cheruiyot would match this feat many years later. I was delirious with exhaustion and joy. My ears were ringing. I couldn't hear a thing. I felt like I was in a dream. I awoke from this dream to suddenly find my marriage crumbling.

Ellen and I had been best friends for seven years, married for five. Our divorce was the hardest thing that had ever happened to me. Maybe it still is.

Gail and I married in 1983. Two years later, we had our first daughter, Elise. In 1990, we had our second daughter, Erika. Those first weeks as a new parent are exhausting, bewildering, and the most exciting, happiest time of your life. I loved being a dad; I still do. I absolutely love it. I adore my daughters. They are the best part of life. Winning a major marathon or building a thriving business—none of those things meant anything, relatively speaking, compared to my children. They are my world.

Going through my two divorces was much tougher than all the marathons I raced put together. The pain of a marathon lasts no more than two hours, the pain of a divorce lasts for years. It's part of your life forever, and that's hard. But you deal with it. Ellen and I had a lot of good times. We were a young couple trying to make our way in the world, and I wouldn't trade the wild, exciting times we had together for anything. I loved Gail, too. We had a long, beautiful relationship. We brought up two bright, lovely, amazing daughters. For this, I'm eternally grateful.

One of the reasons I was able to win road races and marathons for a long while was that, unlike many other long-distance runners, I had a knack for avoiding injuries. For fifteen years, when I was training for marathons at my peak, I never missed more than two consecutive days of running. But in 2003, the day after competing in the Falmouth Road Race, I was on an eight-mile training run when I heard my right tibia snap. I instantly collapsed on the side of the road. I sat on the ground, drenched in sweat, wincing in pain, my thumb in the air. Finally, a teenager came by in his Jeep and gave me a lift.

I didn't sit around too many days asking myself, What if this is it? What if I can't run anymore? My personality is just to keep going—it's that marathoner's personality; no matter what, just try to keep going. Almost immediately, I started to rehab the leg. I always liked the comeback period—it was a quest.

Eventually, I recovered to the point where I was able to attempt my first long run—a fifteen-miler. A friend of mine went with me. We planned to run 8:15 minute miles but once I got out there I started pushing harder. That's just what runners like us do. We can't help it. Suddenly, I was flying along at a sub-eight-minute-mile pace and enjoying that feeling of movement that had been with me since I was a kid. The beautiful part is that there is no age limit on running. The beautiful part of life is there is no age limit on fun.

Four years later, in 2007, I was in Barbados to promote a local race series and run in the 10K. I was down by the pool with a couple of friends, drinking rum and Cokes and having a blast. When I got back to my hotel room, the phone rang. A doctor from Massachusetts General was on the other end. He told me my blood test results were in. I had prostate cancer.

The doctor recommended surgery for the following month. It was a bolt out of the blue. I was in a state of shock. I said, "What? I haven't been in a hospital for surgery since I was ten years old and I had my appendix removed." The doctor told me I needed surgery for the following month. First things first, and I ran the 10K.

Now my thought was, Well, do I have bone cancer? Am I going to be dead in three years? And what does prostate cancer mean? And how serious is this cancer? Cancer is cancer. I was nervous as hell. I wanted to know, after surgery, how quickly I could get back to running. That was the biggest question I had. What was the comeback procedure? If I absolutely could not run anymore, I think I'd be like Clarence DeMar, who, when he was in the hospital, dying with cancer, was running around in the hospital. Or I would be like my uncle, the one who had a heart attack and was literally running around the hospital, yelling, "Get me out of here!" I have a lot of energy. I need to use it up. It's in my DNA.

I had the surgery a month later. A blood test in early June showed no signs of cancer. After that, I set my sights on raising awareness and money for prostate cancer research the only way I knew how—through running. I announced that for the first time in ten years, at the age of sixty-one, I would be running the Boston Marathon to promote prostate cancer awareness.

The last time I had run Boston, back in 1999, I was shooting for my age-group record. It was a hot day. I ended up hitting the wall. I felt light-headed and dizzy. I dropped out at Heartbreak Hill. A replay of my first Boston—only twenty-six years later. It wasn't how I wanted to go out.

The year I ran for cancer I was shot after fourteen miles. I knew I couldn't drop out. There were too many people cheering me on. Too many friends. Too much family. The people running next to me kept me going. If you run with friends, you can always make it. My brother, Charlie, and friend Jason, until his passing this year, have been running alongside me my whole life. I know that's what carried me through to the finish line.

I crossed the finish line in a time of a 4:06:49. Only two hours off my American record time in 1975. But time had never mattered to me before, and it didn't matter to me now. I'd run for something larger than myself. That's what mattered. In a way, it was the most fantastic marathon I'd ever run.

I had discovered that I could come back from a broken bone. I could come back from prostate cancer. Maybe I wasn't the same runner I was before those two incidents, but I still loved the sport as much as ever. When I was younger, I hated to lose any race, particularly a marathon. I don't think like that anymore. Life changes and you get older. Running changes as you get older. You have to adapt. The competitive part fades, but the camaraderie side of the sport grows, and that's a wonderful thing. I love how running for charity has fueled a boom in marathoning. My girlfriend, Karen, participated in the Susan G. Komen Race for the Cure the other day. I run races for prostate cancer awareness. When runners come together as a group, it's amazing the great things that get accomplished.

I've always believed running can be one of the most powerful ways to promote goodwill and tolerance throughout the world. Maybe it's because no man can stand above another when they run. We are all equals on the roads. We are all one people. We are all just kids chasing butterflies.

I'm happy these days going on runs with Karen. She's a good runner; she keeps me on my toes. We run together on the trails in the woods behind our house. Sometimes we'll circle around Walden Pond. We're always looking for wildlife. My mind grows peaceful as I pass by the dew-soaked trees shimmering in the morning sun under a sky of blue.

The other day we were running by this beautiful river and came upon some wild swans gliding together across the water. I moved right along with them. Or as Amby used to say, I was flowing. It was a good run.

Further Reading

CONNELLY, MICHAEL. *26 Miles to Boston: The Boston Marathon Experience from Hopkinton to Copley Square.* Guilford, CT: Lyons Press, 2003.

DERDERIAN, TOM. *Boston Marathon: The History of the World's Premier Running Event.* Champaign, IL: Human Kinetics Publishers, 1994.

MURAKAMI, HARUKI. *What I Talk About When I Talk About Running.* New York, NY: Knopf, 2008.

RODGERS, BILL WITH JOE CONCANNON. *Marathoning.* New York, NY: Fireside/Simon & Schuster, 1982.

SALAZAR, ALBERTO AND JOHN BRANT. *14 Minutes: A Running Legend's Life and Death and Life.* Emmaus, PA: Rodale Books, 2012.

SANDROCK, MICHAEL. *Running with the Legends.* Champaign, IL: Human Kinetics Publishers, 1996.

SEMPLE, JOCK WITH JOHN J. KELLEY AND TOM MURPHY. *Just Call Me Jock.* Waterford, CT: Waterford Publishing Co., 1981.

To view some of Bill's running logs from the 1970s, go online to the Bob Hodge Running Page at www.bunnhill.com/bobhodge/.

Acknowledgments

BILL RODGERS

It has been a unique and fulfilling experience working with you, Matthew Shepatin, on our new book; I learned about the persistence of the long-distance writer; they must have drive and curiosity and an ability to search for the elusive; you have that.

I never would have become a competitive marathoner without the support of my Newington High school cross-country and track coach Frank O'Rourke, and the same holds true for Coach Elmer Swanson at Wesleyan University.

Both coaches guided me forward in a careful way, and allowed me to explore the sport further under Coach Billy Squires of the Greater Boston Track Club, still our country's finest marathon coach.

I will always remember my teammates at Newington High School— James Hall, Craig Schroeder, Chris Chambers, Steve Tonucci, Jim Flynn. I'd like to thank my brother Charlie, who always stood behind me through thick and thin, and my good friend Jason Kehoe, not just a teammate but a lifelong friend. We were on a quest with this running thing; but you, Charlie, and I got to explore the world. Run forever.

To Amby Burfoot, my Wesleyan teammate; high mileage king; keeper of the flame that is the Boston Marathon; thank you for leading me on to the path. And to Jeff Galloway, another Wesleyan runner who aimed high—to the Olympics and beyond, teaching America's runners—always an honor to run and spend time with both of you.

My Greater Boston Track Club teammates; nothing could stop us; especially Greg Meyer, Fred Doyle, Mark Duggan, Scott Graham, Kirk Pfrangle, Alberto Salazar, Dick Mahoney, Don Ricciato, Bob Sevene, Bob Hodge, Randy Thomas, and Walt Murphy. We had strength.

In truth, for me, running is just for fun; I want more importantly to thank the people who I care about most, my family—my mom and dad, my brother Charlie, and my sisters, Linda and Martha. To my daughters Elise and Erika; I always miss you and love you, but I know you have a loving and caring mom in Gail.

So many people in my life helped me out; you know who you are; I'll never forget you.

MATTHEW SHEPATIN

Writing a book is a solitary act, like the marathon. But if this book in any way dispels the myth that a long-distance runner succeeds on his own, allow me to also present this book as evidence that no writer crosses the finish line without the support of family, friends, and teammates.

Thank you, first of all, to my agent Robert Wilson, without whose endless belief and encouragement, this book would not exist.

Second, I owe a debt of gratitude to my editor at St. Martin's Press, Robert Kirkpatrick, for being everything that you could want in an editor—tireless champion, a guiding presence, and an astute voice.

To the entire staff at St. Martin's, especially Nicole Sohl, thank you for your energy and hard work.

I wish to give my love and appreciation to my mom and dad. You have always been there for me.

I raise a tall Berry Hibiscus to my sister, Courtney, the eternal shaman, and my Nana Ruth, a beautiful, strong spirit.

To Bonnie, words cannot express how much you've done for me.

I'd like to thank Anne Fentress Nichols for her literary wisdom and insight, but most importantly her unflagging friendship.

To Roger Ziegler, Constantine Valhouli, Jeff Kurzon, Kyle Smith, David Weintraub, Andrea Syrtash, Dan Peraino, Shawneen Matask, and John and Courtney Brooks—know that I consider myself blessed to have each of you in my life.

To my all-star team of transcribers, Matthew Teti, Jihii Jolly, and especially Andrew Burin, I deeply value your assistance on this book.

Thank you to Jason Kehoe (may you be leading "hate runs" in heaven), Charlie Rodgers, Amby Burfoot, Bill Squires, Bob Sevene, and Tom Fleming for taking the time to share your memories with me.

Finally, I'd like to honor Bill Rodgers with my own laurel wreath. Working on this book with you has been a wonderfully fun and unforgettable experience. You have changed my life for the better, and for that, I express to you my eternal gratitude.